306.6 LYN RES

D1348818

123644

RESEARCH IN THE SOCIAL SCIENTIFIC STUDY OF RELIGION

Volume 6 • 1994

RESEARCH IN THE SOCIAL SCIENTIFIC STUDY OF RELIGION

Editors: MONTY L. LYNN
Department of Management Sciences
Abilene Christian University

DAVID O. MOBERG
Department of Social and Cultural Sciences
(Emeritus)
Marquette University

VOLUME 6 • 1994

Ai JAI PRESS INC.

Greenwich, Connecticut   London, England

CONTENTS

INTRODUCTION

As stated in previous volumes of *Research in the Social Scientific Study of Religion,* this series of books is "interdisciplinary and international in scope, 'ecumenically' encouraging contributions from scholars of diverse religious and ideological orientations, and theoretically eclectic rather than committed to a particular school of interpretation and explanation." The eight articles in Volume 6 vary widely in topic, method, and scope, but each makes a significant contribution to our theoretical and empirical understanding of religion and religious phenomena. Thirteen contributing authors from the United States, England, Northern Ireland, and Canada draw on their extensive backgrounds in sociology, psychology, political science, and religious studies. Catholic and Southern Baptist Christians are examined in detail, and scores of other religious groups are addressed more generally.

If any one transdisciplinary theme has permeated recent scholarly writing, it is that of diversity. Cultural, economic, ethnic, and social differences have moved into the spotlight of multiple disciplines. In several areas, alternative methods and challenging theoretical paradigms fragment scholarship communities. Without any editorial imposition, the diversity motif clearly has emerged in this volume. Diversity in scholarly paradigms, intra- and interdenominational diversity, and diversity posed by the nexus of religion and society are all explored in Volume 6. Yet as chaos theoreticians suggest, diversity does not present a world without form or pattern, but one with complex, interwoven, deep-structure trends and meaning. Several of these diverse patterns of religious dynamics in North America and Europe are explored in this volume.

In the lead article, Matthew Lawson (Princeton University) provides a fresh interpretation of the development of the sociology of religion in America during the twentieth century. He uses Weber's writing as a framework for interpreting thematic pools, waves of scholarship, and methods of research. Lawson explores four phases during the century's research, three of which have diminished but not gone out of existence. These phases are first, 1904 to World War II, when research focused on church and sect differences; second, the post-war period to 1960 when an evangelical revival turned sociological scholars' attention to the possibility of religion's impact on social integration; third, the colorful and socially fragmented 1960s and 70s that brought a growth in new religious movements, neo-pentecostalism, and scholarly inquiry, with foci on religion sustained in community and religion's meaning in everyday life; and finally the last decade and one-half wherein much scholarly examination has been devoted to the relations among culture, society, and religion. Lawson's sweeping historical portrait reflects Weberian themes and vision throughout. It provides a scholarly foundation on which much of a second century of religious and social scientific research will be built.

The next two articles continue the theme of American religious development and diversity. André Nauta (Case Western Reserve University) provides a religious economies reply to the question, Will denominational pluralism die? Using examples of nineteenth and twentieth century denominational schisms and mergers, Nauta argues convincingly that "as long as religious freedom exists in America, the diversity of religious products will persist as well." His insightful and well-reasoned essay uses a macrociological approach to expand the logic of religious economies theory and then sets the stage for empirical tests of these notions.

Kirk Hadaway (United Church Board for Homeland Ministries) and Penny Long Marler (Samford University) carefully unpack the much publicized political conflict in the Southern Baptist Convention (SBC) from the Convention's beginning to 1992. Not only do they document the development of SBC disunity, but they novelly extend elite theory to describe SBC stability and politics. Their article provides a detailed case study illustrating and clarifying the dynamics of denominational conflict wherever it may emerge.

The rising voice of feminist spirituality raises questions about diversity among Roman Catholics. Adair Lummis and Allison Stokes (both of Hartford Seminary) examine the relationship between belief consonant with feminist spirituality and social justice efforts. These researchers surveyed over 3,700 women across thirty-plus Christian denominations and other religions. Catholics form about one-third of the sample and constitute the focus of the article. Lummis and Stokes find that Catholic sisters are the most likely sub-group in the sample to be involved in social justice efforts, although a strong positive correlation exists generally between subscription to feminist spiritual beliefs and social justice actions. They also highlight several other interesting findings about the connection of feminist theology and the practice of social justice.

In the next article, Canadian Augustine Meier (St. Paul University) reveals findings from a sizable and previously ignored community— Catholic charismatics who do not speak in tongues. While up to ninety percent of Catholic charismatics are non-glossolalic, little is said about them in scholarly literature. Meier's dual studies are based on data taken from six psychological and two religious scales. Together they provide an empirical basis on which to strengthen theory building in research on charismatics. From the data, Meier suggests an alternative, psychological differentiation of charismatics based on social and spiritual bonding and separation rather than on psychopathology.

The final three articles focus on the effects of religiosity and religious behavior on family attitudes, drug usage, and views of AIDS policy. From the United Kingdom comes Bernadette C. Hayes (Queen's University of Belfast) and Michael P. Hornsby-Smith's (University of Surrey) comparison of family attitudes and religious identification. Using survey data from over 10,000 respondents in six European nations and the United States, the authors find that religious identification is a significant predictor of family attitudes and that religious independents hold significantly different attitudes toward marriage, divorce, and children, than do active Catholics and Protestants. This study makes a substantial contribution to the religion and family literature as it family religious influences at the macro level.

H. Wesley Perkins (Hobart and William Smith Colleges) expands our understanding of the effects of religiosity on drug usage by unparceling societal, normative influence from religious influence. He discovers some interesting gender effects in this ten-year study and identifies differences of drug usage by level of religiosity when controlling for both actual and perceived peer norms. His findings will be useful for drug researchers as well as for student development professionals.

In the final paper, John K. Cochran (University of South Florida), Jill Garner (University of Oklahoma), and Jeffry A. Will (University of Northern Florida) explore the role of religion on public support for AIDS prevention policies. In a time when AIDS is of concern to broad segments of global societies, its framing is critical. These scholars find that religion has a generally indirect effect, via "traditional values," upon policy support, although conservative Protestant affiliation is tied directly and inversely to governmental approaches to sex education.

Through December 1993 over 175 manuscripts have been submitted to this series of annual volumes, with 35 percent accepted for publication. Each contribution in this volume has been refereed carefully, usually by three or more reviewers, many of whom provided extensive and valuable suggestions for the improvement of individual papers. We are grateful to the sixty reviewers who evaluated the manuscripts accepted, rejected, and under consideration for possible revision for this volume. Their names and institutional affiliations are listed at the back of the book. Additionally, we are grateful for the capable office management of Catherine Slocum and Carole Mahanay, and for the diligent editorial assistance of David Ashmore, John Berryhill, Amanda Bruner, Joella Hayes, Jeff McGuire, and Sunny Jo McNeill in preparing this volume for publication. Finally, we express appreciation to Gayle Jerman of JAI Press for her helpful support and infectious laugh—it seems impossible to catch her on a bad day—and to Lauren Manjoney for excellent production assistance in the weeks prior to publication.

We believe that the numerous implicit and explicit suggestions for further research and theoretical elaboration, along with the numerous references cited in the respective articles and the indexes of subjects and names, constitute an important contribution to further investigations in the social scientific study of religion. Many suggestions for future research can be gleaned from every article in this volume. Comparisons of the findings can be made with those from other cultural contexts and samples of people. Theories proposed here can be elaborated, tested, and refined. Meanwhile, we welcome suggestions about possible future contributions, topics to cover, inquiries, and manuscripts for consideration in subsequent volumes of this series.

Monty L. Lynn
David O. Moberg
Editors

SECTS AND CHURCHES, CONSERVATIVES AND LIBERALS:

SHADES OF MAX WEBER IN THE SOCIOLOGY OF RELIGION IN AMERICA, 1904-1993

Matthew P. Lawson

ABSTRACT

This paper traces the development of the sociology of religion in the United States over the course of this century. A central dynamic in this development stems from Weber's ideal type distinction between church and sect. In the first half of the century these categories oriented work on religious institutions. After mid-century a focus on values consensus led to research on the socially integrative *church*. New religious movements in the 1960s and 1970s led to an emphasis on the subjective meaningfulness of *sect*-like religiosity. A new awareness of history in the 1980s returned attention to a polar conception, though the terms had changed from *sect* and *church* to *conservatives* and *liberals*. The most recent innovations begin to reunite the historical, organizational, and social psychological concerns that interested Weber.

Research in the Social Scientific Study of Religion, Volume 6, pages 1-33.
Copyright © 1994 by JAI Press Inc.
All rights of reproduction in any form reserved.
ISBN: 1-55938-762-9

INTRODUCTION

Over the course of this century, both theory and methodology in the sociology of religion in the United States have developed in response to changes in the field of religion itself. This paper aims to capture these dynamics by considering the contributions of prominent scholarly works. In this task, the work of Max Weber is of central importance because it provides not only a historical starting point, but also a substratum of categories, interpretations, and acute empirical observations that has been repeatedly mined and resifted. In particular, Weber's notion of the distinction between church and sect, with associated distinctions in theology, values, social status and institutional organization, has had an enduring impact on the field.

To prefigure the contents to follow, new initiatives in the sociology of religion since the turn of the century fall, more or less neatly, into four phases. From the turn of the century to its middle, as the fundamentalist/modernist controversy became acrimonious and seemed to yield victory for the modernists, Weber's categories of sect and church were elaborated and refined (Niebuhr 1929, Pope 1942, Yinger 1946). Sects were charismatic and prophetic, offering to deprived status groups salvation out of the world, while churches sought to retain inherited constituencies by accommodating their vision to the world, which meant, in modern times, accommodation to scientific rationality. Later developments along this branch of research extended and elaborated Weber's deprivation explanation for religious affiliation (Aberle 1962, Glock 1964, Wilson 1990[1978]).

In the second period, the post-War ecumenical revival in the mainline churches seemed to vindicate the Parsonian synthesis of Weber with Durkheim: Weber saw value systems, especially religion, as orienting practical activity, while Durkheim thought that uniform values across society provided social integration (Herberg 1955, Bellah 1974[1966]). In contrast to Parsons, Lenski (1961) extended the notion of religious groups as something like Weberian status groups or lifestyle communities.

In the 1960s and early 1970s, with the rise of neopentecostalism and new religious movements like Transcendental Meditation and the Unification Church among middle class youth, deprivation theories were challenged (Gerlach and Hine 1970, Beckford 1975) and a phenomenological emphasis on religion as providing meaning was pushed to the fore, influenced by Geertz (1966) and Berger (1967).

Most recently, as evangelicals have shown renewed vigor, both numerically and politically, there has been a turn to more macro-level questions of American and global social structure and history (McLoughlin 1978, Roof & McKinney 1987, Wuthnow 1988) as well as to historical dynamics at the level of religion and ritual (Warner 1988) or American culture as a whole (Hunter 1991).

Marking these research initiatives as phases conjoined to historical events might raise an objection, with which I would agree, that the sociology of religion does not develop quite so monolithically. Accordingly, the image of the development of the field that I have in mind is not that of geological strata, but of an evolutionary tree, or perhaps better of a river on an alluvial plain, with channels that end or split upon encountering an obstacle, later to rejoin another channel or dry up. Research paradigms that answered questions raised in one period often continued to flourish in later periods, but historical events at times presented challenges and stimulated growth and expansion in new directions. In a paper of this scope I cannot hope to reach out to the twigs of the various branches to include citations from the entire literature. Instead I focus on major limbs or seminal works from which other studies spring. At the end of this paper I will suggest how theoretical developments in the sociology of culture might contribute a new perspective while integrating historical concerns of different periods within the sociology of religion.

CHURCH AND SECT

For the classical social theorists writing at the turn of the century it seemed obvious that democratic politics and capitalist economics had little need of religious legitimation. They saw the influence of institutional religion on social life declining in tandem with the progress of modernization. Within Protestant denominations, in the United States at least, this secularization process was reflected in a theological accommodation to modern science that broke with the previously predominant evangelicalism (for Europe, Reist (1966) describes Troeltsch as a theological leader in this process). By the turn of the 20th century many large urban congregations accepted Darwinian evolution as an established fact and interpreted the Bible in historical context to discover how Christian principles might apply to modern social life. On the other hand, more rural and less affluent congregations resisted interpreting the Bible as anything but eternally relevant and divinely authored, and thus resisted evolutionism. This divide was the basis for the fundamentalist/modernist controversy that split denominations and culminated in the Scopes trial in 1925, in which a Tennessee public high school teacher was convicted of teaching evolution against state law. Press coverage of the defense's ridicule of fundamentalist beliefs did much to discredit fundamentalism, after which fundamentalists largely retreated from the public sphere. With fundamentalists and modernists at the extremes, the majority of Protestants fell somewhere in the middle. Nevertheless, these events at the beginning of the century established clear camps and terms of debate. For canonical accounts of the genesis of these differences, as well as variants and criticisms thereof, see Moberg (1962), Hofstadter (1963), Marsden (1980), Hunter (1983), Wacker (1985), Wuthnow (1988), and Watt (1991).

During the first major phase in the development of the sociology of religion in this century, as the fundamentalist-modernist debate was shaping up, Weber developed his distinction between church and sect. Elaborated by Troeltsch (1931), Niebuhr (1929), and Pope (1942), among others, these concepts have had a lasting influence on the sociology of religion in America (Moberg 1962, Ch. 4,5,11; Beckford 1989, Ch. 2,3). Because of this deep and lasting influence, it is important to outline Weber's use of these concepts.

Weber (1966, p. 59) saw religion's primary function as that of providing a unified and total meaningful interpretation of life and the world.[1] Some questions of meaning are particularly pressing, such as how suffering and death are to be understood. Answers to these questions often involve plans for salvation that have potent effects on practical social activity. Seeking salvation through sectarian rationalism and inner-worldly asceticism, for example (Weber 1930), might lead to such mundane results as the accumulation of capital. But if religions give meaning to the lives that individuals experience, and if different social classes have characteristically different social experiences, then social classes should have "elective affinities" for different religious explanations for the world. The lower classes, Weber thought, would have an affinity for religious meaning systems that provide an explanation for their suffering and a means of salvation out of the world, while the upper classes would be less concerned with salvation but would need to legitimate their position of dominance—something like the opposite of a theodicy of suffering (Weber 1963, pp. 106-107).

These different plans of salvation, associated with social class position, appear to be the ultimate ground for Weber's distinction between sect and church. Sects are religious organizations that provide assurance of salvation to voluntary members, who gain entrance by displaying some evidence of religious virtuosity or charisma. Sect membership is associated with the lower classes because of their need for personal assurance of salvation. Because it proclaims an alternative form of salvation and a vision for a world to come, sect leadership is charismatic and prophetic. In opposition to sects stand more or less bureaucratic churches that dispense grace to members who are born into them, and who may need assurance that they legitimately deserve a salvation they may not have attained by their own merit. As opposed to prophetic or charismatic leadership, churches are more bureaucratic, being led by priests who control access to religious charisma and who accommodate received prophetic visions to the existing world experienced by their members (Weber 1963, pp. 106-108).

For Weber (1963, p. 69; 1946, pp. 270, 287-290), time and history provided linkages between the sect form and the church form of religious organization. If sect members are volunteers who are religious virtuosos, then their religiously "unmusical" children present an organizational problem that must be dealt with—often by moving the organization toward a church form of inherited membership. Sect leaders may prophesy a vision of the world and lead by charisma, but the heirs to leadership may not have the same charismatic abilities. The prophet's disciples tend to "routinize" the prophet's charisma by establishing themselves as a cadre of priests and tempering the prophet's vision to make it attractive to the members they may have come to depend on for their livelihood.

Weber's friend, theologian Troeltsch (1931, I, pp. 331-343), developed Weber's categories of church and sect through an historical analysis of the social teachings of Christian groups through history, showing them equally to be products of applying New Testament teachings to organizations. The "church-type" is organized on the principles of charity and universal love, setting aside hope of divine intervention in worldly affairs, while the "sect-type," based on the model of the early church, sets itself apart from the world as an exemplary community of the saved. For Troeltsch even more than Weber, the sects attracted the socially disinherited and marginalized, while the churches were associated with nationalism and citizenship.

For Troeltsch (1931, I, p. 341), church and sect were "two different sociological types. This is true in spite of the fact (which is quite immaterial) that incidentally in actual practice they may often impinge on one another." Clearly for Troeltsch these types were not exclusive, and thus could not be a means to unambiguously classify religious groups. In this, Troeltsch's "sociological type" was similar to Weber's "ideal-type." Because the conceptual status of these categories differs from their use by American scholars (Swatos 1976), some clarification may be helpful.

Weber first mentioned church and sect (1949[1904], pp. 93-94) as examples of ideal types, which he saw as analytic constructs that meaningfully integrate sociocultural elements into a "complex," or "historical individual," with specific reference to the influence of this complex on other socio-cultural patterns (1949[1904], pp. 89-110, 1930, p. 47). Thus, in *The Protestant Ethic,* inner-worldly asceticism, associated with sectarian religion, had a *causal influence* on the development of capitalism. Constructing an ideal type with reference to its causal influence means that it is not helpful as a classificatory device, though generic or classificatory types may also be constructed. " '[C]hurch" and "sect," for instance, "may be broken down purely classificatorily into complexes of characteristics whereby not only the distinction between them but also the content of the concept *must constantly remain fluid* [emphasis added]. If however I wish to formulate the concept of 'sect' genetically, e.g., with reference to certain important cultural significances which the 'sectarian spirit' has had for modern culture, certain characteristics of both [church and sect] become *essential* because they stand in an adequate causal relationship to those influences" (Weber 1949[1904], p. 93). In the latter usage "church" and "sect" are ideal types constructed for a particular analytical purpose. As particular analytical purposes change, and as the scientific horizon expands and changes, Weber believed that ideal types would have to be reformulated (1949[1904], p. 105). On the American scene the scientific horizon was different from that of Europe because the empirical field of religion was different. This led, over the decades, to transformations in the content of and distinction between the categories of church and sect. This process was perhaps hastened because among Americans the categories lost their status of ideal types to become classificatory types (Eister 1967).

Niebuhr (1929) discussed denominations, churches, and sects as "sociological groups" (as opposed to "sociological types" or "ideal types") in which differences in organizational form determine doctrinal differences. Like Troeltsch, Niebuhr limited his purview to Christianity, and for the most part to the United States, but he was closer to Weber in looking for the sociological (rather than theological) factors that differentiated sects from churches, yet linked them historically. In some ways Niebuhr brought Weber's insights about the relations between sects and churches to logical completion. Weber saw the probability that sect organization and theology would shift to more churchly forms as charisma was routinized and as members needed to accommodate their religiously "unmusical" children into the religious group. What Niebuhr brought to this dynamic transformation of sects into churches, or rather denominations (as he called the disestablished churches in America), was the effect of sectarian asceticism, which had turned Calvinists into capitalists in Weber's *Protestant Ethic*. If the "socially disinherited" joined sects and adopted ascetic lifestyles, then their social condition would improve, leading them to adopt more church-like theologies and practices. The history of Protestantism in America to Niebuhr was a procession of sects turning into denominations, with new sects springing up to meet the needs of the next wave of the disinherited.

Pope (1942), acknowledging a debt to Niebuhr, empirically explored the social class distinctions between sects and churches. In a study of Gaston County, North Carolina, he carefully documented the class differences between the "uptown" and the working class congregations, pointing out the sacramentalism and paternalism of the one and the stress on personal salvation out of the world in the other. He pressed beyond Weber to Marxian themes by examining the institutional linkages between cotton mills and the churches, the role of the churches in promoting labor discipline on an everyday basis, and their role in discouraging unionization. Pope's work in this phase was the closest to what we would now recognize as empirical sociology, using government, church and corporate records to paint a picture of religious group differences and their effects. He also codified dimensions of difference between sects and churches and classified them along a sect-church continuum that continues to be salient, though the type-names have changed.[2]

Other scholars sought to build classificatory schemes on the work of Troeltsch and Niebuhr (for reviews see Moberg 1962, Swatos 1976). Given the fluidity of the concepts as Weber and Troeltsch used them, it is not surprising that categories proliferated as dimensions of difference were isolated and arranged into multidimensional tables. Becker (1950) divided "church" into the ecclesia, or culture-affirming state church, and the denomination, which forms as sects accommodate to the world in the direction of ecclesia. "Sects" on the other hand are smaller and tend to isolate themselves from the world, while cults are informal networks emphasizing a strictly private, personal religion. Wilson (1959) identified four types of sect based on their "response to the world." Yinger's (1957) six-fold scheme created three types each of church and sect (seen as different organizational forms), based on dimensions of inclusion-exclusion and social integration versus personal need. His later effort at systematic classification (1970) used organizational complexity as a third continuous dimension, yielding a classification table with sixteen cells, only half of which had empirical contents; two other necessary categories did not fit onto the classificatory table at all. In the face of this proliferation of types, Johnson's (1963) unidimensional distinction, based on the degree to which groups reject their social environments, was a refreshing simplification that has retained adherents (e.g., Stark & Bainbridge 1985, Finke and Stark 1992). Given the problems with church and sect as classificatory concepts, it is not surprising that they came under severe attack. A series of articles in The *Journal for the Scientific Study of Religion* strongly criticized the church-sect typology as empirically bogus and theoretically bootless (Goode 1967, Eister 1967, Johnson 1971). Demerath (1967), who had built some capital on the concepts, was more reserved in his criticism.

If the concepts of sect and church had a major influence on work in the sociology of religion through mid-century, equally important was the related notion that relative deprivation creates an elective affinity for plans of personal salvation. This was a core theme of much of the early work on church and sect (e.g., Niebuhr 1929, Pope 1942, Dynes 1955), and it continued to flourish even as the focus on churchly social integration developed in the next major phase of theoretical development.

A number of scholars took the relative deprivation thesis seriously and investigated the social consequences of sect membership. In contrast to Pope's (1942) study of co-optation and collusion between business and church leaders as a means of controlling labor (cf. P. Johnson 1978), B. Johnson (1961) and E.P. Thompson (1963) examined how Pentecostalism and early Methodism perhaps unwittingly socialize(d) their members to dominant values such as thrift and work discipline. Bryan Wilson (1959, 1961) disputed Niebuhr's claim that sects tend to transform themselves into churches in two generations, asserting that some sects may not materially change member's social status. Later, Wilson (1990[1978]) suggested that specific forms of relative deprivation may correlate with types of conversion stories associated with different sects. Schwartz (1970) built on Wilson's (1961) work by looking at the different implications for economic behavior of Pentecostal and Seventh-day Adventist "ideologies." The more ascetic Adventists, he found, were more likely to experience upward mobility than the more passively accepting Pentecostalists.

The relative deprivation thesis took a twist with Hofstadter's (1963) interpretation of American evangelicals (i.e., sectarians) as poorly educated, backwater remnant of premodern society, fighting against change. Without acknowledgement, Hunter (1983) essentially reproduced the same argument, though on the basis of a theoretical paradigm of a later period. Both have since been criticized for using fundamentalists as the type case for evangelicals in general (see below). The effect of Hofstadter's interpretation was to look for other ways in which some religious groups may be deprived relative to others, particularly in terms of educational attainment.

Glock and Stark (Glock and Stark 1966, Stark and Glock 1968, see also Selznick and Steinberg 1969) used a national survey to study the relationships among social characteristics, religious beliefs and prejudice. Their main point of reference was Adorno et al. (1950), whose mostly psychoanalytic study of the "authoritarian personality" focused on factors in the family of origin that affect individuals' tolerance of outgroups and image of God. For Adorno, sectarians maintain strict standards of behavior and therefore sharp group boundaries, which correlates with an authoritarian God who is easily displeased. The God of the liberal churches is more distant and forgiving, like the parents of upper class children (cf. Greeley 1981). In a challenge to Adorno, and more in line with Hofstadter's views of the fundamentalist as poorly educated, Glock and his associates found that educational attainment alone, rather than family influence, was the best predictor of religious as well as civic liberalism.

Demerath (1965), a student of Glock, applied quantitative methods to a study of a number of mainline denominations. He constructed measures of churchlike and sectarian individual religiosity and compared these to measures of social status. He found that, even within denominations, social status measures had what were by now predictable effects: Lower status individuals were on average more sectlike, stressing specifically religious aspects of church activity, while higher status individuals were more attuned to the social or clublike aspects of congregational affiliation. A decade earlier, Dynes (1955) had found similar intradenominational differences. Along similar lines, Hoge (1976) studied the theological divide in the United Presbyterian Church USA, and Roof (1978) distinguished individuals on the basis of localism and cosmopolitanism in the Episcopal Church.

Glock (1964, cf. Aberle 1962) extended the relative deprivation hypothesis to its logical extreme when he proposed that *all* religious forms, indeed all organized social movements, have as a precondition some kind of relative deprivation, whether it be economic, social, organismic, psychic or even ethical. Social movements can be categorized on the basis of what deprivation they compensate for. Church members suffer from "social deprivation." Sects, which compensate for economic deprivation, are transformed into churches or disappear as soon as the economic deprivation of their members is relieved, either through improvements in the economy or through the effects of discipline imposed by the sect. The key problem with relative deprivation explanations of religiosity becomes clearly apparent in Glock's formulation: Every individual and probably every group can be identified as relatively deprived in some way. If by definition religious groups function to relieve deprivation, then post-hoc functional analysis will always be able to find some deprivation.

In summary, the first phase of research on American religion in this century built on Weber's formulation of the ideal-type difference between sect and church, mediated through the work of Troeltsch. Sects were associated with fundamentalism, antimodern values, the lower class and the less educated, while the churches were associated with liberalism, accommodation to modern science and the socially dominant middle class. Methodologically, most studies followed Weber's lead of interpretive historical analysis, though beginning with Pope, and flourishing after 1960 with Glock and his students, quantitative methods began to come to the fore.

Because the middle-class churches were culture-affirming and apparently in the process of secularizing, explanatory efforts were directed to a large extent at explaining sectarian religiosity. It was generally thought that economic or other sorts of relative deprivation would induce individuals to look for visions of the world which help to make sense of their plight and offer some sort of eschatological hope or psychological compensation. Aside from offering these compensations, sectarian religion was often thought to provide a plan for attaining salvation which involves an ascetic or disciplined approach to worldly activity. Some scholars saw this new discipline as beneficial for the social status of sect members, while others saw it more pessimistically as a means of labor discipline.

CHURCH TRIUMPHANT: THE AMERICAN WAY OF LIFE

In the post-World War II period, changes on the religious scene presented new problems for sociology. The mainline liberal churches had received less attention in the previous period because they seemed to be generally following the predictions of secularization theory, accommodating themselves to scientific findings and modern rationalism. After the war, however, the mainline churches experienced unprecedented growth and felt a growing influence on culture. Ecumenical movements toward mergers between some denominations, and the unity and strength of the National Council of Churches gave the impression that religion in America spoke with one voice.

Congruent with these changes on the religious scene, social theory came under the sway of Parsons, who had been instrumental in the translation of Weber's works for American audiences. In the "Parsonian synthesis," the sociology of religion gained a basis for understanding the post-war ecumenical revival.

Parsons developed his perspective on a largely Weberian basis, though with an important dose of Durkheim. From the Weberian angle, Parsons saw religion and secular ideologies as providing total, unified explanations for the world that orient social action. Through time these worldviews are rationalized, or brought into logical coherence, which leads to the rationalization of social action. The development of Western civilization for Parsons (1963, 1979) was largely the result of such religious rationalization. What Parsons added from Durkheim (1915) was the notion that collective symbolism, especially "sacred" symbolism, is the ultimate source of social integration—if people are able to coordinate their action, then their action must be oriented toward similar ultimate values, which must be provided by a unified meaning system (Parsons 1949[1937]). Parsons' emphasis on social integration through shared meaning systems led him to downplay, even to disregard, differences among religious systems available within societies, especially as they pertain to different status groups.

The major works which stemmed from Parsons' theory glossed over differences to explore what could possibly be socially integrative about the vast array of often contentious religious groups in the United States. Herberg (1955) made the most important contribution in this regard, building on the work of a Parsons student, Williams. Williams (1951) saw the particular values of the various religious groups in the United States as secondary to a core of basic American value orientations, such as achievement, hard work, morals, practicality and progress. Herberg acknowledged differences among the culturally dominant religious groups in America—Protestants, Catholics and Jews—but saw them as institutional agents of socialization into the "American Way of Life" for the hosts of immigrants who populated the nation. Religious groups acted as buffer communities, teaching newcomers the basic American value system. Bellah, another student of Parsons, suggested that there was a level of religiosity in America's vision of itself that transcended any one denomination or tradition, which he called America's "civil religion" (Bellah 1974[1966], see also Bellah and Hammond 1980, Wilson 1979). Rather than being carried by the churches it involves a minimal appeal to Christian values and a transcendent God.

Studies in later periods that follow on the Parsonian theme of value consensus and social integration include, of course, Bellah et al. (1985) on individualism and community in America. *Habits of the Heart* is a jeremiad, lamenting the increasing individualism and subjectivism on which Americans base their actions, and entreating a return to the Biblical and republican values that had formerly unified the American polity. While the Parsonian language of social and cultural systems is lacking, the theme that social cohesion is based on values consensus is frequently reiterated. Tipton (1982) also worked directly with Parsonian and Bellah-esque themes in his study of the moral philosophies of Pentecostal, Zen and est groups, though he also took up the ethnographic methods and interest in new religious movements that came to the fore in the following period. Finally, Hunter (1991), taking up concerns that became prominent in the final period we will consider, was concerned with the moral philosophies of evangelical and liberal religious groups as they relate to the social integration of the United States, though he sees them, like Lenski, as fundamentally irreconcilable.

Lenski's (1961) quantitative study of survey data from the Detroit area supported some of Herberg's conclusions, but questioned the thesis that religious groups socialized toward uniformity of values and promote social integration. Following up on Weber's Protestant ethic thesis, Lenski's main goal was to establish whether religion continued to have an independent effect on work and other social attitudes, and found that this did appear to be the case. He followed Weber as well in paying close attention to issues of class and status as they relate to religion, and concluded that the various religious groups he analyzed, independent of class, acted like Weberian status groups (Weber 1946, pp. 180-195), each with a particular style of life and set of value orientations which isolates it from and brings it into conflict with other groups. Lenski (1961, pp. 344-359) concluded that the sectarian asceticism of Protestantism accords well with American values of individualism and upward mobility, while the Catholic emphasis on community and family is less at home in capitalism.

In summary, in the early post-war period the Parsonian synthesis of Weber and Durkheim inspired researchers to investigate the ways in which religion in America might serve the function of social integration. In earlier church-sect terms, this meant a de-emphasis on sectarian religion for a focus on the culture-affirming aspects of churchly religion. This shift in emphasis might have been longer lived were it not for new movement on the religious front which initiated a swing in the opposite direction on the church-sect continuum.

The methods used by those who promoted the civil religion and the "American Way of Life" themes were essayist. Lenski, Glock and Stark, and Demerath on the other hand, who pioneered the use of quantitative empirical methods in the 1960s, were less than confident that religion had a unifying function in American social life. The examples they set have had a profound and continuing effect on the sociology of religion down to the present. The journals founded in this period (*Journal for the Scientific Study of Religion* and the *Review of Religious Research*) were initiated with and have retained a primarily quantitative emphasis.

Whether or not sociologists in this period agreed that religion had socially integrative effects, there was a move away from the Weberian interest in the specific life circumstances that require meaningful religious interpretation. Following Parsons, religion was seen as force, *sui generis,* that influences profane behavior. If religion answered questions of meaning, they were ultimate questions, such as the meaning of the cosmos or of death, not the questions about unequal suffering that interested Weber.

PARADIGMS CONTESTED: NRMS AND NEO-PENTECOSTALS

Changes on the religious scene in the 1960s presented such problems for previous theories that there was a decisive break with past paradigms. Along with the counterculture movement of the 1960s came new religious movements (NRMs) and a middle class neo-pentecostal revival. The rise of new religious movements turned staid secularization theory on its head, and the middle class character of neopentecostalism cast grave doubt on the value of relative deprivation theories for explaining sectarian religiosity. Just as important, the Parsonian vision of religious values as socially integrative was presented with a formidable challenge by these movements, which all in some ways were resistant to the values of the dominant culture.

Such a radical break with the past makes intellectual lineages difficult to trace, at best. However, the chaos in the early part of this third phase set the stage for a major change of direction in sociological theories of religion. In some ways this movement was itself sectarian, reacting against recent works for falling away from themes important in the classics. The new direction came to focus on how individuals find meaning for their lives in religious groups, which combines Weber's notion that individuals and groups within society may have elective affinities for different religious forms with Durkheim's emphasis on the religious community. This new direction is hardly exhausted even today, and developments on the religious front in the 1970s and 1980s contributed to it, but also led to a different style of study to be discussed in this section.

New religious movements had a powerful influence on the field beginning in the mid-1960s (Robbins 1988, pp. 190-207). While the literature on cults rejected the notion that deprivation was sufficient to motivate conversion to a sect-like group, deprivation of some sort was often seen as a necessary component in a multicausal model. The Lofland-Stark model of conversion was influential in this regard (Greil and Rudy 1984). Lofland (1977[1966], Lofland and Stark 1965) acknowledged relative deprivation as a necessary precondition for conversion in a value-added or stepwise model. He further modified the notion of deprivation so that it took the form of "tension... best characterized as a [subjectively] felt discrepancy between some imaginary, ideal state of affairs and the circumstances in which these people find themselves" (Lofland and Stark 1965, p. 864). The emphasis on subjective experience encouraged a move away from survey sociology and objective measures of deprivation such as class or status, and a move toward understanding how individuals make sense of the world they experience. Following this logic, Barker (1984) suggested that conversion to the Unification Church may be something of a rational choice, given the conditions of the world as converts experienced it. Other studies investigated how the cult community creates a total way of life. As Bainbridge (1978, p. 14) puts it in his study of a satanist group, "the cult is culture writ small."

The neo-pentecostal revival, which also came to the attention of researchers in the middle 1960s, raised more decisive challenges to deprivation hypotheses. Anthropologists Gerlach and Hine (1970) used ethnographic methods to study Black Power and neopentecostalism as movements for radical social change (i.e., contra Parsons' thesis on religion and values consensus). For both groups, relative deprivation explanations for participation were judged inadequate, since members were drawn from a wide range of occupational statuses. But rather than developing a systematic theory of how religion relates to social context, Gerlach and Hine primarily described the organizational features common to the movements, that is, their schismatic tendencies ("reticular organization"), and recruitment and commitment mechanisms. Their work is notable because it began a wave of ethnographic studies of religious groups conducted by anthropologists which took much more account of religious group life and ritual (see Zaretsky and Leone 1974).

Another important critic of deprivation theory was Beckford, a student of one of the contributors to the deprivation thesis, Wilson. In a study of the Jehovah's Witnesses (1975) Beckford examined three hypotheses for sect affiliation. Like Gerlach and Hine, he found the deprivation hypothesis to be problematic because of the status diversity of sect members, but two other interconnected hypotheses were more compelling. Berger's (1967) theory that groups provide worldviews that give meaning to life, and Douglas's (1973) notion that intentional group life is a means of expressing social solidarity, share the Durkheimian thesis that groups perpetuate particular cultural visions of the world and of group members' relationships with others in society. In considering Berger's and Douglas's perspectives, Beckford found that those who joined the Jehovah's Witnesses had been previously uncertain about their moral commitments and had little social support to help them define or maintain them. The sect gave them both moral certainty and a tight-knit community that would support it.

Lofland and Stark, Gerlach and Hine, and Beckford were early exponents of the shift in theory and methods in this third phase, a shift in theory toward the everyday contexts in which religion is meaningful and a shift in methods toward ethnographic involvement in the everyday lives of research subjects. The contributions of Berger and Geertz have proved to be especially important in this shift (Wuthnow 1987, pp. 18-60; 1992, pp. 9-58). Considering their contributions will help distinguish this period from those previous to it.

Berger (1967) examined religion from the perspective of the sociology of knowledge, building on his work with Luckmann (Berger and Luckmann 1966) which synthesized many themes from classical sociology, especially the German historicist tradition that included Marx and Weber. Berger and Luckmann saw human existence as essentially dialectical, that is, that social life consists of a constant interchange between the subjective internalization of external reality and the externalization or objectification of internal consciousness. This dialectic involves, above all else, historical processes by which social knowledge that was created in one social context is reproduced through time by a community. The perspective thus focuses much of its attention on the social contexts for the perpetuation of forms of knowledge. Religion, as one form of social knowledge, is sustained and transmitted by social groups, from the level of entire societies down to individual congregations. Instead of seeing religion as an autonomous social fact that influences behavior, Berger encouraged researchers to observe and understand how religious worldviews are transmitted in everyday interaction. In practice, applying Berger's perspective meant focusing intensively on how social interaction and religious worldview mutually construct one another in particular groups. The results are often quite Durkheimian, in seeing the religious group as a society in and of itself (cf. Durkheim 1915, p. 59), so that questions of the relation of the group to wider society are de-emphasized.

Geertz was a student of Parsons but abandoned the comparative aspects of Parsons' evolutionary approach for a more particularistic and relativistic one (cf. Parsons 1968). Geertz (1973[1966]) proposed that religion is both a symbolic "model of" the world that answers questions of meaning, as well as an idealized "model for" the world that motivates and coordinates social action. His basic position was that any order found in social life comes not from "reality" but from the coherence of cultural models of the world that order the variety of our experiences. But Geertz did not see cultural knowledge as being composed of basic categories and oppositions, as did some other contemporary anthropologists (e.g., Levi-Strauss 1963, Douglas 1966 and Victor Turner 1967) who were steeped in a Durkheimian rather than a Weberian tradition. Rather, he saw culture as more poetic and creative. Instead of providing analysis and reduction, Geertz saw the task of social science as essentially interpretive, providing enough "thick description" that the reader could participate in the world created and experienced by the natives (1973, Chaps. 1, 15).

In several respects Geertz was restating Weberian themes quite forcefully, for example, in seeing the social sciences as essentially interpretive, human behavior as based on meaningful intention, and religious categories as a basic component of the worldview on which group members base their action. Geertz differed from Weber, however, in that he saw religion as consisting of a "system of symbols" rather than of theological or philosophical constructions like an ethic or a plan of salvation. Moreover, Geertz pointed to rituals as empirical arenas in which symbols are communicated intersubjectively to affect the moods and motivations of individuals.

The effect of Geertz's and Berger's work on the sociology of religion was to encourage an emphasis on how the meaningful visions of the world that are created and sustained in religious groups affect social action. (Each of them also strongly emphasized Weber's notion that religion provides a theodicy of suffering, but this has been largely ignored in subsequent work.) Hunter's (1983) work on *American Evangelicalism*, for instance, followed Berger closely, and looked at how evangelicals had maintained a subculture resistant to the secularizing forces of modernity, composed mostly of less educated rural dwellers who are most distant from those forces. Like Hofstadter (1963), Hunter envisioned evangelicals as throwbacks to preindustrial America who maintain a worldview and a way of life that is under attack. In this characterization he failed to distinguish between fundamentalists and mainstream evangelicals, who are quite varied in their attitudes toward the modern world. Moreover his work rests primarily on content analysis of evangelical literature, bolstered by scant survey data. By and large, it does not provide evidence of how evangelical *community* life reproduces evangelical belief, as Berger's perspective seems to call for.

Tipton's (1982) ethnographic study of three religious or quasi-religious groups (Pentecostal, Zen, and est) laid a much firmer ground for how group interactions provide a context in which their beliefs are supported, but Tipton's thesis was far different from Hunter's. Tipton saw the new religious groups as havens for the rebels of the counterculture movements who needed to be "saved" from the culture of resistance of the 1960s. He investigated social relations within the groups he studied (two of them were communal), but not very much how religion made a difference in relationships with others outside the group. Each religious group essentially socializes individuals to dominant societal values, and it is very clear that values are the issue here. Tipton's open-ended interviews focused heavily on people's moral philosophies, and he compared these to moral philosophies encoded in speeches by politicians and other community leaders, thus developing and refining Bellah's civil religion/ social integration paradigm.

Ammerman's (1987) ethnography of the social life of a fundamentalist congregation was more limited in scope than Tipton's work, but it focused more on how religious beliefs and practices enter the wider social lives of congregation members. More so than most other works in this period, Ammerman showed how religious worldviews are sustained by a community.

Neitz (1987) conducted much the same kind of study as Ammerman but with a charismatic Catholic prayer group,[3] showing how religious group practices create and sustain a vision of the world. She went beyond Ammerman, however, in trying to explain why the neopentecostal revival should have come about. She does so by appealing to other works on culture change in America which assert the rise of expressive individualism and a therapeutic culture (cf. Lasch 1979, Bellah et al. 1985). In contrast to Tipton's subjects, who were "getting saved from the Sixties," Neitz thought that the individualism in the relationship with God in pentecostalism accorded well with expressive individualism, and the pentecostal emphasis on inner healing accords with therapeutic culture.

Earlier than Neitz, Wuthnow (1976) also argued that changes on the religious scene stemmed from changes in the broader culture. He differed from many others who took up Bergerian themes in that he used a sample survey to explore his hypotheses, rather than participant observation of one or several groups. The religious experimentation of the early 1970s, Wuthnow asserted, was a response to long-term changes in American culture. He found that individuals' selections of elements from various meaning systems were based largely on age and education. Selections were influenced to a lesser extent by occupational status, liberalism of parents and religious background. The basic finding was that youth and higher levels of education were correlated with more "modern" meaning systems, including a "social science" perspective (i.e., social determinism) and a mystical perspective, while the older and less educated were more "traditional," holding more frequently to individualistic and theistic perspectives. But rather than being couched in deprivation terms, Wuthnow's point, somewhat like Hunter's, was that age and higher levels of education provide different ways of interpreting socially constructed reality.

In summary, this third period saw a shift away from relative deprivation explanations for sectarian religiosity. Instead there was a movement to understand how religion is sustained in community and gives meaning to everyday life. This meaning is carried, however, not so much in the values or answers to ultimate questions of life that a religious tradition provides, but in collectively shared symbolism of how individuals are related to one another, and collective activities, especially rituals, in which meaning is intersubjectively communicated. Because of the emphasis on the reproduction of religious worldviews in the intersubjective aspects of everyday life, participant observation became the method of choice.

EVANGELICALS AND AWARENESS OF HISTORY

The fourth and most recent trend in research was stimulated by the recognition that evangelical Christianity had become a major force in politics as well as in religion. With the election of a Southern Baptist president, Jimmy Carter, in 1976, and with evangelical moral issues playing an even greater role in the election of Ronald Reagan in 1980, evangelicals announced that they were not dying out as rural hamlets turned into strip malls, but that they could influence core American values as mainline liberals had in the 1960s. Beyond just flexing new political muscles, evangelicals were having just as great an effect in the religious sphere. The neo-pentecostal renewal had become a dynamic force within American denominations, but evangelicals also shifted the balance of membership among denominations. Between 1960 and 1970 the Southern Baptist Convention surpassed the United Methodist Church in size to take first place among Protestant denominations, and other conservative denominations showed high rates of growth. During the same period mainline liberal denominations were suffering from widespread defections. By the end of the 1970s it became clear that these changes were more than the result of 1960s experimentation in religion (cf. Wuthnow 1978) but were part of a larger social movement that sociologists were ill-prepared theoretically to deal with.

In sociology the first warning of this shift came with Kelley's study of *Why Conservative Churches are Growing* (1972). Using Berger's notion that meaningful interpretations of the world are sustained by communities, Kelley suggested that liberal churches no longer attempted to interpret the world and hardly fostered community; conservative churches were strong and could expect further growth because they maintained strict standards of behavior and belief and vilified nongroup members. By 1978 a group of sociologists and denominationally affiliated researchers had gathered to analyze the factors behind church growth and decline (Hoge and Roozen 1979). In a summarizing and interpreting essay, Hoge and Roozen suggested that "a broad cultural shift has hit the churches from the outside, and it has hit the affluent, educated, individualistic, culture-affirming denominations hardest. It was most visible among the affluent young people, especially those on college campuses" (1979, p. 328). If an unexpected culture change had hit the churches from the "outside" it was appropriate that sociology should look outside itself for the source of these changes. The natural place to look was to history.

In sociology's incorporation of historical studies we can see the appropriateness of the metaphor introduced above of a river whose channels split and later rejoin. Weber, Troeltsch, and Neibuhr had been very interested in historical dynamics, but as sociology became more quantitative these concerns receded. After the new recognition of the value of historical scholarship, sociologists generally exchanged the categories of "church" and "sect" for other labels. When referring to differences within denominations or at the individual level, the terms were usually "liberal" and "conservative." When referring to groups, the church-type Protestant denominations were variously "liberals," "mainline-liberals," "public Protestants," or "communitarians," and comprised the older groups which had stood on the modernist side of the fundamentalist-modernist debate in the early part of the century. The terms for sect-type denominations were "conservatives," "evangelicals," "born-again Christians," "Private Protestants," and "individualists," and comprised a variety of old and new Protestant groups which laid a stress on a mature voluntary commitment to accept God's offer of personal salvation and be "born again." The notion that individuals must hear and decide whether to follow God's word frequently corresponds with an emphasis on sharing God's word with unbelievers, or evangelizing; hence the term "evangelicals." Fundamentalists, that is, born-again Biblical literalists who reject aspects of modern culture and militantly struggle to preserve a space for their own religious freedoms, are sometimes seen as the ideal-type evangelical (e.g., Hofstadter 1963, Hunter 1983). In terms of classification, however, fundamentalists should be seen as a sub-type of evangelicals, who as a whole comprise groups ranging quite broadly on attitudes toward modern culture, though all stress the need for a personal decision to follow Jesus (see Pierard 1984, McIntire 1984).

Despite the terminological shift, it seems clear that the trend in this most recent phase has been a return to the church-sect problem complex, armed with better empirical data at the individual, organizational and historical levels. Though the names have changed, the sociocultural contents of the categories touch on similar sets of differences. Perhaps most telling of a continuation of the sect-church problem complex is the way specific denominations are grouped in various studies (compare Pope 1942, p. 124 [sect-church], Stark & Glock 1965, pp. 187-188 [conservative/liberal], Newport 1978, p. 532 [low/ high socioeconomic status], Marty 1970, p. 179 [private/public], Hoge & Roozen 1979, p. 323 ["conservative-disciplined-distinctive from culture" "liberal-pluralistic-culture-affirming"], Roof & McKinney 1987, p. 80 [conservative/liberal], Warner 1988, pp. 14-18 [conservative/mainline]).[4]

The historians whose work became important to sociologists were only tangentially interested in the church-sect problem. In the post World War II era of apparent liberal Protestant hegemony, there was an interest in how this hegemony came about. Smith (1957) explored the historical roots of evangelical religion in the United States in the 19th century and found that evangelical revivalism before the turn of the century had been the predominant religious perspective (cf. Dolan 1977), with what was to become modern liberalism being the deviant newcomer. McLoughlin (1959) carried the story of evangelicalism through to Billy Graham, showing its basic continuities, and it was largely from McLoughlin's research that Hofstadter (1963) painted his picture of fundamentalists as rural hicks, stuck in the 19th century and resisting 20th century modernism. In 1970 Marty published an account of American religious history that looked more deeply at differences between "public" and "private" Protestantism. In Marty's account we can see basic similarities with Weber's original ideal types of other-worldly sect and culture-affirming church:

> One party, which may be called "Private" Protestantism, seized the name "evangelical" which had characterized all Protestants early in the nineteenth century. It accented

individual salvation out of the world, personal moral life congruent with the saved, and fulfillment or its absence in the rewards or punishments in another world in a life to come. The second informal group, which can be called "Public" Protestantism, was public insofar as it was more exposed to the social order and the social destinies of men. Whereas the word "evangelical" somehow came to be part of the description of the former group, the word "social" almost always worked its way into the designations of the latter. They pursued a Social Christianity, the Social Gospel, Social Service, Social Realism, and the like. (Marty 1970, p. 179)

Ahlstrom (1972) later published an influential narrative history of American religion that, while not retrospectively applying Marty's polarized categories, was attentive to countervailing trends in different periods.

These historical perspectives entered sociological discourse through such works as Hoge's discussion of the liberal-conservative division in the Presbyterian Church USA (1976) and Marty's forward to the Hoge and Roozen volume (1979). Marsden's (1980) *Fundamentalism and American Culture,* which explored the logic of the fundamentalist worldview and its social supports, influenced the later qualitative work of Hunter (1983) and Ammerman (1987). None of these sociological works, however, placed a major emphasis on explaining historical dynamics.

In 1978 McLoughlin published a provocative essay in which he proposed that a series of cultural revitalization movements had swept over the United States beginning with the Great Awakening in the 18th century. By referring to "revitalization movements" McLoughlin was adopting Wallace's (1956) name for the process by which new cultural visions of the world are adopted. Ultimately, however, Wallace was restating Weber's vision of the process of creation and routinization of prophetic interpretations of the world. The prophet notices a discrepancy between the going worldview and some aspects of reality and suggests an alternative interpretation. As the new interpretation becomes widely adopted the culture is "revitalized." To Weber it was clear that social change did not necessarily precede or cause cultural change, but for Wallace and McLoughlin the need for new prophetic visions arises because changes in society, particularly in the mode of production, make the old vision inappropriate. McLoughlin (1978) discussed four such episodes in American history since colonization, corresponding to the Great Awakening, the Second Great Awakening, the Social Gospel movement, and the present era of religious disruption. He traced the root causes of the first two movements to changes in authority structures in the family and in the economy. The third awakening, the Social Gospel movement closely associated with modernist liberal Protestantism, was interpreted as an adaptation to industrial capitalism. McLoughlin did not see the resurgence of evangelicalism in recent decades as a creative adaptation, but as a reactionary response to modernization, really only a "traditionalist and backward looking" precursor (p. 186) to the more significant cultural reorganization that is sure to follow, that is, a liberal swing toward more collectivist views of man in society.

McLoughlin's thesis sparked a debate in the sociology of religion (O'Toole 1983, Barkun 1985). Along with growing awareness of the dynamic tension between religious liberals and conservatives, it encouraged a number of sociologists to seek an understanding of the basis for this dynamism.

Warner (1988) studied the swing from post-war liberalism to conservatism in the history of a single Presbyterian congregation. Warner mostly focused his attention on the "idiosyncratic motivations of individuals, including movement leaders" (Warner 1988, p. 29) in a detailed narrative history of the congregation's post-war life. What made his study sociological was his proposal (chapter 2) that religious expressions generally oscillate between individualist (cf. sectarian) and communitarian (cf. churchly) forms. Taken at the level of generality that Warner seems to intend, his scheme outlines a universal logic of self-transformation within which religious forms can be expected to change, a logic he compares with Weber's notions of charisma and routinization (which underlie Weber's distinction between charismatic sect and bureaucratic church).

Similar to Warner in some ways, Hunter (1991) suggested that the liberal-conservative divide, or in his terms progressive and orthodox moral philosophies, entails a basic difference in the cultural logic of how democratic society should be organized and how social resources should be distributed. Unlike Warner, however, Hunter saw these differences not as complementary but as antithetical and irreconcilable. The struggle for dominance by each of the factions results in ongoing "culture wars" in American history. Taken together, Warner and Hunter point toward a cultural dynamic that places moral visions at the base of large-scale cultural change, loosely similar to Weber's alternation of prophecy and routinization or the notion that ideas can be switchmen on the tracks of history.

Roof and McKinney (1987) attacked recent changes with very different methods. They accumulated twelve years of data from the General Social Survey, yielding a sample of over 17,000, to produce a map of the relative positions of American denominations and families of denominations. They based their denominational families largely on Marty's (1970) description of "public" and "private" Protestantism (see above) and found that liberal and "moderate" (i.e., public) denominations were indeed losing members while conservative (private) denominations were growing. They explained this with demographic and cultural arguments, showing that liberals and moderates had lower birthrates and intergenerational retention rates than conservatives. Their cultural argument was that, while pluralism had long been a factor in American religion, the degree of privatism of religious beliefs has been greater since the 1960s. Privatism tended to favor the conservative denominations, they asserted, since those denominations were more concerned with personal salvation and with the personal and experiential aspects of faith. Privatism became a factor in American culture in the 1960s and after because levels of post-war affluence enabled as much as 80 percent of Americans to pursue a quest for personal meaning in life (Roof & McKinney 1987, p. 47).

Wuthnow (1988) also provided an historical account of the religious realignments since World War II, though on a scale somewhere between Warner and Roof and McKinney. Like Warner, he saw the liberal and conservative factions as basically complementary, but their alternation in popular consciousness in recent decades was not idiosyncratic or simply following a cultural logic. Like Roof and McKinney, Wuthnow saw religious change as motivated by economic, demographic and social structural developments after World War II. But rather than seeing affluence as directly affecting culture and religion, Wuthnow analyzed the factors that allowed one movement or the other to mobilize more resources in different periods. In addition to historical analysis, he used data from a nationally representative sample survey to lay out the dimensions of the recent liberal-conservative conflict.

At root, Wuthnow (1988) saw the changing relative power of religious factions as based in changes in the world political economy. After the Second World War the federal government directed unprecedented resources to higher education to maintain leadership in the world economy. The studies of Glock and his students (of which Wuthnow was one) showed a direct correlation between educational attainment and liberal values. While education has an effect on denominational switching (correlating positively with switches to more liberal denominations), the net effect in the 1960s, Wuthnow (1988) showed, was to increase educational attainment in all denominations. This overall increase in education created a liberal/conservative divide within denominations. ·

"[T]he study showed that the public was almost evenly divided between these two camps: 43 percent of those surveyed identified themselves as religious liberals (19 percent as very liberal); 41 percent identified themselves as religious conservatives (18 percent as very conservative); and only 16 percent found it impossible to identify with one or the other of these two labels (Wuthnow 1988, p. 133).

As self-perceived hegemonic moral arbiters, the liberal denominations became more and more closely associated with the problems facing the nation. The liberal-conservative divide was sharpened by reactions to the moral crises of the 1960s. In the civil rights movement and the anti-Vietnam war movement, the highly-educated liberal clergy became especially active, whereas they had been merely vocal on social issues in the previous decade. This activity accentuated clergy differences from their more moderate congregations, and challenged the traditional separation of church and state. The space in the middle abandoned by the clergy on the liberal extreme was left open, to be filled by evangelical coalitions that had been growing in strength since the 1940s.

When the national moral crises of the Vietnam war and Watergate had passed, and Jimmy Carter, one of their own, was elected to the White House, religious conservatives were organized and prepared to lead in a new direction. This direction lay not in door-to-door proselytizing to gather people into congregations, but in using the mass media, direct marketing techniques and special interest groups that had been developed in the 1960s to promulgate the conservative message. If American religious culture had changed, or rather if conservative religionists were more successful in making theirs become the predominant message heard in society, Wuthnow argued, it is because they were better organized and more capable of mobilizing resources.

In summary, the latest period in religious history in the United States has inspired a number of dynamic structural accounts which, after the fragmentation of the 1960s and 1970s, return attention to broad religious groupings and consider social and cultural forces that affect the religiosity of broad segments of the population. Research showed a marked shift from micro-level studies of how religion is meaningful in individuals' or groups' lives to how religion responds to large-scale historical changes. An important element in this shift was the consideration of historical studies by sociologists, which encouraged them to look for larger scale and longer term changes. In Warner's case, it inspired the proposal of a sort of cultural logic which constrains and motivates religious changes along certain general lines. For Wuthnow and Roof and McKinney, it inspired them to look to social changes, ultimately at the level of the global economy, which affect culture and religion. No single method characterizes work in this most recent phase: Historiography, ethnography, and statistical analysis all have been important.

CONCLUSION

To carry forward the metaphor suggested in the introduction, we can see the development of the sociology of American religion as a river that splits into channels as it enters an alluvial plain. In conclusion we may look around to see what channels have been cut and whether they might again converge further downstream.

At the beginning of the century Weber provided a unified vision of the function of religion for individuals and societies: Religious innovators create worldviews that make sense of the world they experience. Differences in the worlds that social status groups experience—not only across societies but across history—lead these groups to have elective affinities for different plans of salvation. Lower status sectarians are concerned with personal salvation out of the world while upper status church members are concerned to legitimate the status quo. These soteriological differences are correlated with organizational differences in religious groups and with different approaches to practical worldly activity. Approaches to worldly activity (always at least partly determined by religious interpretations of the world) have an effect on the patterning of social activities across societies as wholes. Research on American religion in the first half of the century explored and elaborated on these issues by working on the relationship between sects and churches.

In the post-World War II years the study of religious differences within society was largely abandoned for a focus, stimulated by Parsons' integration of Weber and Durkheim, on how religious values provide the basis for social integration across society as a whole. In a sense, this move split Weber's total vision to emphasize only the "church" mode appropriate to the dominant status groups. This came at a point in history when the dominant middle class seemed to include, or would soon include, all members of American society, and religious groups were themselves celebrating the dominant culture and joining forces in ecumenical movements.

In the third period new religious movements threw the discipline into confusion, making room for new paradigms to arise, but also shifting emphasis to studies of sectarian religion, which had been all but forgotten in the previous phase. By and large the field took a turn toward studying the subjective aspects of religious belief and practice at the micro-level, paying attention to how religion is meaningful in people's everyday lives.

In the final period, with a new version of the church-sect dichotomy arising, there has been a return to Weber's motivating questions about historical dynamics and large scale changes in political economy. Social class has more or less dropped out of the equation, its closest analog being differences in education levels. The organizational differences between church and sect that were so important to Weber and his followers have become very much confused, with "sectarian" or "conservative" groups trying to transform the institutional churches from within. Attitudes toward society are also considerably different from Weber's ideal types. The conservatives are not retreating from the world to find compensation in another, but are often struggling for (or against) social changes. If anything, they have been more vocal and uncompromising on social issues than liberals were in previous decades.

Looking up form the channels we have been following we may ask what the prospects are for a convergence of the broad Weberian themes that have been separated over the course of the century. What are the prospects for uniting Weber's macro level questions of the structure of political economy and historical dynamics, with his meso-level questions of institutional differences, and his micro-level questions of the different class-or status-based subjective experiences of individuals? Promising work is currently being done in the sociology of religion and the sociology of culture more generally to unite these questions.

Warner (1993) proposes that a "new paradigm" is shaping up in the sociology of religion. In essence, this paradigm consists of seeing religious groups in America as participating in vigorous free market competition. Berger (1967) first proposed analysis in these terms, and others have taken it up in a more thorough-going fashion (e.g., Finke and Stark 1992; Iannaccone 1988; Stark and Bainbridge 1985). While the pluralism and freedom of American religion has long been recognized as leading to religious vigor (Moberg 1962, p. 89), what is new is a rather straightforward adoption of economic principles to study religious markets, entrepreneurs, competition, and so on. In this market situation, Warner asserts, religious groups are free to divide along ethnic, gender, regional and status lines, thus providing a sense of community and identity in a fragmented and anomic society. Adopting this paradigm unites some of Weber's concerns because self-identity and status characteristics can be linked to religion. The economic model also provides a uniform analytic account of religious and other social institutions. Weber had a similar concern, but his approach was not reductive to economistic utility maximization—other rationalities were possible. His ideal types of authority (legal, traditional, charismatic) and of collectivity (communal, associational) could be applied to religious organizations as well as businesses or states.

A central problem with Warner's "new paradigm" is that it is more or less content free—there is no basis for knowing why *particular* religious conceptions of the world would appeal to different groups. Another problem this paradigm will have to confront is the "as if" status of the economic model on which it is based. Logically, the economic free market model is an ideal-typical construction just as much as church and sect were (Weber 1949 [1904], pp. 89-90). Presuppositions of the economic model and its fit with reality have been under attack by sociologists since at least the time of Weber, and these attacks are likely to persist (e.g., Powell and DiMaggio 1991). Despite these weaknesses, the emerging paradigm Warner points to is promising for its synthetic qualities.

Wuthnow's recent works (1987, 1989) deal with similar institutional questions with a model that incorporates the specificity of meaning systems with more success. To account for macro-level shifts in cultural models of the world, Wuthnow suggests that a population ecology model be applied to the realm of culture. As in the process of speciation, a period of environmental change, including for example economic, political, technological, or structural changes, opens up room for the creation of new ideas and variations on old ones. However, social change in itself may not be sufficient to create new variants that can gain a viable foothold. Generally an expansion of available resources, like opening up new ecological niches, is necessary to support new variations (Wuthnow 1989). These new ideas then compete for adherents and other resources. Some succeed while other die out. This selection marks the start of a process of institutionalization, or adjustment to a niche (cf. Weber's routinization of charisma).

The link of the macro to the micro level in Wuthnow's model takes place at two moments, in the generation of new ideas by movement leaders and in their adoption by followers. In the first moment, the social context for the generation of new moral ideas defines what issues leaders see as problems, and resource distributions among movements help define symbolic oppositions that give a movement identity. These issues and oppositions become elaborated in the movement's discourse, constituting its "social horizon," along with idealized responses, action sequences, or "figural actions." Second, in the selection process individuals come to identify with the problems and oppositions identified in movement discourse and to see the movement's figural actions as applicable in the context of their everyday lives. The movement thus gains adherents and mobilizes them to action. The notion of figural action and a focus on movement discourse retains an emphasis on the meaningfulness of symbols and rituals without appealing to amorphous values or psychological propensities. Linking figural actions to social contexts allows social structural, demographic, and economic factors to be linked with culture. Basing the theoretical model on population ecology allows linkages with other scientific disciplines.

Wuthnow's perspective reunites many of Weber's concerns about the historical creation and transformation of meaning systems at a comparative level across societies and across history (Wuthnow 1989). Wuthnow's notion of social horizon and figural action may also be helpful in regard to different elective affinities for meaning systems among groups within society. His more recent work (1991) is concerned with why individuals choose to orient their actions around particular "stories" (another term for "discourse" that is more accessible to readers). Here let me suggest how his paradigm might be extended to help with the church-sect problem complex as it has developed in the last decade.

Wuthnow (1988) and others have found liberals and conservatives to be most strongly differentiated in regard to educational attainment. Since relative deprivation theories were blasted in the 1970s, the lower education levels of conservatives have been seen, following Hofstadter (1963), as an index of the distance from the forces of "modernity" and modern rationalism. But if education is the only status variable to the emphasized recently, it is one of considerable importance (cf. Blau and Duncan 1967; Collins 1979), especially following the equal opportunity legislation of recent decades. If we follow Weber's definition of class as based on differences in what individuals and groups can offer on the market (Weber 1946, pp. 180-195), then those with educational credentials stand in a different class position from those without, a class position that gives them more choices of lifestyles. These relative differences in the range of choices available may be related to the problems identified and figural actions specified by conservative and liberal religious groups.

Conservative religious groups stress making the *right* choice in conversion: Deciding to learn and follow God's will rather than following the individualistic subjectivism of the modern world (Marsden 1980). If those with fewer educational credentials have fewer choices of lifestyle, then choosing to follow God's will rather than go against it may resonate strongly with their subjective experience. The figural action of diligent labor and acceptance of suffering common to many sectarian religious groups (Ammerman 1987; Beckford 1975; Johnson 1961; Thompson 1963) may improve one's competitive life chances by linking a symbolic rejection of the social system to acceptance of its demands in practice (e.g., the hippy converts in Tipton [1982] and Warner [1988]).

This linkage between subjective experience and figural actions in conservative religion is not restricted to particular class or status groups, despite its probabilistic association with less privileged groups. The wider availability of higher education in the 1960s and 1970s encouraged young people to believe that anything was possible, and that self-expression was the ideal. But the higher proportion of college graduates in the population increased competition for jobs that required a degree (Bell 1976). For almost all groups the economic transformations and dislocations of the 1970s and 1980s further closed down life choices. The lack of choices and the need for personal discipline resulting from *social structural* changes thus may have created affinities for conservative religion in the last several decades.

Liberal or collectivist religious groups are less sure about what the right choices are because they realize (since Schleiermacher's hermeneutics were adopted, see Berger 1979) that historical social configurations shape both phenomenal experience and the interpretation of that experience. Differences in human suffering are not a product of deviance from God's will but of social differentiation and exclusion, which can be mitigated by creating an inclusive and just community. This leads liberals to emphasize figural actions of charity, social outreach, and changing the historical and social contexts that lead to individual suffering. This perspective may be attractive to the more highly educated because they can legitimate the relatively greater choices available to them as due to the structure of society, accidents of fate, and life-directing choices they made which others did not. Since everyone is constrained by these forces, individuals are not sinful just because of the status they may have attained. On the contrary, higher status occupations may be legitimated as a means of serving the community by reducing the suffering of others. Higher education may also create an elective affinity for liberal social engineering because it is compatible with a desacralized scientific or technocratic worldview.

In terms of historical conjunctions that may foster a liberal perspective on a wide scale, the most important may be the apparent bankruptcy of theodicies that suggest that individuals can change their own circumstances. The New Deal grew out of dissatisfaction with Hoover's moralistic individualism as a response to the Depression, just as a recent liberal reconsideration has followed more than a decade of trying to solve social problems by means of individualistic trickle-down economics. The liberal Protestant euphoria of the 1950's, like Galbraith's (1958) *Affluent Society*, was a celebration that the American Way of Life was succeeding in bringing happiness to all. When the limits to success were noticed in the early 1960s, educated liberals worked all the harder to change society, while others decided that their fate was not in human hands, but in God's.

In interpreting conservative and liberal religious perspectives as responses to social conditions I think it is important to point out that, unlike Hunter (1991), I do not see these positions as mutually exclusive or necessarily antagonistic. Liberals can see social structures and history as constraining and still recognize the importance of individual choice. Conservatives recognize structural constraint, though the structures are often a manifestation of God's will. Both individualist and collectivist perspectives are available in many forms in American culture. Recognizing the extremes as ideal types can help us judge the extent to which an individual, group, or period deviates toward one extreme or the other.

Weber's ideal types of church and sect were conceptual constructs that linked social psychological, organizational, and political economic levels of social life. Different phases of research in the sociology of religion in this century have focused in on one or another of these levels. As Weber expected, this has led to a series of changes in, and the eventual abandonment of, church and sect as adequate constructs for making statements about social reality. Weber based his types largely on European history. As sociologists have incorporated the findings of American historians they have been led toward a similar pair of contrasts. As yet there is little consensus about the distinctions between and contents of the categories of "religious liberal" and "religious conservative," though there seems to be agreement that these categories help us understand empirical reality. As we approach the next century, perhaps these categories can be more carefully specified in sociological terms to help us integrate the levels of social reality that concerned Weber.

ACKNOWLEDGMENTS

Work on this paper was supported by a research fellowship from the Center for the Study of American Religion, Princeton University. Thanks to Robert Wuthnow, Gene Burns, Miguel Centeno, participants in Princeton University's Religion and Culture Workshop, and *RSSSR's* reviewers for comments on earlier versions. The author may be contacted at the Department of Sociology, Princeton University, 2-N-2 Green Hall, Princeton, NJ 08544-1010.

NOTES

1.   In this section I am drawing primarily on the section on the sociology of religion from *Economy and Society,* published separately by Beacon Press (Weber 1963). Other works I referred to included Weber (1946, Gerth and Mills' Introduction and Part III), Weber (1930 [1904-1905]) and M.S. Weber (1988).

2.   "Denominations represented in Gaston County fall as follows, in a series ranging from sect type to Church type: Free-Will Baptist Holiness, Pentecostal Holiness, Church of God. Free-Will Baptist, independent tabernacles, Wesleyan Methodist, Baptist, Methodist, Presbyterian, Lutheran, Protestant Episcopal, Roman Catholic" (Pope 1942, p. 124).

3.   The Catholic Charismatic Renewal attracted a great deal of scholarly attention because it conflicted with a number of established theories. It raised the questions: How can an almost ideal-typical sect maintain its linkages to the almost ideal-typical church (Bord & Faulkner 1984; Quebedeaux 1976)? Why should clearly middle-class suburbanites become pentecostals (Neitz 1987)? What are the organizational possibilities of communities based on religious charisma (McGuire 1982)?

4.   Compare Roof and McKinney's groupings to Pope's (see note 2): *Liberal Protestants* (Episcopalian, United Church of Christ, Presbyterians); *Moderate Protestants* (Methodists, Lutherans, Disciples of Christ, Northern Baptists, Reformed); *Black Protestants* (Methodists, Northern Baptists, Southern Baptists); *Conservative Protestants* (Southern Baptists, Churches of Christ, Evangelicals/Fundamentalists, Nazarenes, Pentecostals/Holiness, Assemblies of God, Churches of God, Adventists); *Catholics; Jews; Others* (Mormons, Jehovah's Witnesses, Christian Scientists, Unitarian-Universalists).

REFERENCES

Aberle, D.F. 1962. "A Note on Relative Deprivation Theory as Applied to Millenarian and other Cult Movements." Pp. 209-214 in *Millennial Dreams in Action: Essays in Comparative Studies,* edited by S.L. Thrupp. The Hague: Mouton.

Adorno, T.W., E. Frankel-Brunswik, D.J. Levinson, and N. Sanford. 1950. *The Authoritarian Personality.* New York: Harper Brothers.

Ahlstrom, S.E. 1973. *A Religious History of the American People.* New Haven, CT: Yale University Press.

Ammerman, N.T. 1987. *Bible Believers: Fundamentalists in the Modern World.* New Brunswick, NJ: Rutgers University Press.

Bainbridge, W.S. 1978. *Satan's Power: A Deviant Psychotherapy Cult.* Berkeley: University of California Press.

Barker, E. 1984. *The Making of a Moonie: Choice or Brainwashing?* Oxford: Blackwell.

Barkun, M. 1985, "The Awakening-Cycle Controversy." *Sociological Analysis* 46(4): 415-424.

Becker, H. 1950. *Systematic Sociology: On the Basis of the "Beziehungslehre" and "Gebildelehre" of Leopold von Wiesse.* Gary, IN: Norman Paul Press.

Beckford, J.A. 1975. *The Trumpet of Prophecy: A Sociological Study of the Jehovah's Witnesses.* New York: John Wiley.

_____. 1989. *Religion and Advanced Industrial Society.* London: Unwin Hyman.

Bell, D. 1976. *The Cultural Contradictions of Capitalism.* New York: Ballantine Books.

Bellah, R. 1974[1966]. "Civil Religion in America." Pp. 22-44 in *Civil Religion in America,* edited by R.E. Richey and D.G. Jones, New York: Harper and Row.

Bellah, R.N., and P.E. Hammond. 1980. *Varieties of Civil Religion*. San Francisco: Harper and Row.

Bellah, R.B., R. Madsen, W.M. Sullivan, A. Swindler, and S. Tipton. 1985. *Habits of the Heart: Individualism and Commitment in American Life*. New York: Harper and Row.

Berger, P.L. 1967. *The Sacred Canopy: Elements of a Sociological Theory of Religion*. Garden City, NY: Anchor Doubleday.

_____. 1979. *The Heretical Imperative: Contemporary Possibilities of Religious Affirmation*. Garden City, NY: Anchor Doubleday.

Berger, P.L., and T. Luckmann. 1966. *The Social Construction of Reality: A Treatise in the Sociology of Knowledge*. Garden City, NY: Anchor Doubleday.

Blau, P.M., and O.D. Duncan. 1967. *The American Occupational Structure*. New York: John Wiley.

Bord, R.J., and J.E. Faulkner. 1984. *The Catholic Charismatics: The Anatomy of a Modern Religious Movement*. University Park, PA: Pennsylvania State University Press.

Bruce, S. 1984. *Firm in the Faith: The Survival of Conservative Protestantism*. Aldershot: Gower.

_____. 1988. *The Rise and the Fall of the New Christian Right*. New York: Oxford University Press.

Collins, R. 1979. *The Credential Society*. New York: Academic.

Cross, W.R. 1950. *The Burned-over District: The Social and Intellectual History of Enthusiastic Religion in Western New York. 1800-1850*. Ithaca, NY: Cornell University Press.

Demerath, N.J., III. 1965. *Social Class and American Protestantism*. Chicago: Rand McNally.

_____. 1967. "Comment: In a Sow's Ear." *Journal for the Scientific Study of Religion* 6(1):77-84.

Dittes, J.E. 1971. "Typing the Typologies: Some Parallels in the Career of Church-Sect and Intrinsic-Extrinsic." *Journal for the Scientific Study of Religion* 10(4):375-383.

Dolan, J.P. 1977. *Catholic Revivalism: The American Experience, 1830-1900*. Notre Dame: University of Notre Dame Press.

Douglas, M. 1966. *Purity and Danger: An Analysis of Concepts of Pollution and Taboo*. London: Penguin.

_____. 1973. *Natural Symbols*. Hammondsworth: Penguin.

Durkheim, E. 1915. *The Elementary Forms of the Religious Life*. New York: Basic Books.

Dynes, R.R. 1955. "Church-Sect Typology and Socioeconomic Status." *American Sociological Review* 20(4):555-560.

Eister, A.W. 1967. "Comment: Toward a Radical Critique of Church-Sect Typologizing." *Journal for the Scientific Study of Religion* 6(1):85-90.

Finke, R., and R. Stark. 1992. *The Churching of America, 1776-1990: Winners and Losers in Our Religious Economy*. New Brunswick, NJ: Rutgers University Press.

Galbraith, J.K. 1958. *The Affluent Society*. Boston: Houghton Mifflin.

Geertz, C. 1973[1966]. "Religion as a Cultural System." Pp. 87-125 in *The Interpretation of Cultures*. New York: Basic Books.

Gerlach, L.P., and V.H. Hine. 1970. *People, Power and Change: Movements of Social Transformation*. Indianapolis, IN: Bobbs-Merrill.

Glock, C.Y. 1964. "The Role of Deprivation in the Origin and Evolution of Religious Groups." Pp. 24-36 in *Religion and Social Conflict*, edited by R. Lee and M. Marty. Oxford: Oxford University Press.

Glock, C.Y., and R. Stark. 1966. *Christian Beliefs and Anti-Semitism*. New York: Harper and Row.

Goode, E. 1967. "Some Critical Observations on the Church-Sect Dimension." *Journal for the Scientific Study of Religion* 6(1):69-76.

Greeley, A. 1981. *Religion: A Secular Theory.* New York: Free Press.

Greil, A.L., and D.R. Rudy. 1984. "What have we Learned from Process Models of Conversion?: An Examination of Ten Studies." *Sociological Focus* 17(4):306-323.

Hadden, J., and A. Shupe. 1988. *Televangelism: Power and Politics on God's Frontier.* New York: Henry Holt.

Herberg, W. 1955. *Protestant-Catholic-Jew: An Essay in American Religious Sociology.* New York: Doubleday.

Hofstadter, R. 1963. *Anti-Intellectualism in American Life.* New York: Knopf.

Hoge, D.R. 1976. *Division in the Protestant House: The Basic Reason Behind Intra-Church Conflicts.* Philadelphia: Westminster.

Hoge, D.R., and D.A. Roozen (Eds.) 1979. *Understanding Church Growth and Decline 1950-1978.* New York: Pilgrim Press.

Hunter, J.D. 1983. *American Evangelicalism: Conservative Religion and the Quandary of Modernity.* New Brunswick, NJ: Rutgers University Press.

————. 1991. *Culture Wars: The Struggle to Define America.* New York: Basic Books.

Iannaccone, L.R. 1988. "A Formal Model of Church and Sect." *American Journal of Sociology* 94(supplement):s241-s268.

Johnson, B. 1961. "Do Holiness Sects Socialize to Dominant Values?" *Social Forces* 39:309-316.

————. 1963. "1963. "On Church and Sect." *American Sociological Review* 28:589-599.

————. 1971. "Church and Sect Revisited." *Journal for the Scientific Study of Religion* 10(2):124-137.

Johnson, P.E. 1978. *A Shopkeeper's Millennium: Society and Revivals in Rochester, New York 1815-1837.* New York: Hill and Wang.

Kelley, D.M. 1972. *Why the Conservative Churches are Growing.* New York: Harper and Row.

Kellstedt, L. 1991. "Religious Interest Groups and Political Behavior." *The Evangelical Studies Bulletin* 8(2):6-8.

Lasch, C. 1979. *The Cullture of Narcissism.* New York: Warner.

Lenski, G. 1961. *The Religious Factor: A Sociological Study of Religion's Impact on Politics, Economics and Family Life.* New York: Doubleday.

Levi-Strauss, C. 1963. *Structural Anthropology.* New York: Basic Books.

Liebman, R.C., and R. Wuthnow (Eds.) 1983. *The New Christain Right: Mobilization and Legitimation.* Hawthorne, NY: Aldine.

Lofland, J. 1977[1966]. *Doomsday Cult: A Study of Conversion, Proselytization, and Maintenance of Faith.* New York: Irvington.

Lofland, J., and R. Stark. 1965. "Becoming a World-Saver: A Theory of Conversion to a Deviant Perspective." *American Sociological Review* 30:862-875.

Luckmann, T. 1967. *The Invisible Religion: The Problem of Religion in Modern Society.* New York: McMillan.

Luker, K. 1984. *Abortion and the Politics of Motherhood.* Berkeley: University of California Press.

Marsden, G. 1980. *Fundamentalism and American Culture.* Oxford: Oxford University Press.

Marty, M. 1970. *Righteous Empire: The Protestant Experience in America.* New York: Dial Press.

McGuire, M. 1982. *Pentecostal Catholics: Power, Charisma and Order in a Religious Movement.* Philadelphia: Temple University Press.

————. 1988. *Ritual Healing in Suburban America.* New Brunswick, NJ: Rutgers University Press.

McIntire, C.T. 1984. "Fundamentalism." Pp. 433-436 in *Evangelical Dictionary of Theology,* edited by W.A. Elwell. Grand Rapids, MI: Baker Book House.

McLoughlin, W. 11959. *Modern Revivalism: Charles Grandison Finney to Billy Graham.* New York: Ronald Press.

_____. 1978. *Revivals, Awakenings and Reform: An Essay on Religion and Social Change in America, 1607-1977.* Chicago: University of Chicago Press.

Moberg, D.O. 1962. *The Church as a Social Institution: The Sociology of American Religion.* Englewood Cliffs, NJ: Prentice-Hall.

Neitz, M.J. 1987. *Charisma and Community: A Study of Religious Commitment within the Charismatic Renewal.* New Brunswick, NJ: Transaction Books.

Newport, F. 1978. "The Religious Switcher in the United States." *American Sociological Review* 44(4):528-552.

Niebuhr, H.R. 1929. *The Social Sources of Denominationalism.* New York: Henry Holt.

O'Toole, R. (Ed.) 1983. "Symposium on Religious Awakenings." Special issue of *Sociological Analysis* 44(2):81-122.

Parsons, T. 1949[1937]. *The Structure of Social Action* (2nd ed.). Glencoe, IL: Free Press.

_____. 1963. "Christianity and Modern Industrial Society." Pp. 33-70 in *Sociological Theory, Values, and Sociocullltural Change: Essays in Honor of Pitirim A. Sorokin,* edited by E.A. Tiryakian. Glencoe, IL: Free Press.

_____. 1968. "Commentary on 'Religion as a Cultural System.' " Pp. 688-695 in *The Religious Situation, 1968,* edited by D.L. Cutler. Boston: Beacon.

_____. 1979. "Religious and Economic Symbolism in the Western World." *Sociological Inquiry* 49(2-3):1-48.

Pierard, R.V. 1984. "Evangelicalism." Pp. 379-382 Evangelical Dictionary of Theology, edited by W.A. Elwell. Grand Rapids, MI: Baker Book House.

Pope, L. 1942. *Millhands and Preachers: A Study of Gastonia.* New Haven, CT: Yale University Press.

Powell, W.W., and P.J. DiMaggio (Eds.) 1991. *The New Institutionalism in Organizational Analysis.* Chicago: University of Chicago Press.

Quebedeaux, R. 1976. *The New Charismatics: The Origins, Development, and Significance of Neo-Pentecostalism.* New York: Doubleday.

Reist, B.A. 1966. *Toward a Theology of Involvement: The Thought of Ernst Troeltsch.* Philadelphia: Westminster.

Robbins, T. 1988. *Cults, Converts and Charisma: The Sociology of New Religious Movements.* London: Sage.

Robertson, R. and W.R. Garrett (Eds.). 1991. *Religion and Global Order.* New York: Paragon House.

Roof, W.C. 1978. *Community and Commitment: Religious Plausibility in a Liberal Protestant Church.* New York: Elsevier.

Roof, W.C. and W. McKinney. 1987. *American Mainline Religion: Its Changing Shape and Future.* New Brunswick, NJ: Rutgers University Press.

Schwartz, G. 1970. *Sect Ideologies and Social Status.* Chicago: University of Chicago Press.

Selznick, G.J., and S. Steinberg. 1969. *The Tenacity of Prejudice: Anti-Semitism in Contemporary America.* New York: Harper and Row.

Smith, T.L. 19957. *Revivalism and Social Reform in Mid-Nineteenth Century America.* New York: Abingdon Press.

Stark, R., and W.S. Bainbridge. 1985. *The Future of Religon: Secularization, Revival, and Cult Formation.* Berkeley: University of California Press.

Stark, R., and C.Y. Glock. 1968. *American Piety: The Nature of Religious Commitment.* Berkeley: University of California Press.

Stromberg, P. 1986. *Symbols of Community: The Cultural System of a Swedish Church.* Tucson: University of Arizona Press.

Swatos, W.H., Jr. 1976. "Weber or Troeltsch?: Methodology, Syndrome, and the Development of Church-Sect Theory." *Journal for the Scientific Study of Religion* 15(2):129-144.

Thompson, E.P. 1963. *The Making of the English Working Class.* New York: Vintage Books.

Tipton, S.M. 1982. *Getting Saved From the Sixties: Moral Meaning in Conversion and Cultural Change.* Berkely: University of California Press.

Troeltsch, E. 1931. *The Social Teaching of the Christian Churches* (2 vols.), translated by O. Wyon. New York: MacMillan.

Turner, V. 1967. *The Forest of Symbols: Aspects of Ndembu Ritual.* Ithaca, NY: Cornell University Press.

Wacker, G. 1985. "The Holy Spirit and the Spirit of the Age in American Protestantism, 1880-1910." *Journal of American History* 72(1):45-62.

Wallace, A.F.C. 1956. "Revitalization movements." *American Anthropologist* 58: 264-281.

_____. 1988. *New Wine in Old Wineskins: Evangelicals and Liberals in a Small Town Church.* Berkeley: University of California Press.

Warner, R.S. 1993. "Working in Progress toward a New Paradigm for the Sociological Study of Religion in the United States." *American Journal of Sociology* 98(5)1044-1093.

Watt, D.H. 1991. *A Transforming Faith: Explorations of Twentieth Century Evangelicalism.* New Brunswick, NJ: Rutgers University Press.

Weber, M.S. 1930[1904-5]. *The Protestant Ethic and the Spirit of Capitalism.* London: Unwin Paperbacks.

_____. 1946. *From Max Weber: Essays in Sociology,* translated and edited by H.H. Gerth and C.W. Mills. New York: Oxford University Press.

_____. 1949[1904]. ' "Objectivity' in Social Science and Social Policy." Pp. 49-112 in *The Methodology of the Social Sciences,* edited and translated by E.A. Shils and H.A. Finch, Glencoe, IL: Free Press.

_____. 1963. *Sociology of Religon,* translated by E. Fischoff, edited by T. Parsons. Boston: Beacon.

_____. 1973[1910]. "Weber on Church-Sect and Mysticism." *Sociological Analysis* 34(2):140-149.

_____. 1988. *Max Weber: A Biography,* translated and edited by H. Zohn. New Brunswick, NJ: Transaction Books.

Williams, R. 1951. *American Society: A Sociological Interpretation.* New York: Knopf.

Wilson, B.R. 1959. "An Analysis of Sect Development." *American Sociological Review* 24(1):3-15.

_____. 1961. *Sects and Society: A Sociological Study of the Elim Tabernacle, Christian Science, and Christadelphians.* Berkely: University of California Press.

_____. 1990[1978]. "Becoming a Sectarian: Motivation and Commitment." Pp. 176-200 in *The Social Dimensions of Sectarianism: Sects and New Religious Movements in Contemporary Society.* Oxford: Clarendon.

Wilson, J.F. 1979. *Public Religion in American Culture.* Philadelphia: Temple University Press.

Wuthnow, R. 1976. *The Consciousness Reformation.* Berkeley: University of California Press.

_____. 1978. *Experimentation in American Religion.* Berkeley: University of California Press.

_____. 1987. *Meaning and Moral Order: Explorations in Cultural Analysis.* Berkeley: University of California Press.

_____. 1988. *The Restructuring of American Religion: Society and Faith Since World War II.* Princeton, NJ: Princeton University Press.

_____. 1989. *Communities of Discourse: Ideology and Social Structure in the Reformation, the Enlightenment, and European Socialism.* Cambridge, MA: Harvard University Press.

_____. 1991. *Acts of Compassion: Caring for Others and Helping Ourselves.* Princeton, NJ: Princeton University Press.

_____. 1992. *Rediscovering the Sacred: Perspectives on Religion in Contemporary Society.* Grand Rapids, MI: Eerdmans.

Yinger, J.M. 1957. *Religion, Society and the Individual.* New York: Macmillan.
———. 1970. *The Scientific Study of Religion.* New York: Macmillan.
Zaretsky, I., and M.P. Leone (Eds.) 1974. *Religious Movements in Contemporary America.* Princeton, NJ: Princeton University Press.

"THAT THEY ALL MAY BE ONE":
CAN DENOMINATIONALISM DIE?

André Nauta

ABSTRACT

This article examines the premise that denominationalism in America must continue because a "critical number" of denominations must exist in order to meet the diverse spiritual, emotional, psychological, and social needs of a pluralistic society. The premise is examined from a religious economies perspective, with the primary focus on the occurrences and explanations of denominational schisms and mergers. It is argued that an excessive number of mergers leads to too little diversity in the religious "products" being offered, while too many schisms results in religious organizations duplicating services. Thus, as long as religious freedom exists in America, the diversity of religious products will also persist.

The study of religion in the United States is somewhat unique from that in other countries of the world, in no small part due to the denominational nature of American Protestantism. Niebuhr (1957[1929]) attempted to explain how this denominationalism occurred by focusing on four social factors that

Research in the Social Scientific Study of Religion, Volume 6, pages 35-51.
Copyright © 1994 by JAI Press Inc.
All rights of reproduction in any form reserved.
ISBN: 1-55938-762-9

he believed led to the formation and growth of denominations. Thus, he posited the impact of race, ethnicity, social class and regionalism on the religious makeup of American society.

More recently, some have shifted to the use of economic models (Finke 1990; Finke and Iannaccone 1993; Finke and Stark 1988, 1989, 1991, 1992; Iannaccone 1991, 1992). The terms "religious markets" and "religious economies" are used, along with other economic concepts, to describe the changing face of American religion. These studies deal with religion as a product, produced by a variety of organizations (the "supply side"), in order to meet the needs of a variety of groups (the "demand side").

This article focuses on the changes brought about by recent mergers of some U.S. denominations, particularly in the last three decades. Using a religious economies approach, the question is raised as to whether these mergers represent a fundamental shift toward a continued unification of American Protestantism. Particular emphasis is placed on explaining why mergers (as well as schisms) occur, from the perspective of a religious marketplace. The premise to be argued is that a "critical number" of denominations must exist in any pluralistic society, such as the United States. This critical number represents the minimum number of denominations necessary to meet the diverse spiritual, emotional, psychological, and social needs of a pluralistic society. It may also represent a maximum number of denominations, beyond which there is too much competition for the same "consumers." If this is an accurate depiction of the American religious marketplace, then denomination-alism in the United States is likely to remain strong.

THE RELIGIOUS ECONOMIES APPROACH

The religious economies model makes extensive use of the terminology of economics. Iannaccone (1992) makes note of the fact that many are quick to see this as a passing fad, resulting from a materialistic age in which the language of economics is applied to a variety of situations. He argues that this is not a fad, that it is instead an approach that "offers a new paradigm in the sociology of religion" (Iannaccone 1992, p. 123). The dominant feature of this approach is the consideration of the individual as a religious "consumer," attempting to maximize profit by weighing the anticipated costs and benefits of a religious choice. The assumption is that individuals approach the choosing of a religious affiliation in much the same way that they would choose any other product. They seek out the religious organization that produces the product they feel most meets their needs.

Such an approach presumes a high degree of religious freedom, such that the individual feels free to choose a religious affiliation without fear of being punished for that choice. Stark and Bainbridge (1987, p. 147) make note of this fact with the proposition that "the greater the degree of coercion the external society imposes on religious deviance, the weaker the tendency for deviant religious organizations to form."

Historically, a high degree of religious freedom was not the case in the United States. In fact, the immigrants who came to the colonies to escape religious persecution did not necessarily want religious freedom for all (Finke 1990; Finke and Iannaccone 1993). On the contrary, "the various groups of religious immigrants sought to create enclaves in which their own religion, such as Puritan Congregationalism, enjoyed preeminent status" (Finke and Iannaccone 1993, p. 29). Most of the colonies had their own established church, one that received direct support from the government through tax revenues and positions of authority, and indirect support through persecution of those of dissenting faiths (Mead 1956). For a variety of reasons, the situation changed; first to religious toleration, and finally (with the adoption of the Bill of Rights and the signing of the Constitution) to religious freedom (Finke 1990; Finke and Iannaccone 1993; Mead 1956). Gaustad (1987) refers to the time between the Declaration of Independence in 1776 and the deaths of Thomas Jefferson and John Adams in 1826 as "years of momentous option and crucial decision" (p. 1), a period of time in which many questions were raised regarding the relationship of church and state.

The choice for religious freedom was indeed "momentous." Finke (1990) notes that there are a variety of consequences of this new freedom for the individual, for the religious organization, and for the religious market. At the individual level, deregulation of the market meant: (1) that each person had the freedom to choose a religious affiliation, (2) that the cost of joining a "dissenting faith" would not be inflated because of persecution and loss of privileges; and (3) that the individual became more active in the support and operation of the church. For religious organizations, deregulation meant: (1) that they had to rely on the resources of their adherents, rather than on the state, to survive, (2) that all religious organizations were free of persecution, with no one group receiving special privileges, and (3) that religious institutions and government institutions were now separate entities. Finally, the consequences for the religious market were: (1) an abolishing of regulatory agencies for religion, which was especially beneficial to new religious groups, (2) an increase in both religious diversity and competition, and (3) an increase in the level of religious mobilization (or adherence).

This last consequence contradicts the widely held belief that religious pluralism and competition in cities is a threat to the continued existence of religion (Berger 1967, 1979; Durkheim 1951[1897]). Finke and Stark (1988) are in agreement with Berger that pluralism forces religious organizations to compete; however, they "view competition as a stimulus for religious growth and not an avenue for its demise" (p. 42). They go on to show, using U.S. Census data from 1910, that religious diversity has a positive impact on the rate of adherents. Historical evidence also shows an increase in adherence rates nationally, with 17 percent adherence in 1776, 37 percent in 1860, 45 percent in 1890, 58 percent in 1926, and 62 percent in 1980 (Finke 1990, p. 623). Thus, the evidence indicates that religious pluralism, and the competition that results, is beneficial in maintaining the existence of religion.

Much of the preceding discussion focuses on the "supply side" of the religious marketplace. Finke and Iannaccone (1993) argue that this aspect of the religious economies approach is often neglected; that typical explanations for changes in the religious marketplace focus on the consumers' demand for a religious product. They cite as evidence the explanation of the surge in Asian-style cult membership during the 1960s as being due to a "new religious consciousness." They attribute this surge to the rescinding of the Oriental Exclusion Acts by President Johnson in 1965, resulting in a jump in the supply of Asian teachers. They conclude that "it was not so much that Eastern faiths had struck a new chord in the American counterculture as that their growth had been artificially thwarted until then" (Finke and Iannaccone 1993, p. 37).

It would be a mistake, however, to conclude that one should focus only (or primarily) on the "supply side" of the picture, for the increased supply of a product does not guarantee an increase in demand. Deregulation may have opened up the possibility of new products being offered, or old products being more accessible, but it is still the choice of the religious consumer as to whether to "buy" the product.

The "demand side" of the religious marketplace consists of the needs of the religious consumer. Niebuhr's (1957[1929]) work, while looking at social sources of denominationalism (a seemingly supply-side issue), provides one means of examining the demand side of the religious economy. His concept of regionalism explains why certain churches thrived in the new frontier, while others faltered. He suggests it is the individualism that was so pronounced in the frontier, due to the overwhelming need to simply survive under rugged conditions, that determined whether a religion would flourish or not. In contrast, the eastern U.S. housed a culture characterized by affluence, with very little emphasis on survival. Finke and Stark (1989, 1992) note how these different needs shaped the approach of the religious suppliers, such that those denominations that were most successful in the frontier (Baptists and Methodists) had a more congregational polity and ministers who were uneducated (like the people they served), unpaid (or paid very little), farmers serving as part-time preachers. These denominations recognized the different viewpoint of the frontier people, and were able to provide a product suitable for their religious needs. In addition, Niebuhr (1957[1929]) notes that the frontier people were largely unbound from prior commitments to a religious organization. They were free to choose a church in a society that allowed them a variety of choices.

Wallace (1975) also examines the demand side of the religious marketplace, focusing on the ways that religious affiliation fills a deficiency in the lives of individuals. Her study considers four hypotheses, each pertaining to a different religious motivation. Nauta (1991) summarizes these four motivations as: (1) a need for meaning, (2) a need for social support, (3) a need for goal attainment, and (4) a need for escape. Each of these needs is emphasized (or de-emphasized) differently by the religious denominations, thus providing a variety of religious experiences suitable for a diverse population.

Religious needs are also considered by Moberg (1984) in the context of considering the functions of religious activities. He notes that the manifest function of worship is the praise and adoration of God. However, a latent function of worship is meeting human needs. Moberg (1984) states that:

> God is often worshipped in the hope or faith that man's needs will therefore be met more easily and surely, that the lot of man on earth will be lightened, that his prospect in the present and the future life will be bright.... Worship for many people is partly or wholly homocentric. We worship God to serve human needs.... (p. 161)

His subsequent discussion of the variety of social, recreational, aesthetic, economic, and ethical-moral functions of religious bodies offers insight into the variety of needs humans have that are satisfied within the context of religious affiliation. The church provides the individual a way of determining the will of God, experiencing fellowship with God, a sense of security, meaning for life, as well as many other needs.[1]

It is also possible that a demand can be "created" by charismatic leaders who appeal to the needs of disgruntled followers within a particular denomination. Moberg (1984, p. 96) notes such examples as Father Divine's Peace Mission and the International Church of the Foursquare Gospel (founded by Aimee Semple McPherson). More recently, the Branch Davidian sect came out of the Seventh-day Adventist church due to the charisma of David Koresh. These examples indicate the ability of the charismatic leader to capitalize on a demand not being met by creating a new religious group (i.e., adding to the supply side of the marketplace).

What exists in the religious marketplace of America is a variety of religious bodies that to some extent attempt to meet religious needs. It would be difficult at best (perhaps impossible) for one religious group to satisfy all the needs of all people. A variety of religious organizations, each focusing on one need (or a few needs), while not totally ignoring the other needs of members, provides individuals in American society with religious options from which to choose. Moberg (1984) notes that the relative strength of religion in our society compared to most European countries is likely due in great part to this variety of options: "The individual's opportunity to find a religious group he likes is much greater when there are fifty or more distinct groups to choose from than it is when an established church dominates the entire religious scene" (pp. 88-89).

Thus, we have a situation in which religious organizations, because of the deregulation of religion in the United States, operate to satisfy particular demands on the part of the consumers. Given this situation, I now examine the main premise of this article; that a critical number of denominations must exist in order to meet the diversity of religious needs of the population. This "critical number" may represent both the minimum and maximum number of denominations needed, with the actual number fluctuating above and below this number. In order to examine this premise, I will begin by considering the circumstances that lead to schisms and mergers among American Protestant denominations, followed by a discussion based on the religious economies approach.

SCHISMS AND MERGERS IN AMERICAN PROTESTANTISM[2]

American history is rife with examples of denominations splitting for a variety of reasons. Niebuhr (1957[1929]) noted the impact of differences in culture between the northern and southern U.S. in the breakup of several denominations prior to or during the Civil War. These splits were not simply the result of a dispute over slavery, but were due to cultural and economic differences that existed between the primarily industrial northern states and the primarily agricultural southern states. The slavery issue provided a symbolic context within which these differences could be expressed.

At least four denominations (the Christian Church, the Presbyterian Church in the U.S., the Associate Reformed Presbyterian Church, and the Methodist Episcopal Church) were produced by regionalistic schisms during the 1800s. In addition, although Baptists did not form denominations as such, the cooperative efforts in missionary societies and in tract publishing were also discontinued due to the regionalistic dispute. Goen (1985) provides a detailed summary of how the dispute over whether missionaries could be slave owners eventually led to the creation of the Southern Baptist Convention as a separate organization from the Northern Baptists.

In addition to schisms caused by regional issues, Niebuhr (1957[1929]) indicates that race also has played a role. One example of a racially motivated schism is that which produced the African Methodist Episcopal Church. This denomination split from the Methodist Episcopal Church in 1816 not because of heresy or doctrinal dispute, but because of racial problems. During the time before the split, blacks were treated as second-class members, who were often required to sit in the balcony—apart from the white members, who sat below. Because black leaders in the church were unable to change this policy, the only options were to tolerate the situation or to leave the denomination and form a new church for the black members.

The preceding paragraphs should not be misconstrued as implying that all schisms are motivated by nontheological problems. Certainly the issues of slavery and discrimination are important from a theological/doctrinal point of view. In addition, other schisms have occurred primarily because of doctrinal issues. The formation of the Association of Evangelical Lutheran Churches (AELC) as a separate group from the Lutheran Church-Missouri Synod in 1976 is one example. Wuthnow (1988) notes that this split resulted "after a conservative faction captured control of the Lutheran Church-Missouri Synod and forced a number of the denomination's liberal seminary professors to resign their positions" (p. 165). The AELC was formed out of the 245 local congregations that opposed these changes.[3]

While such "snapshots" provide some important information regarding schisms, it is also useful to consider the big picture. The work of Sutton, Wuthnow, and Liebman (1988) provides one way of doing so. Their focus is on the effect of prior schisms and prior mergers on the founding rate (measured as the number of schisms occurring during a given decade). They hypothesized, based on population ecology models, availability of resources, and level of competition, that the relationship between prior foundings (number of denominational schisms reported in the previous ten years) and founding rates would exhibit an inverted U-shaped association. In other words, they believed that an increasing number of schisms in one decade would increase the founding rate in the following decade until the increased competition among denominations would drive the founding rate down. (I will consider the relationship of prior mergers to the founding rate later in this section.)

In contrast to the hypothesis, Sutton et al. (1988) found that prior schisms had a U-shaped association with founding rates. They conclude that

> Schisms are the product of intradenominational conflict; they may, in addition, reflect tensions that affect groups or networks of denominations, or perhaps all Protestant denominations at once. The occurrence of a few schisms might ameliorate these tensions, allowing grievances to be articulated and inviting members to sort themselves out among new organizations. At some point, however, perhaps due to exogenous historical events, the tendency to schism might become contagious, leading to a large-scale reorganization of the institutional terrain (Sutton et al. 1988, p. 12).

They argue further that the Protestant Reformation was an early example of this type of phenomenon, that the schisms resulting in the various Protestant denominations took part in an era of reorganization.

Recent Mergers in the Religious Marketplace

Reorganization, however, can also occur through the process of mergers. In the past three decades (1960-1990) there have been a number of mergers involving a significant number of denominations; three of these mergers have involved Lutheran churches. An examination of these mergers is warranted,

paying particular attention to the reasons given by some of the participants
for the organizations coming together.

The United Church of Christ was organized in 1961 by the merging of the
Congregational and Christian Churches with the Evangelical and Reformed
Church. Each of these denominations was formed in the 1930s by prior mergers.
The preamble of the UCC Basis of Union states:

> We, the regularly constituted representatives of the Congregational Christian Churches and
> of the Evangelical and Reformed Church, moved by the conviction that we are united in
> spirit and purpose and are in agreement on the substance of the Christian faith and the
> essential character of the Christian life;...Confronting the divisions and hostilities of our
> world, and hearing with a deepened sense of responsibility the prayer of our Lord 'that
> they all may be one'; Do now declare ourselves to be one body....(Gunnemann 1977, p.
> 207)

Gunnemann notes that if there was a single event that began the merger
movement, it was the formation of a study group of ministers from the two
denominations in St. Louis in 1937. Their meetings "led to the recognition of
common bonds and responsibilities" (Gunnemann, 1977, p. 21).

Seven years later the United Methodist Church was organized by the merging
of the Methodist Church (1939-1968) and the Evangelical United Brethren.
Each of these churches was also the product of a prior merger. This merger
was basically a "reunion" of the three main schismatic groups from the
Methodist Episcopal Church.

Washburn (1984) was a participant in the unity talks. He indicates that the
Commissions on Church Union first met jointly in 1958, and that they:

> ...listed nine reasons why union should be pursued: 1) union is God's will for the
> churches; 2) theological positions are alike; 3) emphasis on human dignity and social
> action is similar; 4) histories run along parallel lines; 5) common terminology is used
> in polity; 6) more effective ministerial education programs could be conducted; 7)
> petitions for union with the Methodist Church were submitted by Evangelical United
> Brethren Conferences in Illinois and Kansas; 8) there are potential economies in
> administrative costs; and 9) there could be a possible strengthening of witness and mission
> (Washburn, 1984, pp. 64-65).

The Presbyterian Church (USA) was organized in 1983 by the merging of
the Presbyterian Church in the United States (PCUS) with the United
Presbyterian Church in the USA (UPC). This merger was, in a sense, a reunion
of the split caused by regional differences during the Civil War era.

The primary reason for the merger of these two denominations was an easing
of potential tensions between the southern group (PCUS) and the northern
group (UPC). Loetscher (1983) notes that "in the twentieth century, the South
has moved increasingly into the mainstream of American national life and
power, and was swept by the same forces of theological and social innovation,

[and as a result] differences between Northern and Southern churches noticeably decreased" (p. 123).

The most recent denomination to be formed by a merger is the Evangelical Lutheran Church in America (ELCA). In 1988 the ELCA was formed from three groups: The American Lutheran Church (ALC), the Lutheran Church in America (LCA), and the Association of Evangelical Lutheran Churches (AELC). The formation of the AELC was noted earlier in this section. The ALC and LCA mergers resulted from a reduction in the importance of ethnicity as a divisive factor. Nichol (1986) notes that Lutherans "discovered that old differences of nationality, chronology, and geography were not so divisive among a people increasingly at home in America" (p. 19). The ethnic churches had formed because of the desire of immigrants to worship in their native tongues. With English as a common language, the language barrier that had hindered these churches from merging was removed.

The reasons for the ELCA merger can be found in various writings. The faculty of Trinity Lutheran Seminary (1981) endorsed a statement favoring the merger that included the following:

> We Lutherans must become—if we are not already—painfully aware of the negative witness which we constantly give because of our organizational disunity ... We expend inordinate time and energy in coordinating enterprises which ought to be one ... some form of maximal organizational unity is imperative as soon as it can be effected (p. 23).

Dr. James R. Crumley, Jr. (1981) concurs when he states:

> ...the church needs to keep its priorities straight. To serve the world and maintain the faith of its people, worship, evangelism, teaching, serving and stewardship will continue to be of the highest importance for the church.... Maintaining our separate organizations could serve as a detriment to our task of strengthening each other and serving our fellow human beings.... For the sake of God's mission and to carry out our ministry in the world, it seems clear to me that a united church would be a far more appropriate instrument than one that is divided (p. 23).

Moving once again to a consideration of the big picture, it is useful to look at the second part of the study by Sutton et al. (1988). They hypothesized that prior mergers would have a U-shaped association with founding rate. It was expected that increasing numbers of prior mergers would lower the founding rate to a point at which the lower number of competitors would increase the probability of schisms.

As with the previous finding regarding prior schisms and the founding rate, the actual relationship was opposite that hypothesized—an inverted U-shape. Sutton et al. (1988, p. 13) posit that:

within denominations, mergers are likely to create pockets of discontent among members suffering the loss of a familiar denominational identity. Across denominations, a wave of mergers would reduce the number of relocation options available to discontented members, and might thereby increase the likelihood that insurgent groups will strike out on their own and establish new organizational structures. The subsequent decline in the effect of prior mergers suggests that at some point the founding of new denominations meets the demand for relocation options.

Having considered some anecdotal evidence regarding schisms and mergers, I now examine these cases using a religious economies approach. Particular emphasis will be placed on the commonalities of the various accounts, as well as on the differences that I believe exist in the reasons given for why schisms and mergers occur. I will then present my argument in support of the premise that a "critical number" of denominations must exist in the United States, and that significant deviation above or below this number is unlikely to continue for an extended period of time.

SCHISMS, MERGERS, AND THE RELIGIOUS MARKETPLACE

When one looks at the various accounts of schisms and mergers summarized above, it is difficult to see what commonalities exist, since the reasons given for these changes appear to defy generalization. However, I believe that the religious economies approach does offer one means to make sense of these diverse stories.

Schisms Reconsidered

Looking first at the schisms, one sees several churches broke apart for geopolitical reasons, another for primarily racial reasons, and yet another for theological/doctrinal reasons. The common feature of these accounts is that the denomination's stand on a given issue led to problems with those who did not agree with the denomination. In essence, the precipitating factor leading to the schism was a change in the religious needs of a major part of the denomination, along with "a refusal by one or more factions to change when most of the denomination shifted."[4]

Consider again the case of the split between northern and southern Baptists. Both antislavery northerners and proslavery southerners attempted to have the General Missionary Convention support their point of view (Goen 1985). As late as April 1844 the General Convention made every attempt to remain neutral, neither supporting nor condemning slavery. However, in November of 1844 Alabama Baptists addressed a resolution to the Acting Board of the General Convention (the executive committee that oversaw the work between the triennial meetings). They demanded that the Board explicitly avow that slave holders were equally eligible and entitled to be appointed as missionaries. While the Board attempted to evade the issue, they were finally forced to declare:

> ...if, however, any one should offer himself as a missionary, having slaves, and should insist on retaining them as his property, we could not appoint him. One thing is certain, we can never be a party to any arrangement which would imply approbation of slavery (Goen 1985, p. 95).

What is seen here is a need on the part of southern Baptists to have their "right" to own slaves approved by the national Board. It is possible to see this as both a need for social support and for meaning. Southern Baptists wanted to feel that the General Convention approved of their choice to support slave owners as potential missionaries. In a sense, the owning of slaves could be seen as reflecting a particular world-and-life-view, one in which blacks were seen as subhuman and not image bearers of God. The decision of the Board clearly challenged this view, thereby making it difficult for southern Baptists to be a part of the missionary society. The Southern Baptist Convention, formed in May of 1845, provided a new organizational format to supply the needs of those who supported slavery.

A similar analysis can be made of the schism of the Methodist Episcopal Church (MEC) in 1816. Although the issue here was racism, with black worshippers being treated less favorably than their white counterparts, the essential needs were much the same as for the Baptists. Blacks in the MEC needed to have the social support of the church on the issue of racial equality, not simply because of a need to feel welcome in their local congregations, but because accepting less would have been to accept a world-and-life-view that considered them as lesser beings in the eyes of God. Being unable to change the churches' position on the issue, they created a new denomination to meet these needs for black worshippers.

The breakup of the Missouri Synod Lutherans in 1976 can also be seen in this way. When the denomination was "taken over" by conservatives who forced liberal professors in the seminary to resign, a threat was perceived by those in the church whose views were in concordance with those liberals. It was not simply a protest of these "resignations" that spurred the split, but more so a recognition that the denomination would not accept the views these professors espoused, views that a significant number of adherents found compelling. Given the fact that their views were not going to be recognized as legitimate, they felt the need to create a denomination that would accept their "liberal" point of view.

The thing that these accounts have in common is that there was a discrepancy between the needs of some of the denomination's adherents and the ability (or willingness) of the denomination to meet those needs. In these cases, it appears that schisms arise primarily as a result of a change in demand on the part of some consumers within the denomination, a change that the denomination cannot or will not meet. As a result, the demand must be met by the creation of a new religious organization, one that is able to supply the needs of those consumers. Thus, the anecdotal evidence indicates a change in religious "demand" preceding a change in the religious "supply."

The study by Sutton et al. (1988) offers further support for such an argument. Recall that they found, in contrast to their hypothesis, that prior schisms had a U-shaped association with founding rate. One may conclude that the decline in founding rate associated with increasing numbers of prior schisms (to a certain point) is representative of the manner in which these prior schisms have acted to increase the supply of religious products, meeting the demands of religious consumers. Thus, a moderate number of prior schisms creates enough variety in the religious marketplace that the needs of the consumers are being met, and so fewer foundings occur.

Beyond this moderate level of prior schisms, Sutton et al. (1988) argue that schismatic tendencies become contagious. It may be that the recognition that a substantial number of new schismatic groups in the marketplace that appear to have found a target group of consumers might lead others to see the creation of a new group as a more viable alternative. This suggests that, while schisms appear to be primarily demand driven, the shape of the religious marketplace, in the form of prior schisms (a change in supply), also has a profound impact.

Mergers Reconsidered

The situation for mergers appears to be directly opposite that of schisms. Rather than being driven primarily by demand, mergers seem to be primarily related to supply. In particular, there is a recognition on the part of adherents in two (or more) denominations that their organizations are serving the same type of consumers, that they are offering essentially the same product.

Consider, for example, some of the writings by participants in these mergers, cited earlier in this article. Gunnemann's (1977) quote regarding "common bonds and responsibilities," along with the portion of the *UCC Basis of Union* which reads that they were "moved by the conviction that we are united in spirit and purpose and are in agreement on the substance of the Christian faith and the essential character of Christian life" (Gunnemann 1977, p. 207), reveals that those involved in the formation of the United Church of Christ were well aware that they served the same consumer needs.

Similar kinds of positions were taken by participants in the other mergers discussed earlier. Of the nine reasons cited by Washburn (1984) for why the UMC union was pursued, several reflect the emphasis on commonalities: "...Theological positions are alike; emphasis on human dignity and social action is similar; common terminology is used in polity" (pp. 64-65).

The Lutheran mergers were also supported using a similar approach. This is particularly evident in Nichol's (1986) statement regarding the reduction in importance of ethnic differences in facilitating the mergers that formed the ALC and LCA denominations. Since these churches used English in worship services, rather than the language of their ancestors, there was a commonality that did not exist before. Crumley's (1981) statement that separate organizations were detrimental indicates a recognition that the general needs served by the separate organizations were similar enough that a single organization would be more effective (see previous discussion of ELCA merger).

Unfortunately, the study by Sutton et al. (1988) does not look at the merger rate to determine whether prior mergers have any effect on merger rate. Therefore, it isn't possible to directly relate their study to the present thesis. However, one might infer from the fact that prior mergers tend to increase the founding rate (up to a certain point), that the impact on merger rate would therefore be negative (a U-shaped curve). From a religious economies perspective this would make sense, since a certain number of mergers would act to limit duplication in the marketplace, thus making further mergers less likely.

The conclusion one can draw from the preceding discussion is that schisms and mergers appear to be driven by different aspects of the religious economy. Schisms are primarily the result of changing demands on the part of consumers, such that a new producer is established to meet these demands. Mergers, on the other hand, are primarily supply motivated. They occur when there is a recognition that two or more organizations are offering a similar religious product, along with the recognition that there is more to be gained by joining together than is lost, that staying apart results in a less effective ministry.[5]

A CRITICAL NUMBER OF DENOMINATIONS?

Taking into account the evidence presented regarding the religious marketplace, I am led to conclude that a critical number of denominations must be present in the United States in order to serve the needs of consumers. Several factors lead me to this conclusion.

First, one must acknowledge the great diversity of the U.S. population. We are a people with a wide variety of ethnic and national backgrounds. The diversity of backgrounds, along with such variables as race, social class, and education, imply a variety of needs to be satisfied by religious organizations. It would be unreasonable to expect that any one religious group (or even a few select groups) could meet these needs for all people. For example, those of lower social status tend to seek out churches that emphasize other-worldly goals (getting to heaven) and that provide a way to understand and gain meaning for the injustices they suffer in this world. Those of higher socioeconomic status are attracted to churches that emphasize inner-worldly goals (worldly accomplishment), churches that provide a justification for their higher status while others suffer (Nauta 1991). It would be difficult, at best, for any one organization to provide such diverse products to very different consumers. Considering the other factors involved, it is clear that some level of pluralism is needed in the religious marketplace.

Second, as Finke (1990) makes clear, the deregulation of the religious marketplace in America makes the choice of different religious options more plausible, since no one religion is state supported. As a result, the variety of needs present in the diverse population can be more easily addressed by a variety of religious organizations. As long as the practice of religion, and the presence of religious options, are protected as rights, it is unlikely that any significant drop in the number of choices in the religious marketplace will occur.

Third, the findings of Sutton et al. (1988) regarding the relationship of prior schisms and prior mergers to the founding rate also suggest the need for a critical number of denominations. It is interesting to note that a recent history of mergers tends to increase the rate of denominations founded by schisms. This indicates that mergers reduce the diversity of products available, despite the fact that most mergers occur between very similar religious organizations. Apparently there are some in every merger who feel their needs are not being met by the larger denomination created, such that new churches are formed by schism. Thus, it appears that it is possible for the number of churches to become too small, with too little diversity to meet consumer demands. When this happens, new organizations arise to supply their needs.

Conversely, a recent history of schisms tends to decrease the founding rate. Since schisms act to increase the diversity of products offered in the religious marketplace, the declining founding rate after a decade of schisms indicates that at some point there is a sufficient number of religions available, perhaps even too many. When too many exist, then there is a greater likelihood that religious organizations will be offering essentially the same product to similar consumers. Under these circumstances, mergers should occur to reduce competition. This last thought is speculative, since there is no study that has looked at the merger rate and its associations with prior schisms and mergers.

Fourth, the available statistics support continuity (or a slight increase) in the number of religious organizations. Wuthnow (1988) notes that there is "little evidence that mergers have significantly reduced the number of different denominations" (p. 83). In fact, he indicates that the numbers of denominations within the major Protestant families have not changed substantially since World War II. This includes the Lutherans, who were divided into 19 different denominations in both 1950 and 1980, despite the mergers cited earlier.

Therefore, I believe that the available evidence supports the premise that there is a critical number of religious organizations necessary to supply the diverse demands of the American population. When the number of denominations drops below this "critical number," then the demand side of the religious economy drives the market to create new alternatives. Conversely, when the number of denominations exceeds this "critical number," then the supply side kicks in, limiting the duplication of services provided by organizations serving the same target market by encouraging religious organizations to merge.

Whether this critical number can change as the result of major societal changes needs to be addressed in future studies. For example, one might hypothesize that a major regionalistic conflict (such as that which occurred around the time of the Civil War) would lead to an increase in the critical number, since denominations might split on the basis of regional differences. Similarly, any major change in race relations or social class composition of the population could cause the critical number to rise or fall considerably. An influx of immigrants might raise the critical number, as new religious traditions are brought in or created to meet the needs of these new citizens. An analysis of religion in America focusing on the times in our history when new religious traditions arise in large numbers would be useful in illuminating the types of social changes that might lead to a change in the critical number of religious organizations.

However, assuming there is relative stability in American society, the premise regarding a critical number deserves further consideration. Specifically, it is important to contemplate how one might empirically test this premise, and by testing it determine what the actual critical number might be. The study by Sutton et al. (1988) provides some insight in this regard. Their approach involved noting the relationship between prior schisms and mergers on the founding rate. The results of their study suggest a cyclical pattern for both schisms and mergers, with high numbers of mergers being associated with low numbers of schisms, and vice versa. Thus, if one examines the number of religious groups across time, the pattern should also be cyclical, with the actual number of denominations remaining consistently close to the "critical number." If simple regression were used, one would hypothesize that the slope for the relationship between year and number of denominations should be zero, with the intercept representing the critical number. This is the next logical step to be taken in a future study.

ACKNOWLEDGMENTS

Special thanks to Roger Finke (Purdue University) for his assistance in providing reference materials for this paper, and to Carl Roberts (Iowa State University) and Randy Johnson (CWRU) for their critical comments on earlier drafts of this paper. Thanks as well to Rodney Stark, Robert Liebman, and an anonymous reviewer for their helpful critiques. Please direct any correspondence to André Nauta, Department of Sociology, Case Western Reserve University, 10900 Euclid Avenue, Cleveland OH 44106-7124.

NOTES

1. For a complete listing of the functions of churches and the needs that they satisfy see chapter 7 ("Functions and Dysfunctions of Church Activities") of Moberg (1984).

2. The accounts of schisms and mergers presented in this paper. are necessarily limited in number. It is not my intent to empirically test the main arguments presented at this time. Thus, the schisms and mergers chosen are used only to illustrate my thesis.

3. The AELC was short-lived, for it was part of the 1988 merger that formed the Evangelical Lutheran Church in America. See Hillis (1991) for a more detailed account of this schism.

4. Quoted from comments by an anonymous reviewer of this paper.

5. I am aware that this discussion ignores the possibility that individuals may switch religious affiliation as their needs change. While this certainly occurs, the overall needs of the population tend to be more constant, requiring a constant supply of the various religious products. That is, while the needs of an individual may change, for example, as the result of an increase in income, it is much less likely that all people living with inadequate incomes in our society will see such an increase. Thus, while individuals' life circumstances do change, leading to a change in religious needs, the variety of religious needs in a society are much more stable.

REFERENCES

Berger, P. 1967. *The Sacred Canopy*. New York: Doubleday.

————. 1979. *The Heretical Imperative: Contemporary Possibilities of Religious Affirmation*. New York: Doubleday.

Crumley, J. R. 1981. "Crumley Favors United Church." *The Lutheran Standard* (March 20,· 1981):23.

Durkheim, E. [1897] 1951. *Suicide: A Study in Sociology*. Translated by J. A. Spaulding and G. Simpson. Glencoe, IL: Free Press.

Finke, R. 1990. "Religious Deregulation: Origins and Consequences." *Journal of Church and State* 32(3): 609-626.

Finke, R. and L. R. Iannaccone. 1993. "Supply-Side Explanations for Religious Change." *The Annals of the American Academy of Political and Social Science* 527(May): 27-39.

Finke, R. and R. Stark. 1988. "Religious Economies and Sacred Canopies: Religious Mobilization in American Cities, 1906." *American Sociological Review* 53(1): 41-49.

————. 1989. "How the Upstart Sects Won America: 1776-1850." *Journal for the Scientific Study of Religion* 28(1): 27-44.

————. 1991. "Ecumenical Movements in the 1920's: Why Unification Failed." Paper presented at the annual meeting of the Society for the Scientific Study of Religion, Pittsburgh.

————. 1992. *The Churching of America, 1776-1990: Winners and Losers in Our Religious Economy*. New Brunswick, NJ: Rutgers University Press.

Gaustad, E. S. 1987. *Faith of Our Fathers: Religion and the New Nation*. San Francisco: Harper and Row.

Goen, C. C. 1985. *Broken Churches, Broken Nation*. Macon, GA: Mercer University Press.

Gunnemann, L. H. 1977. *The Shaping of the United Church of Christ*. New York: United Church Press.

Hillis, B. V. 1991. *Can Two Walk Together Unless They Be Agreed?: American Religious Schisms in the 1970s.* Brooklyn, New York: Carlson Publishing.

Iannaccone, L. R. 1991. "The Consequences of Religious Market Structure: Adam Smith and the Economics of Religion." *Rationality and Society* 3(2): 156-177.

_____. 1992. "Religious Markets and the Economics of Religion." *Social Compass* 39(1): 123-131.

Loetscher, L. A. 1983. *A Brief History of the Presbyterians.* Philadelphia: Westminster Press.

Mead, S. E. 1956. "From Coercion to Persuasion: Another Look at the Rise of Religious Liberty and the Emergence of Denominationalism." *Church History* 25: 317-337.

Moberg, D. O. 1984. *The Church as a Social Institution: The Sociology of American Religion.* Grand Rapids, MI: Baker Book House.

Nauta, A. 1991. "Trends in American Religion, 1964-1986: Implications for the Future." Unpublished doctoral dissertation, Iowa State University. *Dissertation Abstracts International* 52: 3438A-3439A. (University Microforms Order No. DA9207251).

Nichol, T. W. 1986. *All These Lutherans: Three Paths Toward a New Lutheran Church.* Minneapolis: Augsburg.

Niebuhr, H. R. [1929] 1957. *The Social Sources of Denominationalism.* New York: Henry Holt.

Stark, R. and W. S. Bainbridge. 1987. *A Theory of Religion.* New York: Peter Lang.

Sutton, J. R., R. Wuthnow and R. C. Liebman. 1988. "Organizational Foundings: Schisms in American Protestant Denominations, 1890-1980." Presented at the meeting of the American Sociological Association, Atlanta, Georgia.

Trinity Lutheran Seminary. 1981. "Single Church Endorsed by Trinity Profs." *The Lutheran Standard* (March 20, 1981):23.

Washburn, P. 1984. *An Unfinished Church.* Nashville, TN: Abingdon Press.

Wallace, R. A. 1975. "A Model of Change of Religious Affiliation." *Journal for the Scientific Study of Religion* 14(4): 345-355.

Wuthnow, R. 1988. *The Restructuring of American Religion.* Princeton, NJ: Princeton University Press.

THE POLITICS OF ELITE DISUNITY IN THE SOUTHERN BAPTIST CONVENTION, 1946-1992

C. Kirk Hadaway and Penny Long Marler

ABSTRACT

Research on political conflict and stability suggests that "powerful actors" or elites play a pivotal role into the direction and shape of national polities. Indeed, the work of Field, Higley, and Burton indicates that elite unity or consensus is essential for political stability in modern nation states. Disunity, by contrast, increases the likelihood of serious political conflict and regime overthrow. The purpose of this research is to apply the insights of elite theory to a quite different political organization: A large-scale denominational polity. It is our view that the actions and posturing of elites have implications for interpreting not only the rise and fall of political regimes, but also the stability and instability of non-state polities. A case in point is the Southern Baptist Convention. Recent political upheavals in this denomination are best understood as by-products of elite disunity. We trace the history of the conflict in the SBC from one form of unity (based on cooperation among elites), to the breakdown of elite unity, to the establishment of another form of unity (based on coercion). The "federated" nature

Research in the Social Scientific Study of Religion, Volume 6, pages 53-102.
Copyright © 1994 by JAI Press Inc.
All rights of reproduction in any form reserved.
ISBN: 1-55938-762-9

of the Southern Baptist Convention and the threat posed by continued presence of disgruntled moderates and their churches should keep the current political elite focused on the need for tight ideological and practical control for the near future.

"Order, order, I call this group to order," McCarty shouted above the noise in New Orleans' Cafe Du Monde June 13, at the end of the second day of the SBC annual meeting. "After all, I am the parliamentarian...." The presentation was the gift of framed certificates of appreciation to Houston judge Paul Pressler and Dallas educator Paige Patterson, who met years ago in that cafe and planned the strategy to control the SBC. During the New Orleans meeting, their forces won the SBC presidency for the 12th straight year.... Some Southern Baptists expressed their displeasure with McCarty and the conservatives, even during their celebration. "Shame, shame, shame," they shouted, before being drowned out by conservatives, who sang a verse of "Victory in Jesus" (Knox 1990a, p. 1).

Symbolic gavels are raised in unusual forums in pursuit of organizational power. An improvised call to order in a French Quarter eatery is no more odd, however, than the gavel-wielder or those who have conspired to capture the gavels of national, political pulpits. Whether the result is "Victory in Jesus" or "Victory for the party"—all is politics. And lest the ascendant party become smug in their victory, the crowd in the background chants a partisan response.

The Southern Baptist Convention has been embroiled in a well-publicized power struggle for more than a decade. The "Great Controversy," as it has been termed by interpreters on both sides, captured the interest of a nation and inspired numerous books. Yet this ideological tug-of-war has moved in a spotlight that it did not create. Indeed, the arena of greatest attention was the conservative resurgence in American politics—"the new right"—and so observers have viewed this "holy war" as an expression of a larger sociocultural trend (Ammerman 1990; Leonard 1990; Rosenberg 1989; Barnhart 1986). And while it is true that cultural forces *do* affect organizational fortunes, the real story behind the "Great Controversy" seems closer to home. The protagonists in *this* story are a relatively small group of persons who affect Convention outcomes "individually, regularly, and seriously" (Burton and Higley 1987, p. 296).

"Powerful actors" or elites play pivotal roles in the direction and shape of national political organizations. Recent research suggests that unity among elites is *essential* for political stability in nation-states (Burton and Higley 1987; Higley and Burton 1989). Conversely, the more typical situation of elite disunity is seen as a determinative factor in regime instability—increasing the likelihood of factious conflict and political overthrow. It is also plausible that the actions and posturing of elites have implications not only for interpreting the rise and fall of political regimes, but for understanding the stability and instability of other organizations, particularly those that are governmental in function and national in scope.

Religious denominations, for example, represent a type of organization *qua* nation-state. The Southern Baptist Convention is not a centralized bureaucracy. Although the denomination contains a number of highly bureaucratic organizations, the Convention itself is a polity—a governmental structure. Convention agencies and boards are guided by decisions mandated at a once a year, three-day meeting of "messengers." At these annual events, trustees and committee members are elected who control a massive infrastructure of educational, publishing, and missionary agencies whose treasuries and constituencies easily rival smaller nation-states. With the increasing size, wealth, and influence of denominational bureaucracies, the stakes have grown proportionately—both for the national elite within Convention agencies and institutions and for the political elite "at the top."

A revised version of Field, Higley, and Burton's elite paradigm provides the starting point for an investigation of the politics of elite disunity in a large, nonstate organization. The suggested model addresses a number of interrelated factors that condition elite activity including: The degree of unity/disunity in the elite structure, the active mode of political engagement, the presence or likelihood of unconventional political activity, the severity of political sanctions, and organizational stability. The paradigm is applied to an elite transformation occurring within the Southern Baptist Convention.

POLITICAL ACTIVITY IN NON-STATE ORGANIZATIONS

The application of political theory is typically restricted to the "public realm" in which people struggle for office and power (Leftwich 1984, p. 62; Moodie 1984, p. 23). Political activity also occurs in other areas of society and in societies that lack a fully formed state. According to Leftwich (1984, p. 69), "whenever one finds social groups, one finds such collective activities: all of them, productive or social, in some way involve activities concerned with organizing the use, production or distribution of resources. That's politics." Indeed, Leftwich (1984, p. 63) argues that politics is found "in all formal institutions—such as churches, factories, bureaucracies, universities and clubs...and in all the relations which may obtain between them."

Obviously, political activity occurs within organizations as well as in the public realm. But according to Zald and Berger (1978), however, politics in some organizations resemble those within nation-states more than others. This is especially true of "federated organizations" like trade unions, most religious denominations, charitable institutions and other organizations that lack a command-oriented hierarchy. Zald and Berger (1978, p. 853) observe that it is possible to "move the whole apparatus of political sociology analysis into these polities with even less modification [than for hierarchical organizations]." They conclude, "The processes are the same and only the scale is different" (Zald and Berger 1978, p. 856).

Federated organizations are composed of members rather than employees. Their members, or constituency, are at least hypothetically able to elect their own leadership and control the structure and direction of the organization. In such organizations, unconventional political activity including protest, bribery, and violence is frequently, and sometimes successfully, employed. Conventional political activity including campaigns and petitions is also widespread. In hierarchical organizations, however, conventional political activity is virtually useless because leaders are not elected nor are they accountable to employees. Unconventional political activity is also minimal since management retains the right to hire and fire. Regime takeovers by employees are impossible in nearly all hierarchical organizations because they are illegal.

Protestant religious denominations are federated organizations. Some, such as the Episcopal Church, contain major elements of hierarchical structure, but the Southern Baptist Convention was designed, as a rather pure form of the federated style. Because of this federated structure, religious denominations are more likely to exhibit open, factional disputes. Not surprisingly, this often results in the breakup or splintering of various segments of the organization. Indeed, the great diversity of religious denominations in the United States is the result of schisms and secessions within federated denominational structures. Because of the similarities between such political activity and that within nation-states, it is possible—and should prove fruitful—to use theory based on nation-state politics to interpret political activity within denominational polities.

ELITE UNITY AND POLITICAL STABILITY

The elite paradigm developed by Field, Higley, and Burton addresses the problem of regime stability in modern nation-states. In their view, current political theories that emphasize economic, cultural, or social-structural explanations for political stability do not adequately explain why periodic seizures of power occur in some nations and not in others. Instead, Higley and Burton (1989, p. 21) propose that the *structure of elites* in a society should be "viewed as logically and factually prior to regime stability." Whereas social conditions may create the opportunity for political instability, the determining factor is the presence or absence of unity among elites. In simplified form, the elite paradigm states that societies with *unified elites* will exhibit stable political systems and societies with *disunified elites* will correspondingly exhibit unstable political systems (Field and Higley 1985). Elite unity is a precondition for political stability.

Elites are defined as "people who are able, through their positions in powerful organizations, to affect national political outcomes individually, regularly, and seriously" (Burton and Higley 1987a, p. 296). They are persons who can make "substantial political trouble" for persons in authoritative positions "without being promptly repressed" (Field and Higley 1973, p. 8). Thus, the elite structure of a nation-state includes elites both of the "establishment," as well as "counter-elite" factions, who, although not in control of the government, do control substantial power bases that allow them regularly to affect political outcomes and to cause "political trouble."

Most nation-states exhibit a *disunified* elite structure in terms of the "attitudes, values, and interpersonal relations among factions making up the elite" (Burton and Higley 1987a, p. 296; Field and Higley 1985). Elite factions do not trust one another; they have little interpersonal contact across factional lines; and they do not cooperate to avoid political crises (Burton and Higley 1987a, p. 297). A nation-state with a disunified elite structure is inherently unstable. This instability results from the fact that elites in power systematically exclude other elite factions from powerful positions and take coercive measures to ensure that they do not gain (or regain) control (Higley and Burton 1989, p. 19).[1] Excluded elite groups have no stake in such a system. Thus, these factions try to gain power by any means possible—including direct seizures of power and/or the mobilization of non-elites. Politics becomes war, and in such nations seizures of power occur frequently or are widely expected (Burton and Higley 1987, p. 297).

Conversely, stable political regimes are characterized by elite unity. And, according to the theory, there are two basic ways in which elites can be unified. The first is through ideologically justified coercion and the second is through consensus.

In an *ideologically unified* elite structure a single defined ideology is professed by all elites. There is one party in power and no rival party. In such societies, "there exists an apparatus of power sufficient to force all current and aspiring leaders to harmonize their public statements with the views that are momentarily orthodox" (Field and Higley 1973, p. 13). This allows unity to be enforced and maintained. What is considered orthodox is decided by a few elites who occupy the highest positions. Political stability characterizes such nation-states because the elites are able to prevent anyone who does not accept the legitimacy of the current system from achieving elite status, and thus from causing "political trouble." Those who do not conform are silenced, banished, purged, or otherwise separated from the bases of power which allow them to be elites.

Nation-states with a *consensually unified* elite structure are also characterized by political stability. The unity of this elite does not depend on a single ideology, but rather on an "agreement to disagree." There may be competing ideologies, and the cleavages among elites may be deep. However, the inevitable conflicts that occur among elites (and among non-elites who respond to elite criticism, posturing, and mobilization efforts) are never allowed to get out of hand. Why? Simply because, in a consensually unified elite structure, all parties have a vested interest in preserving the existing political structure and institutions. As Field and Higley (1973, p. 15) note, power is distributed "...so that all or most [elites] can still have an impact on political outcomes sufficient to deter them from translating their oppositions into attempts to seize power by force."

In a society with either unified elite type, political instability is very unlikely because elites have no need to: (1) seize power through a coup d' état, or (2) mobilize a mass movement to topple the existing regime. Field, Higley, and Burton conclude that a unified elite structure of either type tends to be self-perpetuating (Field and Higley 1985, p. 37; Higley and Burton 1987, p. 297; Field and Higley 1979, p. 142). Because of this self-perpetuating nature—and due to the fact that few examples of transformation from unity to disunity were apparent prior to breakdown of communist regimes in Europe—the authors focus on transformation from disunity to unity. They see three possibilities: (1) a sudden elite settlement, (2) a slightly more gradual "two-step" elite settlement, and (3) a "revolutionary elite transformation to ideological unity" (Higley and Burton 1989, p. 27).

REFINING THE ELITE PARADIGM

There are several problems with the Field-Higley-Burton paradigm. First, unity and disunity are described in absolute terms. According to the theory, an elite structure is either unified or disunified. There is no possibility for "greater or lesser" unity. In other words, unity (or disunity) is treated as a *descriptive characteristic* exhibited by certain nation-states, rather than as an analytic dimension. Second, as noted earlier, elite transitions are described as moving only in the direction of unity, rather than from unity to disunity. Finally, transitions from one type of elite structure to another are presented as relatively abrupt historical shifts rather than longer, more gradual processes.

The first step in revising the elite paradigm is to separate the analytic dimensions that are explicit and implicit in the model. The first of these dimensions is elite unity/disunity. We do not define elite unity in terms of either a shared ideology or a prevailing "agreement to disagree." These are *characteristics* exhibited by elites in certain stable nation-states, but they are inadequate for defining the dimension of unity. Instead, we look to the central element in *both* types of elite unity and determine that what they have in common is a *consens US* that (1) the system of government *is valid*, and (2) *it works* (for the characteristics of "consensus" in totalitarian and democratic systems, see Morris 1966, pp. 43-75). Elites are unified to the extent that such a consensus exists.

The *validity* of the current system is judged on a number of criteria: Its legitimacy (based on societal norms); the acceptability of the formal procedures and rules through which power is obtained and exercised (and resources allocated); and the basic values and assumptions guiding the regime. Whether the system *works*, on the other hand, is judged by whether or not the structure operates as designed; and whether or not it is being used in a manner deemed acceptable by elites in the current regime. How are rules interpreted and policy determined? And how are political appointments made and other discretionary political actions taken? The answers to such questions determine whether or not a system of government "works."

In a *disunified* elite structure many elites believe that the governmental system is not valid or that the way in which it works is unacceptable (or both). A repressive regime that has control by virtue of a seizure of power may be seen as invalid (because of its illegitimacy), but a regime that is inefficient, arbitrary, or unwieldly may be seen as merely unacceptable by elite factions who think that a better system of government is possible. In still other cases, elites may accept the legitimacy of the current system of government, but be very dissatisfied with the way the system is being used by the current ruling party.

Unity is eroded when a regime that may have been accepted as valid and as working properly comes to be seen as neither due to changing circumstances or a shattering ideological disconfirmation. In all cases of elite disunity there is the belief among elites that something is wrong with the system or in its operation, and that something should be done about it—either by changing the system itself or by overthrowing the current ruling party.

The second analytical dimension is the dominant mode of political engagement. Acceptance of the system and its operation can be based primarily on *coercion*—in which case consensus among elites is forced. Or, it can be based on *cooperation*—in which case elites *voluntarily* come to see the system as valid and are basically satisfied with the way it works. In a coercive elite structure the emphasis is on conformity and uniformity. Those in power believe that they have the right and duty to force compliance. Sharing of power is inconceivable because those out of power are not seen as fit to lead. Sanctions are used to keep the ruling party ideologically "pure" and to keep rival elites from sharing in the decision-making process. This includes efforts to remove the power base of rival elites in order to deprive them of elite status. In a cooperative system, on the other hand, there is little emphasis on uniformity. Factional divisions are recognized, accepted, and are not used as a basis for denying access to political power. The system may or may not work very well but there is a certain civility about the process. Elites in power are prepared to "talk things out" rather than to "fight for our rights."

Two kinds of elites are found in modern nation-states: Political and national elites. *Political elites* are persons who hold top-level positions within the formal political structure.[2] *National elites* are persons outside the political elite circle who nevertheless wield considerable power by virtue of their position, personal charisma, connection to certain political elites, or relation to a potentially powerful non-elite faction. National elites are found inside and outside the formal political structure. According to Field, Higley, and Burton, both elite groups have important roles to play in the stability/instability of any regime. In a discussion of the dynamic relationship between elite unity, regime (or organizational) stability, and modes of political engagement, however, a choice must be made as to "which group" is the proper focus of analysis. Our point of reference is the *political elite*. It is their resistance to change, their unity, and their actions towards *national elites* that drives this model. The rhetoric and actions of national elites, we believe, illumine the process of elite transformation only when analyzed *in relation* to those of the political elite.

The revised model yields four types of elite structure (see Figure 1). It is not a static model. Elite structures may change in the direction of either unity or disunity, and elite structures exhibit varying degrees of unity as they move from one "cell" to another. Field, Higley, and Burton document many cases of transitions from disunity to unity, but in the 1980s and into the 1990s—from the Southern Baptist Convention to the former Soviet Union—the dominant mode of transition has been from unity to disunity. Further, recent experience suggests that nation-states and non-state organizations do not move directly from one form of elite unity to another. In all cases, disunity is a necessary transitional step.

Four Types of Elite Structure

The *unified-cooperative* elite structure is similar to the consensually unified elite in the Field-Higley-Burton paradigm (see also, Elder 1982). In such a structure, elites may not have unity in any area other than agreement that the system of government is valid and that it is being used properly by those in power. Elites may hold differing ideological positions and factional interests; yet they are allowed to express these differences and influence policy. Stable democratic governments exhibit this form of elite structure, but the dynamics also obtain in non-state organizations. In a unified-cooperative structure there is widespread agreement among organizational leaders (elites) to work within existing written rules and unwritten norms of political conduct rather than engaging in unconventional political activity.

Political sanctions are low in organizations or nation-states with this type of elite structure because there is no need to force compliance. Instead, it is recognized that those who cooperate will have access to power and those who do not cooperate will be left out. Still, there is no move to silence critics of the system through coercive means (nor to banish them). Control is much more subtle and civil. It works, however, because elites recognize that they will retain access to power through cooperation.

Elites also recognize that the viability of the cooperative system is in their hands. The precarious balance is threatened when political elites exclude certain

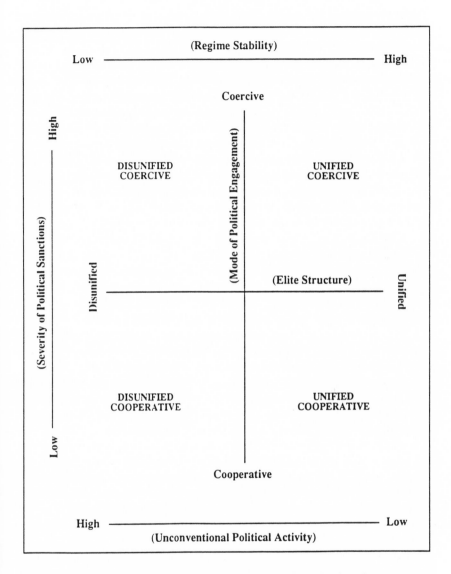

Figure 1.　Revised model of elite structure and modes of political engagement

elites from power or when efforts are made by elites to seek power outside accepted political channels. Democratic ideals normally undergird such an elite structure. Not only do elites realize that the system allows them access to political power, but they believe that all factions have the right to some say (and usually some participation) in the governing process.

Even though this type of elite structure tends to produce political stability, it can become unstable. This may occur when an ideological faction—inside or outside the political elite—begins to value orthodoxy over harmony and political suitability over representative politics. Consequently, a faction (or factions) in a unified-cooperative elite structure may come to see other elites as unworthy of power and the governance of current political elites as no longer valid. If this occurs, the elite structure moves towards a disunified-cooperative state as elites in powerful institutional positions try to maintain the cooperative structure, while opposing elites reject cooperation and begin to engage in unconventional political activity. In other cases, dominant political elites may precipitate the breakdown by using the system in a manner that seems to violate the spirit of cooperation. Frustrated by their inability to work within the system to produce change or to oppose the actions of top decision-makers effectively, excluded elite factions may be forced to work outside the system to oust top political elites and/or to alter the system. Elite disunity results, in this case, because the adjudged system no longer works.

The second type of elite structure is the *disunified-cooperative* elite.[3] This type may seem unlikely, but in fact, it occurs quite regularly as nation-states go through what Higley, Burton, and Field (1990) call, "elite convergences." Further, it provides an answer to the problem of regimes which avoid seizures of power for many years, and thus appear stable, only to experience a constitutional crisis or a non-violent regime breakdown. In nation-states and non-state polities with this type of elite structure, most political elites believe that cooperation makes more sense than coercion, and they are supported in this belief by norms that reject harsh political sanctions and respect "civility." Nevertheless, among certain elite factions there may be widespread dissatisfaction with the system or with the way it is being used.

In some cases, the development of a disunified-cooperative elite structure is the first step in the destabilization of a once-stable polity. Increasingly, the system is viewed as invalid and unworkable. Often, institutional arrangements for the control and distribution of resources are viewed as inefficient, arbitrary, or inadequate. For instance, the organization may have outgrown its polity structure to such an extent that a great deal of political activity must operate in the gray areas between the rules; or efforts may have been made to change the polity structure without the consent of all elite factions. Dissatisfaction may also arise when the system is seen as valid and acceptable, but the political elite is apparently using the cooperative nature of the system to exclude other elite factions from meaningful access to power. The situation may not be severe enough to lead immediately to a revolution, however. Even though disgruntled elites continue to work within the system to change it or its operation, their frustration and dissatisfaction also leads them to work outside the system.

In other cases a disunified-cooperative elite structure may be seen as a stage in the development of a stable democratic regime (Morlino 1987). After an elite settlement is made or soon after a new organization is formed, there may be *hope* that the cooperative mode of political engagement will work but complete confidence and trust has not yet been established. Disunified elites may also be hampered in their efforts to govern because the accompanying mechanisms are not yet in place to insure a new mode of political engagement (see for example, Hagopian 1990 and McDonough 1983). Elites take a "wait and see" attitude toward the new regime, but do not have complete confidence that the institutional arrangements for the sharing of power and for the distribution of resources are workable. Nor do they have complete confidence in the commitment of their former adversaries to cooperation. Thus, the structure remains disunified-cooperative until confidence and trust are sufficient to achieve unity.

In a nation-state or a non-state polity characterized by a disunified-cooperative elite structure, coercive efforts are not made to control criticism by elites. However, unconventional political activity of a subtle and civil sort may be used to "rein in" other elites who are inside or outside the political elite. The rift between elites may emerge among formerly cooperative political elites or it may appear between regime elites and elites who are not part of the regime (national elites). Even in the latter case, however, it is likely that rival elite factions will include a few elites who are currently or were formerly members of the political elite.

Obviously, a disunified-cooperative elite structure can change in various directions. An elite faction which desires to monopolize power may topple a regime dominated by elites who have operated in a cooperative mode. Or, in order to retain control, elites in power might abandon cooperation with a powerful and threatening rival faction in favor of coercion. In either case, the system would then become disunified-coercive. Alternatively, elites could work together to "fix" an unwieldy and inefficient system of government; opposition could provoke political elites to share more power with rival factions (thus restoring all elite groups to a cooperative mode); or rival elite factions could topple a regime and institute reforms which would restore cooperation. In all of these cases, the elite structure would move from disunified-cooperative to unified-cooperative.

In a *disunified-coercive* elite structure contesting elite factions have substantial institutional bases of support and can regularly cause "political trouble" for the dominant elite faction. The political trouble may come from within the political elite itself or among the national elite. Contesting factions may take various forms: For example, elite-led movements seeking to overthrow the current regime; political parties pressing for shared power; or subcultural groups contesting the ideological or practical bases of power. Rather than involve these factions in a cooperative effort at government, the political elite fights to maintain the status quo.

Efforts may be made by the dominant political elite to suppress, outlaw, or even to exterminate rival factions. In one possible scenario, a disunified-coercive elite structure may result from the breakdown of a unified-coercive order. In another scenario, this structure emerges when a disunified-cooperative order dissolves and destabilization intensifies. Either way, a disunified-coercive elite structure is typically a *transitional* stage. The political elite retain a tenuous control while rival faction(s) cause plenty of "political trouble." In some cases, the dominant faction does not have the means (or the will) to eliminate elites who do not accept the validity of the system. This may be due to a governmental structure which does not allow for complete centralized control (or meaningful cooperation), to the fact that the ideological justification for such control (or cooperation) does not exist in the society or organization, or to the failure of a revolutionary movement to seize control of all bases of power.

The political processes in nation-states or non-state polities with disunified-coercive elite structures can be quite disruptive. In its effort to suppress and remove other elites from power, the ruling political elite tends to use rather severe political sanctions. And because it does not have absolute control of the society or the organization, it tends to resort to unconventional political activity to achieve its own aims. Thus, political elites may break the rules they created or interpret them in an unconventional manner for their own purposes. Rival elite factions, on the other hand, have little stake in the system and in many cases are suffering under sanctions imposed by the dominant elite faction. Rival elites are unable to work within the system so they also resort to unconventional political activity to oppose top elites. In the most extreme cases, this leads to such chaos that the regime is no longer able to govern effectively. Elite factions fight it out, and no one is able to gain the upper hand.[5]

A *unified-coercive* elite structure is similar to the ideologically unified elite in the original model. There is a consensus among elites concerning the validity of the existing governmental system and the way the system is being used. However, elites have little choice. In order to avoid being purged or to gain elite status, they must express support for the regime and its ideology, and they must refrain from political activity directed against it.

The focus is on uniformity in this type of elite structure. The "party line" is sharply drawn and deviation typically provokes harsh reactions. In nation-states an elite critic may be sent to a forced labor camp or to a "hospital" for political retraining and, in some religious bodies, an elite critic may be excommunicated. Typically, however, critics simply lose access to power. They forfeit their status and their jobs. Whether the setting is a nation-state or a non-state organization, the political goal of top elites is the same: To use coercive action to ensure that power is restricted to those who accept and support the current regime and its procedures for the distribution of resources (see for example, Gross 1989, pp. 208-209). Normally, the justification for this restriction has an ideological base.

In order to maintain a unified-coercive structure, the top political elite must enforce compliance in its own ranks and, at the same time, restrict access to political power. This necessarily requires a great deal of power on the part of political elites—power which must be centralized if the control is to be effective. Without such power, opposing factions may emerge and fragment the ruling party from within; individual elites may break with the ruling party and openly question the validity of the current system; or rival elite factions may form outside the regime and openly oppose the government. In all cases, the unity of the elite structure would be eroded.

A unified-coercive elite structure tends to produce political stability within a nation-state or a non-state organization. Powerful elites critical of the system and its operation are unlikely to rise from within a unified-coercive regime. Further, in the absence of powerful rival factions, potential elites also are unlikely to rise from outside. Unconventional political activity among elites is kept to a minimum; opposition is not allowed to reach the point where it poses a serious threat to those in power. In fact, control is so tight that even the suggestion of political activity outside official channels is dealt with swiftly and harshly.

The structure of an organization naturally influences the extent to which elite unity can be maintained through coercion. In federated organizations, such as religious denominations, political elites may move to tighten control through any available channel. The segmented nature of these organizations, however, results in a lack of centralized control. Therefore, a sufficient level of control is not achieved easily or, if achieved, is difficult to maintain. Opposing elites may be deprived of status by various institutional means. Still, as long as potential power bases exist which cannot be suppressed totally by the ruling elite, it will be possible for rival elites to emerge or reemerge and undermine the unity of the elite structure. Faced with this situation, the political elite in a unified-coercive system may attempt to force former elites out of the organization along with their constituencies. If that occurs, the possibility of abandoning a coercive posture and lowering sanctions could lead (eventually) to a unified-cooperative elite structure. Alternatively, the top political elite can try to change the structure of the organization and achieve greater control. Failing this, a unified-coercive elite structure may dissolve into a state of disunity.

THE SOUTHERN BAPTIST CONVENTION: DISUNITY IN DIXIE

An analysis of elite transformations in the Southern Baptist Convention departs from previous interpretive foci and accordingly, comes to alternate conclusions. Ammerman (1990), Leonard (1990), and Rosenberg (1989), for example, begin with assumptions about the *unity of Southern culture* and trace present Convention conflict to the dissolution of cultural hegemony. This kind of analysis assumes parallel effects on non-elites and elites. In addition, failure to distinguish between Southern Baptist elites and non-elites blurs the significance of Ammerman's observation that the Convention is an appointive oligarchy. Finally, the approach underestimates historic regional tensions in the supposed "solid South."

The following analysis, on the other hand, begins with the fact of *disunity in the elite structure* of the Convention. First, the social and historical roots of elite disunity are explored. Then, the flow of power and authority through the organizational polity is traced. Finally, the period leading up to and including the present elite transformation is examined. Particular attention is given to unity/disunity, cooperation/coercion, "regime" stability, the presence of unconventional political activity, and sanctions imposed on "uncooperative" elites and non-elites by those in power. Not surprisingly, interpretations of the crisis through this lens provide a different picture of the relation between culture and the machinations of Convention elite.

The Roots of Elite Disunity

The roots of elite disunity in the Southern Baptist Convention are deep. According to Baptist historian, Walter Shurden, the founders of the SBC were nurtured by four distinct theological, ecclesiological, and even regional traditions (Shurden 1981). Shurden points to the fact that the combination of these perspectives created the "synthesis" that became the Southern Baptist Convention. However, this synthesis has always been tenuous and frequently its more contentious components have threatened to upset the fine balance of cooperation and civility (Leonard 1990, pp. 37-39).

A survey of early Baptist histories surfaces two distinct types of Southern Baptist elites. The first type we call a "founding elite" or cultural elite. The founding elite were well-educated and highly involved in the new denomination. Many also held key political and business positions in the South. A review of biographical data on the early Southern Baptist Convention Presidents is telling (*Encyclopedia of Southern Baptists*, p. 1958; Routh 1976). Fifteen Presidents serving from 1845 through 1925 included graduates of Brown, Columbia, Harvard, Amherst, Princeton, and Mercer. Seven of the fifteen were full-time pastors of large, prestigious churches such as First Baptist Richmond, Virginia; Second Baptist, Richmond Virginia; and First Baptist, Nashville, Tennessee. Among the laymen who served as President of the Convention were two Governors of Southern states (Georgia and Arkansas), a judge, the chancellor of the University of Georgia, an editor and publisher, and a coffee importer who was the Prohibition candidate for the President of the United States in 1896.

All but three of the first Presidents were from states that were instrumental in the founding of the Southern Baptist Convention. Three of the early presidents—whose total tenure was twenty-two years attended the founding meeting in 1845. Other presidents participated in Southern Baptist life as editors of state Baptist papers, presidents of state conventions, trustees of Baptist colleges and seminaries, and mission board trustees. By far the most influential institution in the elite circle was The Southern Baptist Theological Seminary: Two SBC Presidents were heavily involved in its founding; one was President of the Southern Seminary Board of Trustees for many years; two were Presidents of Southern Seminary itself; and two were pastors with Southern Seminary degrees.

The Southern Baptist founders were cultural elites. They represented the best of the Reconstruction-era South. The traditions which shaped their stance on church governance were the Charleston and the Georgia tradition (Shurden 1981, pp. 3-4, 6-7). Influenced by the Philadelphia confession, the "Charleston tradition" was characterized by order, civility, and cooperation. Informed by two prominent Southern Baptist leaders, the "Georgia tradition" was personified in intense sectional pride. Together, these strains yielded the ideal Southern Baptist elite: The quintessential Southern gentleman whose primary concern was rebuilding a safe and sanctified Southland.

Zeal for order and civility was the special legacy of these Southeastern, founding elites. P.H. Mell of Georgia who was President of the Georgia district association for twenty-nine years, President of the Georgia Baptist Convention for twenty-five years, and President of the Southern Baptist Convention for fourteen years epitomized this brand of Southern Baptist elite (Routh 1976, p. 16). In a commentary about the SBC Convention meeting in Waco, 1883, a Texas newspaper reported:

> The Southern Baptists can never cease to admire the genius of Dr. Mell as a presiding officer. He rules with the inflexible rigor of a tyrant, and yet with a spirit so genial and sympathetic that no reasonable man can ever be embarrassed by his presence (Barnes 1954, p. 90).

Indeed, throughout the first century of its founding, Southern Baptist controversies were dealt with in efficient, parliamentary order and in the spirit of Christian civility.

Regardless of the issue, the gravest sin in Convention life was non-cooperation. Dr. L. R. Scarborough, President of Southwestern Theological Seminary (who attended Southern Seminary), President of the SBC, and Director of the Seventy-Five Million Dollar Campaign, concluded in his 1920 annual report to the Convention:

In our unswerving stand for the truth as we see it, we must maintain the spirit of brotherhood and Christ-likeness everywhere. We cannot maintain New Testament orthodoxy in a spirit foreign nor at cross-currents to the spirit of our Master. A sound theology manifested in an unchristian spirit is the most dangerous heresy (*SBC Annual* 1920, p. 57).

No doubt his comments were directed at another contemporary Baptist elite: J. Frank Norris. Indeed, Norris represents a different kind of Southern Baptist elite. This elite had equally deep roots in the ecclesial Southland soil.

The second Southern Baptist elite type, like the first, is representative of a certain style. These elites generally hailed from one of the Southwestern states. By geography and character, the Southwestern states belie the illusion of a solid South. An example of the independence of Southwestern Baptists is the fact that they convened their own "Western Baptist Convention" in 1833 though little actually came of it (Barnes 1954, p. 18). Later, in deliberations over the name of the 1845 Southern schism, the first title suggested was the "Southern and Southwestern" Convention. The "Southern Baptist Convention" won after much debate because it was "shorter and more expressive" (Woodson 1950, p. 127).

The traditions in Southern Baptist ecclesiology that characterized the Southwestern elite are the Sandy Creek and the Tennessee traditions (Shurden 1981, pp. 5-6, 7-8). The "Sandy Creek tradition"—while originating in the southeast—embodied the spirit of the frontier areas. Rising out of English separatism, this tradition is characterized by revivalism, charismatic fervor, a rugged independence, and a strict biblical literalism. The tradition was anti-intellectual (in favor of pietistic experience), anti-connectional (in favor of local church autonomy), and anticonfessional (no creed but the Bible).

The Tennessee tradition shared some of the same characteristics and has had a direct regional effect. J.R. Graves, a contentious Southern Baptist elite, was the originator of this stream of Baptist thought known as "Landmarkism." Landmark emphases included the conception of the local church as "visible and local only"; the identification of Baptist churches with the Kingdom of God; and the claim that Baptist churches can be literally traced to the time of Christ (successionism) (Tull 1975). Landmarkers were fiercely independent and waged a small war within Southern Baptist life during the late 1850s over whether or not local churches should appoint, support, and direct overseas missionary work (as opposed to the Convention-run Foreign Board) (McBeth 1987, pp. 445ff).

The influence of Landmark independence and pride spread primarily through the "Landmark belt" including Tennessee, parts of southern Kentucky, Arkansas, Texas and Oklahoma. Much of this influence can be traced to the skilled rhetoric and pens of a "triumvirate" of Southern Baptist elite: J.R. Graves, editor of *The Tennessee Baptist*; A.C. Dayton, associate editor of the same paper; and J.M. Pendleton, pastor of the First Baptist Church of Bowling

Green, Kentucky (Tull 1975; McBeth 1987, pp. 445ff). At the Convention level, the threat of Landmarkism was defeated by a "coalition composed of some of the most outstanding leaders of the Convention" including long-time President P.H. Mell (Tull 1975, p. 13).

Nevertheless, "open politics" in the federated structure of the Convention guaranteed that further Landmark conflict would erupt. In the late 1890's the President of Southern Seminary, William Whitsitt, resigned after a three-year battle with Landmarkers across the Convention over the question of the historicity of successionism. Baptist historian, W.W. Barnes noted that Whitsitt's "phrasing of the questions involved" had more to do with his eventual downfall than his intellectual position (Barnes 1954, pp. 138-139). Once he became the center of controversy, Whitsitt was sacrificed in the name of cooperation and peace-keeping.

Barnes concluded, that the airing of successionist views at least helped the Baptist populace clarify the issues. So in the end, "Landmarkism won the battle [with Whitsitt], but lost the war" [Landmarkers left the Convention] (Barnes 1954, p. 138). Indeed, it seems that engaging controversy was frowned upon by the Southern Baptist founding elite. Graves was a maverick and Whitsitt made the mistake of directly engaging him and his constituency. To be pulled into prolonged, uncivil strife and to fail to cooperate (which in the case of denominational elites apparently meant, "compromise" or even "conciliate") was to resist the preferred mode of political engagement.

Perhaps the most infamous of the Southwestern elite was J. Frank Norris. The "tornado from Texas" was the bane of the local Baptist association, the state convention, and the larger Southern Baptist Convention (Russell 1976; Entzminger, n.d). In the beginning, however, J. Frank Norris was an elite on the right track. Like other successful Southern Baptist elites, he was educated at The Southern Baptist Theological Seminary and quickly, pastor of large and prestigious churches. He was also editor, for a time, of the *Baptist Standard* in Texas.

But J. Frank Norris was at cross-purposes with the current Southern Baptist regime at several levels: He was outspoken and uncivil; he was fiercely independent and dogmatic about certain theological fundamentals; he was, in essence, countercultural. As a result, the usual career path for denominational elites was closed to him. Norris and his church were eventually expelled from their local Baptist association, and later, from the Texas Baptist Convention (Thompson 1982, pp. 137ff).

Norris and his constituency, however, were not without influence in the open politics of the Convention. In fact, Norris's complaints about the denominational "machine" and its collusion with "liberalism and modernism" provoked calls from the Convention floor for a confession of faith in 1925. Still, his ultimate influence on Southern Baptist life was muted by two factors. First, Norris responded to his ouster by forming the World Baptist

Fellowship—effectively taking his rhetoric and resources out of the Convention (Thompson 1982, p. 141). Second, the Convention elite at the time were heavily involved in the push toward financial centralization through the Cooperative Program (McClellan 1975). This mammoth undertaking drew some of the "limelight" away from Norrisite clamour.

The resulting statement of faith was a version of the New Hampshire confession and, when it was read, there were very few comments. According to McBeth, the statement was well-received although many thought there was "no great call for such an utterance" (Mcbeth 1987, p. 678). It is not incidental that the compromise confession was engineered by The Southern Baptist Theological Seminary President, E.Y. Mullins. Here was a denominational elite with the civility of the founding elites (educated at Southern Seminary) *and* the ardor and Biblical orthodoxy of the nonfounding faction (reared in Mississippi and Texas) (Barnes 1954, p. 138).

In sum, the founding or cultural elites of the South shaped the ethos of Southern Baptist Convention life: Civility and cooperation (Spain 1961, pp. 9-10). The nonfounding or counter-cultural elites of the Southwest provided the tension with their more aggressive and independent (anti-institutional) style. To be a *political* elite in Southern Baptist life during the first century of its existence, several characteristics were needful: An advanced education, a history of denominational involvement (early on, as a "founder"), a high status vocation in public life or in a prestigious pastorate, "Southern gentleman" style if not Southeastern breeding, and some connection with The Southern Baptist Theological Seminary.

However, to be a *national* elite in the Convention proper, the best criteria was a pastorate because the local church was (and is) the basic unit of Convention life—and, the larger the church, the larger the constituency, the larger the reputation, the more the power. Indeed, counter-cultural elites who have worked their way into the ranks of the political elite have done so primarily through success in the local church. Yet, as the previous two cases illustrate, the political elite have been willing to employ some sanctions to constrain "noncooperating" or "noncooperative" individuals and churches. And until the 1970's, at least, noncooperative factions have either compromised with the current regime or left the Convention.

The Flow of Elite Authority and Power: A "Pebble in the Pool"

"We, the Delegates from Missionary Societies, Churches, and other Religious bodies of the Baptist denomination in various parts of the United States, met in Convention, in the city of Augusta, Georgia, for the purpose of carrying into effect the benevolent intentions of our constituents, by organizing a plan for eliciting, combining and directing the energies of the whole denomination in one sacred effort for the propagation of the Gospel...." Styled 'The Southern Baptist Convention,' and designed to "promote Foreign and Domestic missions and other important objects connected with the Redeemer's Kingdom," the

Convention made provision for membership, based on contributions, for officers and boards (Woodsen 1950, pp. 127-128).

When the Southern Baptist Convention was constituted, the polity devised was different than that of the parent body, the Triennial Baptist Convention. Under the leadership of William B. Johnson of South Carolina, the gathering chose a more centralized polity with a number of boards and agencies falling under the direct authority of officers and trustees duly elected at a regular Convention of cooperating Southern Baptists (Barnes 1954, pp. 12ff). Initially, almost any entity that contributed was eligible to send "delegates" to a Convention: Individuals, churches, associations, missionary organizations, and state conventions.

In the late nineteenth century, churches and church contributions became the basis for representation through "messengers." Every cooperating (contributing) church has at least one messenger. Additional messengers (up to ten) are apportioned for each additional 250 members as well as for each additional $250 contribution (McBeth 1987, pp. 615-616). At Convention, messengers elect a President who in turn appoints a Committee on Committees. The Committee on Committees then nominates a Committee on Nominations. The Committee on Nominations is then responsible for nominating the Boards of Trustees for all Convention agencies and institutions (James 1989, pp. 12-13).

The power of the President is obvious. In a kind of "ripple effect," the personal choices of the President for one committee starts a three-tiered nominating process (see Figure 2). At the end of the two-year appointive cycle, those choices result in the selection of hundreds of Board and Committee persons who oversee segments of a large denominational bureaucracy.

Over the years, the rules have changed and the structure has been altered. For example, .in 1917 an Executive Committee was added to conduct the business of the Convention between sessions (Barnes 1954, pp. 177-179; Torbet 1950, p. 406). Since 1927, the Executive Committee has sole authority in the Convention "for fixing total objectives, for allocating funds to its various agencies and recommending same to the Southern Baptist Convention for adoption" (Routh 1954, pp. 429-433). Also in 1927, the Executive Committee employed its first full-time secretary. Thus, this powerful Committee has its own "denominational bureaucrats" with longer tenure than any single committee member. These high-level bureaucrats became important conduits of the formal and informal rules and models for aspiring elites.

As noted earlier, Ammerman calls Southern Baptist polity an "appointive oligarchy" (Ammerman 1990). While the largest number of positions are nominated, the fact is that the large slates of nominees from these committees are, for all intents and purposes, appointed. Few nominees have ever been successfully challenged or replaced. Time for business on the Convention floor

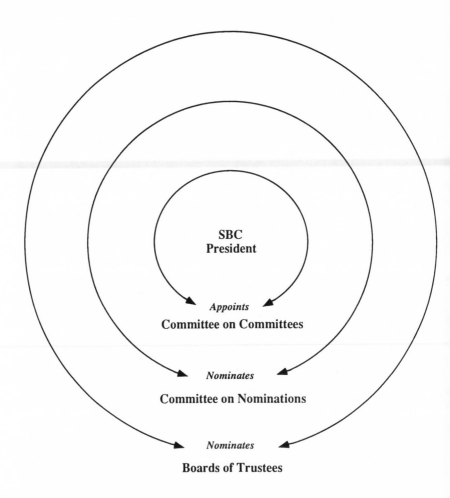

SBC President

Appoints

Committee on Committees

Nominates

Committee on Nominations

Nominates

Boards of Trustees

Figure 2. Appointments and nominations: A "pebble in the pool"

is relatively brief. In addition, a 1986 revision of Bylaw 16 made it virtually impossible for a majority of messengers at an annual meeting to make changes in a slate of nominees. The bylaw "prohibits a messenger from nominating an alternative slate of trustees from the floor. A messenger can only propose changes one name at a time" (James 1989, p. 12). At the 1990 Convention, for instance, this allowed for only two failed attempts to replace an individual trustee out of a slate of nominations before time for business had expired.

Regardless of slight changes in organizational structure, the effect was always the same: Convention leadership inevitably was composed of a small circle of friends of the political elite. There were no formal rules for admission into this political circle, but tacit guidelines were firmly in place. As the previous review of Convention Presidents revealed, there were a few necessary rungs in the denominational authority ladder. Besides serving as pastor of a large church, it seems that some connection with Southern Seminary was a key informal criteria.

The cumulative power and authority perpetuated through an appointed circle of friends was reinforced by the simple geography of the annual Convention. Because of distance and some Convention apathy, annual meetings were attended by those who lived near the meeting site (which changed each year) and those already involved formally in Convention decision-making. So, the network tended to feed on itself: Convention regulars were the likely leadership. This process assured that a certain type of Southern Baptist cultural elite became a member of the political elite. And this remained true even after the Convention membership, as a whole, became more Southwestern in composition.

Elite Disunity and Shifting Power: The "Big Church" Phenomenon

Denominational unity around *method* (cooperation) and *mission* (evangelization at home and abroad) is the stackpole of Southern Baptist Convention life (Shurden 1981, p.7; 1978, p. 225). In this biblically-conservative denomination, theological struggles did rock the denominational boat from both the right and the left. Nevertheless, such challenges were rebuffed. In the early twentieth century, for example, Southern Baptists resisted both modernism and fundamentalism with a statement against evolution in 1923 and a mild, nonbinding confession of faith in 1925 (Thompson 1982). Organizational cooperation was one thing: Theological or ideological conformity was quite another.

Mattingly argues that "since Southern Baptists do not have an articulated church tradition or creed they usually end up debating truth in terms of growth rates and trends." Essentially, what is left is a "sociological, statistical creed." As a result, Southern Baptist church tradition is "usually whatever is popular at the moment in the nation's biggest SBC churches" (Mattingly 1986, p. 11).

Indeed, there has long been a shared feeling in Southern Baptist life that "bigger is better." But how, exactly, does a large church pastorate translate into political power in the Convention? Reviews of early biographies clearly demonstrate that certain pastorates were considered "prestigious"—such as First Baptist Richmond, Virginia. Most were also among the largest churches in the Convention. In 1872, for instance, the five largest SBC churches included First Baptist Richmond, Nottoway, and Leigh Street in Virginia, Walnut Street in Louisville, Kentucky and Seventh Baptist in Baltimore, Maryland. Convention officers and national elites from the pool of large church pastors in the early years of the SBC included Andrew Broaddus, J.L. Burrows, M.E.

Dodd, Richard Fuller, S.L. Helm, Basil Manley, Jr., George W. McDaniel, George W. Truett, and many others.

The previous section traced elite unity and threats to unity through a historical survey of early SBC Presidents and other SBC elites involved in significant controversies in the Convention. The picture of the founding political elite was one of Southeastern lineage, denominational and civic involvement, an advanced education, and some connection with the first Convention Seminary. Most often, these early elites were from one of the nine founding Southeastern states. From 1845 to 1925, SBC Presidents were dominated by civic leaders, Seminary and University Presidents, and prominent pastors in almost equal numbers. From 1925 to 1935, however, the trend shifts not only to pastors—but to pastors of largest churches.

Figure 3 traces the location of the twenty-five largest SBC churches for selected years. In 1852 all of the twenty-five largest SBC churches were located in founding states. The number of largest churches located in nonfounding states grew steadily, however. By 1922 the number of largest churches in the nonfounding states exceeded the number in founding states. From that time onward, the Southeastern region, generally, lost its former power base of large churches. In 1989 only three out of the top twenty-five SBC churches were located in founding states.[5]

Since 1923, twenty-six of thirty-four SBC Presidents have been pastors.[6] Of those twenty-six, *twenty-three* were pastors of largest churches. From 1924 to 1951, of the six SBC Presidents who were pastors, *all* served a largest church. And, despite the increasing dominance of largest churches in nonfounding states, three of the six SBC President-pastors were from founding states. Of the eleven SBC Presidents during this period, six were from founding states. From 1952 to 1977, the SBC Presidential profile began to change. First was a transitional period (1952-1959) in which only one of four Presidents was a largest church pastor and two were from founding states. In 1960, with the Presidency of Ramsey Pollard, a new pattern developed. From 1960 to 1977 all SBC Presidents except one attended Southern Seminary. Seven out of ten were pastors of largest churches and only two were from founding states. A connection to Southern Seminary essentially replaced the founding state criteria for disproportionate access to the SBC Presidency.

From 1978 to 1992, there is a rather abrupt shift in the elite structure of the Convention—particularly as reflected in the SBC Presidency. Of the nine SBC Presidents elected during this period, all are pastors of largest churches, eight are serving in a nonfounding state, and *none are graduates of Southern Seminary*. The constituency of the political elite, finally, reflects the Southwestern "large church" power base.

Reviewing the data above, four factors are of particular note: First, the original reversal in "big church" power occurs precisely in the years preceding the Norrisite controversy and the first adopted confession of faith; second,

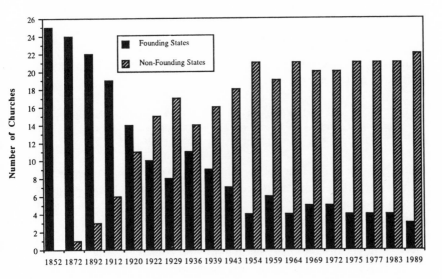

Figure 3.   Location of the 25 largest SBC churches in selected years

during the years when the founding states were realizing fewer and fewer largest churches, denominational bureaucrats and pastors of "not largest" churches were still securing SBC President seats in disproportionate numbers; third, from 1960 to 1977, 90 percent of SBC Presidents attended Southern Seminary; and fourth, during the years of the controversy 1979 to the present—no SBC President was a denominational elite or a graduate of Southern Seminary.

The following section will examine the real effects of the shift in the elite structure of the Southern Baptist Convention—particularly from 1946 to the present. Even from this cursory review, it is apparent that elites followed an implicit career track in the denomination. It is equally apparent that the majority of SBC constituency (and their leaders) shifted from the old Southeastern power base to the Southwest. Perhaps most amazing is the fact that the founding elites held power so long *after* the numerical center changed. How these Southern Baptist cultural elites finally fell to the ineluctable pressure of this growing rift is the rest of the story.

FROM COOPERATION TO COERCION: ELITE TRANSFORMATION IN THE SBC

What we have been observing in the Southern Baptist Convention for the past 11 years is a revolution. A somewhat entrenched bureaucracy and a "good old boys" club had closed their eyes to a gradual erosion of orthodoxy within our ranks.... Thousands of Baptists, rightly or wrongly, felt disenfranchised. Some institutional leaders were unresponsive to calls for a mid-course correction....(Corts 1990, p. 3).

So writes conservative North Carolina pastor, Mark Corts. Corts is one of many who support the redirection of Southern Baptist Convention life. Reflecting on the current situation, he states:

The time has come for true denominational loyalists who have long shared concerns, if not the zeal and methods, with conservative leadership, to support the revolution, bring it to maturity and cease the confrontational atmosphere (Corts 1990, p. 3).

Since most perceive that the revolution *is* over, conservatives across the Convention are calling for an end to unconventional political activity and a reconsolidation of power under the banner: "unity with doctrinal integrity" (Hefley 1990, p. 159).

The older Southern Baptist banner-cry of cooperative unity in theological diversity has changed to theological unity *over* cooperative diversity. Why has the basis for unification in this large, nonstate polity changed? The obvious answer is: Because the banner-carriers have changed. An elite transformation has occurred in the Southern Baptist Convention.

As the previous section shows, signs of an impending elite transformation have been brewing since the 1920's when the power base of largest churches shifted from the Southeastern to the Southwestern states. The rift between the Southwestern and Southeastern elite has been exacerbated by a polity that encouraged the appointment of a circle of friends.

The result was a burgeoning organization managed by long-time bureaucrats and governed benignly by volunteer, short-term political elites. The political elite generally trusted the organizational bureaucrats because they knew them: They went to school with them, served in their churches (or knew someone who had), sat on denominational committees and boards with them, and depended on them to keep the massive bureaucracy running smoothly. The organizational bureaucrats, on the other hand, had tremendous power within their organizations and institutions—but little real authority (see Ammerman 1990). They were equally dependent on the goodwill and continued trust of those political elite who held ultimate authority. Disunity among the elite necessarily imperiled this fragile symbiosis. Most elites agreed that the system was valid. Indeed, baptizing the decisions of early founders was a part of Baptist historiography. However, some began to sense that the system was "not working." What is important to understand up front, however, is what Southern Baptists construe as "not working."

As Mattingly observed, in place of a theological creed, Southern Baptists had a kind of statistical creed. Since evangelization was their cooperative goal, the success of the denominational system was measured by numbers: Of baptisms, new members, churches, and new missionary outposts. This pragmatic interpretation met the needs of both elite groups. Denominational bureaucrats built bigger and better "businesses," and pastors built bigger and better "churches" (Givens 1988). Despite theological differences, if the numbers were good, "things were working" in the respective fiefdoms of Southern Baptist elite.

Post-War Consolidation: Unity in Diversity (1946-1960)

The post-War period was good to Southern Baptists—as it was for many other denominations. The Southern Baptist Convention entered a period of unprecedented organizational expansion. Porter Routh, long-time Executive Secretary of the Executive Committee, described the significant changes inaugurated at the 1946 Convention:

1. Austin Crouch, the first Executive Secretary of the Executive Committee (1927-1945) retired and Duke McCall was elected. A Ph.D graduate of Southern, McCall left the Executive Committee in 1951 to succeed Ellis Fuller as President of his alma mater.
2. The Convention adopted a new policy to meet capital eeds of agencies and institutions. By 1952, $14,000,000 in Cooperative Program funds were distributed.
3. The "Convention machinery" was changed during this period. In 1946, the Convention voted for a rotational system for all members of the Executive Committee and Boards. In addition, members were added to each board for states having 500,000 members and another additional member for each 250,000 members in excess of 500,000. The Executive Committee was also expanded.
4. The Southern Baptist Foundation was established under the leadership of Duke McCall.
5. J.M. Dawson was elected the first secretary of the Joint Conference Committee on Public Relations whose mandate was "to enunciate, defend, and extend the historic, traditional Baptist principle of religious freedom with particular application to the separation of church and state...." (Routh 1954, p. 299).

It is not surprising that Southern Baptists' most significant periods of organizational expansion followed the World Wars. Post-war "rebuilding" energy served as a culture-wide impetus for new growth.

From 1946 to the mid-1950s, two other areas of expansion are notable. During this time a commission was formed to look into the situation of theological education. First, the Convention approved the incorporation of an existing seminary in California and made funds available for a "new seminary in the East" (Routh 1954, pp. 291ff). Second, a dispute in the mid-1940s with the Northern Baptists over California led to the end of a long-held comity agreement between the two denominations. At the 1951 Convention in San Francisco, Southern Baptists voted to remove all territorial limitations on evangelization in the United States (Routh 1954, p. 291). By 1964 Southern Baptists had churches in all fifty states. In effect, the SBC became a "national denomination" (McBeth 1987, p. 623).

Membership and new church growth was also marked in the early to mid-fifties. In 1956, the HMB inaugurated the "Thirty Thousand Movement" to form thirty thousand new SBC churches and missions. Significantly, McBeth concludes that this territorial expansion (most of it Westward) reawakened the "fading embers of Landmarkism into a raging fire" (McBeth 1987, p. 632). The fierce independence and pride of Landmarkist traditions was particularly attractive to struggling mission churches in "pioneer" SBC territory. Again, the issue was a basic difference in style as well as orthodoxy.

Pointing to rising statistics, most Southern Baptist elites would have agreed that the Convention was "working." The ranks of the political elite were also swelling. The growth and territorial expansion of the Convention meant that more people were being included from outside traditional Southeastern states. Indeed, the Southeastern cultural elite were proud of their denominational growth. Increasing inclusiveness was only a sign of the success of "cooperation" and "unity in diversity." Those who differed were allowed to express their opinions and influence policy through Convention meetings and through membership on ever-expanding Boards and Committees. The elite structure was decidedly "unified-cooperative" (see Figure 4).

Real power in the institutions was wielded by a cadre of cultural elite with long and stellar records in many areas of Convention life. Because the polity was based on appointments, it was more "relationship-based" than "representative." While the inclusion of new constituency was well-intentioned, the real effect was a kind of tokenism. The norms of cooperation and diversity required the inclusion of "others," but it became clear to new insiders who was "in control."

If knowledge is power, those who shaped and maintained the bureaucracy had the power: They knew the system best. And because the "litmus test" for status in Southern Baptist life was involvement in the denomination, those who had been involved the longest had the highest status (for further explanation of Baptist "activism," see Leonard 1990, pp. 110-113). In a real sense, positions of authority in the Convention membership on Boards, Committees, and election as officers were an "award" for involved and cooperating Southern Baptists.

Hefley, a conservative chronicler of the controversy, provides a description of how the "control group" operated in those days. He observes that these "well-

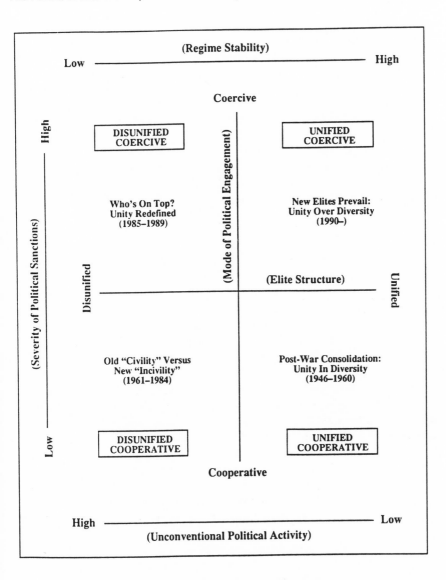

Figure 4. Elite transformations: The Southern
Baptist Convention, 1946 to the present

intentioned kingmakers politicked in informal but successful ways, to get men
elected to the presidency" (Hefley 1990, p. 17). The tone and fact of the account
itself points to the perception of exclusion and control by rival elites as much
as the intention of exclusion and control by the political elites.

As early as 1960, Hefley says, then-President Ramsey Pollard stated in a letter that a group of Convention bureaucrats were interested in nominating Hobbs as SBC President the following year. The group apparently included: A past President of the Convention, the President of the Woman's Missionary Union, and two SBC Presidents-to-be. Other correspondence showed that additional candidates were to be nominated but Hobbs was preferred, particularly because one candidate, although "greatly admired," was inattentive to "denominational activities" (Hefley 1990, pp. 18-19).

Cooperation was one of the unwritten gateways to political power in the SBC. However, the viability of this cooperative system rested primarily in the hands of a small group of elites, of a certain type, who acted as gatekeepers. This worked well in an earlier era, but by including more persons in the overall political elite network, more and varied elite were exposed to the system. Those new elites who had not been socialized into the system either felt excluded and resentful or patronized and dependent. Thus, a counter-cultural (Southwestern) elite like W.A. Criswell laments that while he was President of the Convention, he asked the Executive Secretary of the Executive Committee to "give me a list of people you think best qualified to serve" because "you know the Convention better than I do" (Hefley 1986, p. 65). Years later, Criswell translated his ignorance and the Executive's willingness to help as an instance of perpetuating the system.

Three other occurrences in the late fifties also contributed to a growing dissatisfaction with the way the system was working. First, seminaries began to experience a slow-down in enrollment. This was exacerbated by an internal crisis in the flagship seminary. In 1958, Southern Seminary lost 12 tenured faculty (McBeth 1987, p. 668; Barnhart 1986, pp. 27ff; Southwestern and Southern Seminary catalogues 1957-1961). Both circumstances are significant in that the seminaries had been the "nurseries" of the denominational and political elite. Southern Seminary, in particular, had produced a disproportionate share of denominational dignitaries. It is suspected that the loss of faculty during this period contributed to a decrease in the number of graduate students in subsequent years—prospective elite for prestigious pulpits and top-level denominational positions.

In addition, after that time, there seemed to be an implicit shift in seminary emphases and perceptions. So that by the seventies, enrolling students knew "you go to Southern if you want to teach" and "you go to Southwestern if you want to preach." Thus, during the critical decades following the "1958 crisis" at Southern Seminary, there were theoretically fewer potential candidates with the Southern Baptist cultural elite profile. And, concurrently, the balance of "largest churches" were in nonfounding states closer to Southwestern Seminary (the largest SBC seminary since the mid-fifties).

Second, Southern Baptists were beginning to experience a decrease in their overall growth rate, "the percentage membership gains in 1950 were 4.7 percent;

in 1965, 1.6 percent; and in 1978, 0.9 percent" (Hadaway 1990, p. 15). Thus, by pragmatic standards alone, the system was beginning to look like it "wasn't working." Indeed, strategists for the conservative movement pointed to declining baptisms as indications that the SBC was going the way of the "liberal mainline" (Hawkins 1990, p. 17; Patterson 1985, pp. 3-4; Pressler 1985, pp. 16-17). And, when things aren't working—Southern Baptists looked for "reasons why." Exclusion from the political elite by "back-room" politicking was one example. Enrollment decreases at the Seminaries was another. But in true Norrisite fashion, the suspected cause was spiritual failure and "liberal theology" provided the source.

Third, in the late fifties, the Convention went through an organizational evaluation by a New York firm. The result was the institution of "big business" practices throughout the Convention (Givens 1988). At least at Southern Seminary, this administrative reorganization brought in significant tensions. The faculty and administration had previously operated in an informal, family style—but had outgrown that configuration. The effect of the reorganization was to formalize procedures and add administrative layers.[7] The kind of distancing that the faculty experienced in this period of change was akin to the alienation nonfounding elite felt when they entered organized Convention life. Indeed, one of the two self-identified "strategists" of the takeover movement later concluded that the "super-corporate" organization also contributed to growing problems in the SBC:

Those formerly spoken of as "denominational servants" are increasingly distant from the constituencies they serve, surrounded by burgeoning bureaucracies, which continue to demonstrate lack of sensitivity to many of those who actually provide funding (Patterson 1985, p. 6).

New elites began to question the use of the system by those in power. They interpreted it as impregnable: The "gray" areas of camaraderie and informal politics were difficult to penetrate. Pastor-elites with a markedly different style— independent, aggressive, and unabashedly orthodox—were not readily accepted in the genteel boardrooms of elder statesmen or the "ivory towers" of seminaries with aspirations of divinity school rigor and status. Nor did they feel at home.

Despite the illusion of democracy, the polity was not representative in the classic sense. And although many "cooperative" elite still felt good about the system, it did not seem to be working very well. "Harmony" or cooperation was not enough. Indeed, cooperation tended to salve over more important issues like ideological orthodoxy. So, in 1961 when Broadman Press published Elliott's book, *The Message of Genesis*, the rival faction finally had a "hard" issue: Here was evidence of liberalism and it came from the pen and press of the denomination's elite. Many "cooperative" elite began to value political suitability over representative politics.

Old Civility Versus New Incivility (1961-1984)

In 1961, the Sunday School Board's Broadman Press published 4,000 copies of Elliott's *The Message of Genesis*. Hefley observes that this book "would become a time bomb to disrupt the unity of the SBC and set the stage for the crisis which is shaking the denomination today" (Hefley 1986, p. 49). A review of the episode along with the interpretations of two different elite-types highlights the movement from unity to disunity within the "rules and norms" of cooperation.

Ralph Elliott was a professor at Midwestern Seminary and according to Hefley, his book "plainly declared the stories of Adam and Eve, Cain and Abel, Noah and the Flood, the Tower of Babel and some events in the life of Abraham [were] nonhistorical and error-prone" (Hefley 1986, p. 49). K.O. White, pastor of the First Baptist Church in Houston Texas, called the book "liberalism, pure and simple" (Shurden 1972, p. 106).

At the 1962 Southern Baptist Convention, White made a motion reaffirming "faith in the entire Bible as the authoritative, authentic, infallible Word of God." It was passed unanimously. A related motion also passed. It affirmed "abiding and unchanging objection to the dissemination of theological views in any of our seminaries which would undermine such faith in the historical accuracy and doctrinal integrity of the Bible...." In addition, the motion called on trustees to "remedy at once those situations where such views now threaten our historic position" (*SBC Annual* 1962, pp. 65-68).

Other motions instructing the Sunday School Board to "stop publishing the Elliott book and to recall all copies in distribution were defeated" (Hefley 1986, p. 50). Nevertheless, the Board administration did cease publication and recall the copies. Further, Midwestern Seminary's trustees met with Elliott and told him to "go easy on the higher-critical method" as well as instructed him "not to republish his controversial book with another publisher." When he failed to abide by this agreement, he was dismissed for "insubordination" (Hefley 1986, p. 50).

An ultraconservative observer of the controversy who teaches at Bob Jones University, observed that "Elliott's dismissal was not a repudiation of his Modernism; it was a means to stop the rocking of the ecclesiastical boat." As in the Whitsitt controversy: "Liberals have shown their willingness to 'sacrifice' an occasional sacred cow like Elliott in order to quell the trouble waters of controversy" (Beale 1985, pp. 78-79).

Another outcome of the Elliott Controversy was the formulation of a new confessional statement: The Baptist Faith and Message. Conservative leaders, however, viewed the statement as little more than a compromise for the sake of denominational peace. Hefley concludes that the 1963 statement "plowed little new ground beyond previous confessions." The statement on the Bible was merely "lifted" from the 1925 confession and "in a bow to moderates" the committee added, "The criterion by which the Bible is to be interpreted is Jesus Christ" (Hefley 1986, p. 51).

After the controversy over the Elliott book, Convention conservatives were further "appeased" by the election of K.O. White to the SBC Presidency. Although, Hefley notes whereas "White took a stronger personal stand...[he] had no great influence in the agencies" (Hefley 1986, p. 52). And, the two following Presidencies were filled by Wayne Dehoney and Franklin Paschall— both with strong Southern Baptist cultural elite profiles. The following year another conservative, W.A. Criswell was supported by the "control group" for the SBC Presidency. Again, Hefley records that this nomination was the action of the political elite who "saw themselves as a sort of benevolent junta who worked to hold the denomination together" (Hefley 1990, p. 21).

Interestingly, by most indices White and Criswell had done the right things to earn a place in the political elite circle. They were graduates of Southern Seminary, pastors of "largest churches," and promoted strong Cooperative Program giving. Yet, their Southwestern style and restricted network of denominational elite contacts put them on the margins of the Convention elite.

Members of the cultural elite group did not interpret the inclusion of Criswell and White as "patronizing" or "conciliatory." In response to such charges, Southern Seminary historian, Bill Leonard remarked that:

> Fundamentalists were not excluded from service on boards of trustees and other convention offices. In fact, the 1960s and 1970s witnessed the election of a series of well-known conservatives to the SBC presidency, among them fundamentalists W.A. Criswell and K.O. White (Leonard 1990, p. 133).

Nevertheless, the fact remains that this was the way the countercultural group interpreted these actions.

Given the Convention-wide stress on church growth and evangelism, it seemed incongruous that the pastors who were most successful were not happily included in the denominational bureaucracy. Pressler accounted for the rift in involvement and regard in this way: "Conservatives had been out winning people to Christ and not attending Conventions, and not paying attention to the convention institutions" (Pressler 1985, p. 18). By the late sixties, however, disgruntled pastors and laypersons spurred by the dissatisfaction of marginalized elites like Criswell and White began to pay very close attention.

Frustrated by their inability to affect change in the Convention, unhappy elites began to mobilize outside the Convention structures. In 1973, the Baptist Faith and Message Fellowship was formed and a new journal was begun, *The Southern Baptist Journal*. The editor, William Powell, was a long-time Home Mission Board employee and staunch biblical conservative. Hefley states that Powell "came out swinging" by "quoting from books of 'liberal' professors and printing letters to denominational teachers and executives asking them if they believed in Adam and Eve, Cain and Abel, Noah and Jonah...." Powell urged conservatives not only to "take a stand," but to "take action!" (Hefley 1986, pp. 59-60).

The course of that action was largely dictated by two "Texas Baptist bluebloods"—Judge Paul Pressler and Paige Patterson. Both Pressler and Patterson fit the "cultural elite" pattern in every respect except for their Southwestern brand of orthodoxy and style. Pressler was a Texas Appeals Court judge, deacon and Sunday School teacher at the Second Baptist Church of Houston. Patterson was a seminary student at New Orleans when he first met Pressler. Patterson's father was Executive Director of the Baptist General Convention of Texas for many years and Patterson would subsequently receive a Th.D from New Orleans, become Criswell's associate, and the president of the Criswell Center for Biblical Studies. Pressler's primary concern was "liberalism" in the universities and seminaries; Patterson's was the denominational bureaucracy and elitism (Patterson 1985; Pressler 1985; Hefley 1986, p. 139).

Pressler and Patterson are the acknowledged architects of the "takeover" strategy.[8] Pressler described the process in this way:

> ...I began to study the structure of the Convention because I felt that the conservatives had been fighting battles without knowing what the war was. The liberals had analyzed the Convention structure and manipulated it for their own purposes.... We studied the constitution, studied the by-laws, and, not wanting to be dissident, we decided that we would work within the system to effectuate the changes that needed to be made, and obviously needed to be made, by working within the system (Pressler 1985, p. 18).

Thus, beginning with the 1979 Convention, a group of conservatives consciously targeted the Presidency. Their plan was to place someone in that position who would appoint "like-minded" persons on the Committee on Committees, who in turn, would nominate like-minded persons to the Committee on Nominations—and likewise to the Executive Committee and Boards of agencies and institutions. Because of the structure of the polity, this process would take at least ten years during which the rival faction must win every SBC Presidency.

The old system of informal politics based on trust and friendship was challenged by an upswing in conventional political activity, a partisan campaign. The counterculturalists mobilized messengers through the channels that they knew best. They "took to their pulpits" and preached to their people. They also cultivated and nurtured an expanding network of conservative pastors in smaller churches who shared their distrust of religious bureaucracies. Spreading the word about "liberalism" in the seminaries and "corruption" in the denominational agencies was not difficult, and was made easier through the emergence of several fundamentalist journals and newspapers. In addition, education about the Convention machinery and a new emphasis on Convention involvement resulted in commensurate increases in attendance.

Overtly politicizing the Convention meant attracting scores of "first-timers." And these newcomers did not know the "old rules" at all. Carefully socialized "civility" paled in the face of fiery evangelists who stood in the pre-Convention Pastor's Conference pulpits and described liberalism's "slippery slope."

From 1979 to 1984, the rival elites successfully ran and elected their candidates. Shurden, a long-time denominational elite, noted that the "fundamentalist activities of 1979, however, did not issue into a knee-jerk response" (Shurden 1985, p. 11). Indeed, the response of the long-time elite was slow. Leonard described the dominant perception of the political elite: "old convention 'pros' insisted that this was merely another rightward swing of the denomination that would wear itself out in five to seven years..." (Leonard 1990, p. 138). They took a "wait and see" attitude, generally; and in some cases, the political elite actually worked to defeat efforts to revise the appointive process—all in the hope that a cooperative approach would quell the rhetoric of the ascendant elites and restore harmony to the Convention.

Responses to growing disunity and the mobilization of rival elite took the form of more "informal networking" and politicking in the same old elite networks. Again, Leonard reflects on the rather loosely organized (and largely ineffectual) early attempts to counter the rival faction:

> there were often several identifiably "moderate" candidates nominated at the same convention, thereby enhancing the electability of the lone fundamentalist. For a time moderates turned to denominational statesmen, individuals whole lifetime service to the convention made them highly respected and widely known. These included Grady Cauthen, the executive director of the Sunday School Board, and Duke K. McCall, the president of Southern Seminary. Neither candidate was able to overcome the fundamentalist machine. It was the day of the preachers, not the "bureaucrats," as fundamentalists call convention leaders (Leonard 1990, p. 140).

Leonard observed that it took about "five years" to mount "anything resembling a united front." Once they did, however, the old political elite took the unusual step of contesting the rival faction's candidate during the customary incumbent year. In addition, denominational agency heads made public statements disavowing support for the incumbent. So, the old elite began to break their own informal rules and risked the charge from the rival faction that they weren't "playing fair." Hefley observes that the "opposition to Stanley's re-election by the agency heads created a backlash that brought thousands of conservative messengers to Dallas who might otherwise not have taken the trouble to come" (Hefley 1990, p. 34).

Up until 1984, the rival faction was still testing its power in tentative ways. Beale, again, who represents a more conservative, independent position, viewed the conservatives early attempts as "too cooperative"—and not nearly incivil enough. Throughout the seventies and early eighties, the rhetoric of the rival faction concentrated on images like "parity" and time and again, they insisted that they did not intend to "fire anyone" (Beale 1985, pp. 154, 161, 165, 175; Patterson 1985, p. 10; Pressler 1985, p. 19). At the beginning of the elite transformation, the rival faction Presidents sounded not unlike old elite. Disunity in ideology was clear—but a coercive mode of political engagement was not.

While it is true that some of the early rival elites were "in the system"— many aspiring elites that they attracted to their cause were not. Further, as the ideology of the movement took hold, even those who were formerly cooperative began to rethink their support of the system. This effect is seen clearly in giving patterns to the Cooperative Program. During the years of the controversy, the average SBC church dropped slightly in the percentage of total gifts which are used to support the Cooperative Program. As shown in Figure 5, however, the drop in percentage gifts from the largest SBC churches was much more serious.

The old political elite seized on this issue. Cooperative Program giving was the real "test of faith"—not doctrinal orthodoxy or membership growth. Still, this defense was only partially successful because examples of healthy giving could be found among the countercultural elite and examples of poor giving could be pinpointed in strong denominational bastions (Hefley 1986, pp. 20-21). Nevertheless, the data do demonstrate the nature of the rift: Loyalty to "cooperation" and the program versus commitment to "doctrinal orthodoxy" and church growth.

Most observers agree that by the 1985 Convention, the rival faction was well on its way to controlling the political elite of the SBC. Gaining a sense of their own power and putting in five years of on-the-job experience in the President's seat, the rival coalition changed their approach and rhetoric. Indeed, for the first time, they changed the "look" of the Convention platform. Long-timers at the Convention saw many more new faces than old ones on the simulcast screens in the halls. One tract on the "takeover" described a controversial ruling effectively "cancelling" a successful vote to overrule the chair in this way:

> Dr. Charles Stanley aided by Parliamentarian Wayne Allen rolled over an SBC business session with a clear moderate majority. This heavy-handed action generated more conflict. Suits were filed asking that the officers of the SBC be directed by the courts to follow the SBC Constitution (Watkins 1987a).

The new elites had the voice and the votes to risk more coercive moves.

On the other hand, after five years of waiting for the "tide to turn"—the old political elite also shifted into a more active mode. The next four years witnessed escalating sanctions from the new political elite and increased

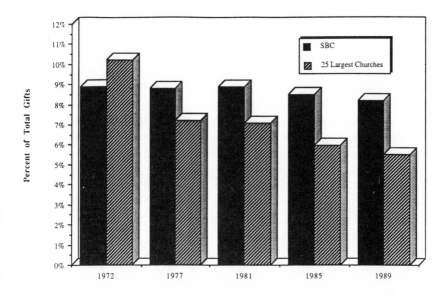

Figure 5.   Cooperative program gifts to SBC as a percentage of total gifts

political activity on the part of the old faction. For at least four years, "outside" journals for both sides of the controversy predicted an impending victory. In the case of the old political elite the hope was that "this year we'll win the Presidency and start to turn things around." In the case of the new political elite the hope was that "this year we'll finally realize a majority of trustees on boards and agencies and start to make some real changes."

Who's on Top? Unity Redefined (1985-1989)

After two decades of disunity in the SBC elite structure, a new regime with a clear ideological goal and a coercive mode of political engagement began to dominate. The SBC, subsequently, endured four years of conflict punctuated by increasing unconventional political activity all-around and sanctions from the now-partisan platform at annual Convention meetings. As long as the older political elite maintained power positions in the agencies and institutions, the conflict teetered on the brink of complete takeover and consolidation or recovery through de-escalation and, at least, a return to cooperative disunity.

As McSwain and Wilkerson (1987) observe, the old cultural elite were averse to "public confrontation." A more aggressive, coercive mode "frightened the long time advocates of the bureaucratic approach to conflict." Roy Honeycutt reflected on the position of the elite now out-of-power in a 1986 address to the Southern Seminary Alumni Luncheon, "We may have to do as they did in Rome, when they survived the Dark Ages, by creating pockets of civility, intelligence, and morality." Indeed, the old regime supporters did begin to "create pockets"—more pockets of deliberation than action.

In response to the threat of eminent board-takeovers, a number of channels outside the system were formed. In 1983, a group of self-identified "traditionalists" began *SBC Today*. The paper is the primary news vehicle for Southern Baptists with views akin to the older political elite group. In addition, between 1985 and 1989, the older political elite supported the formation of two "alternative" organizations. The first, the Southern Baptist Alliance, was organized in 1987 as "an alliance of individuals and churches dedicated to the preservation of historic Baptist principles, freedoms and traditions and the continuance of our ministry and mission within the SBC" (James 1989, p. 56). The Alliance's primary contributors were initially concerned North Carolinians—many with connections to Southeastern Seminary.

The second Baptists Committee was formed in 1988 by older denominational elite and a few "new entries" into the former political circle conservative Southwesterners who serve "largest churches" that are heavy Cooperative Program supporters (James 1989, pp. 54-55; Hefley 1988, p. 222; Hefley 1990, p. 63). In fact, the new elite of the "old" political circle fit the profile of the Southwestern counterculturalists more than the Southeastern founding elite. But, these particular pastors—including Winfred Moore, Richard Jackson, and Daniel Vestal—were either disenchanted with or disenfranchised by the new political elite. Interestingly, in the years of the "holy war,"[9] the former elite circle conceded the importance of the biblical issue (which they had previously resisted) by promoting these "inerrantists" for the SBC Presidency.[10]

It is clear, however, that more aggressive action by the former political elite came too late in the game. Two developments in 1986 made political mobilization both difficult and ultimately ineffectual. First, at the suggestion of an ex-SBC President from the old elite camp, the Dallas Convention voted to form a "Peace Committee." The intent, from the perspective of the former political elite, was to effect an "elite settlement"[11] and put the Convention back on a less volatile and more acceptable track. Leonard observes that these "denominational leaders" refused to "believe that the divisions were irreconcilable" and "that the old art of compromise no longer prevailed" (Leonard 1990, p. 143). The second development was a conciliatory statement on the Bible by the six SBC Seminary Presidents.

The twenty-two member Peace Committee was composed of elite from both sides of the Controversy. While the organizers may have had hope of compromise, it was clear to most that the new elite were in no mood to "give in" on any point of theological diversity. Hefley reported that Bill Sherman (an opponent of the takeover group) was not optimistic that "the Peace Committee could bridge the chasm." Sherman stated:

> I met with Adrian Rogers [Peace Committee member] and told him, "I don't see eye to eye with you theologically, but I can work with you and you interpret Scripture as you wish." Quick as a flash he snapped his finger and said, "Bill, that's good enough for you, but I will not work with liberals" (Hefley 1986, p. 131).

Indeed, that would be the case: The new elite would not "work with" anyone outside their camp. The Peace Committee investigations merely served to validate the contentions of the new elite that "liberalism" did exist in the seminaries. And, in response, the Seminary Presidents produced a 1986 "Glorieta Statement" on the Bible as a kind of "olive branch" to the new elite. The statement included this phrase: "the 66 books of the Bible are not errant in any area of reality" (Hefley 1987, pp. 118ff; Leonard 1990, pp. 143ff; Knight 1987).

This compromise move ultimately back-fired because it disappointed the old elite who still contended that "theology is not the issue" and it gave the new elites something they could hold over the seminaries. Peace Committee member, Adrian Rogers concluded after reports that Honeycutt and others were elusive about whether "not errant" meant the same thing as "inerrant" in the areas of "science, philosophy, history and so forth":

> The only way we can take the Glorieta Statement is literally. They assured us that this is not slippery language: "not errant in any area of reality." I say if "not errant" and "inerrant" don't mean the same thing, then language has no meaning at all and there's no need to discuss anything. Not errant and inerrant are absolute synonyms. Absolute. And you can't tell me that history is not an area of reality (quoted in Hefley 1987, pp. 120-121).

In the end, the Peace Committee report (which was accepted after limited floor debate punctuated by many "points of order") included a short laundry list of literal Biblical interpretations as examples of "where the majority of Southern Baptists stand." In addition, the report recommended that Southern Baptist institutions recognize these basic Bible beliefs and build their future staffs with like-minded persons (*SBC Annual* 1987; Hefley 1988, pp. 80ff). Two Peace Committee members, Cecil Sherman and Winfred Moore, resigned from the group prior to its official closure in protest because the committee became "an agent for the work of the Fundamentalists" and a "watchdog" group (Leonard 1990, pp. 145ff).

As Leonard remarked: "the Peace Committee was too little, too late" (Leonard 1990, p. 149). By 1986 the Pressler-Patterson coalition had elected a string of SBC Presidents and the balance of power on Boards and Committees was already "swinging" their way. The Peace Committee process began at a time when the new elite were gaining power on all the boards. Given the structure of the polity—the "pebble in the pool" flow of authority—it was only a matter of time until the "new" political elite circle was fully formed. And because the Peace Committee also included a strong statement against denominational leaders' "political involvement"—any direct action from those quarters could now be labeled as "uncooperative." Thus, again, the old political elite were put in a position to break their own rules to recapture power.

A review of the actions of the new political elite demonstrate that both political sanctions and unconventional political activity were running high from 1985 to 1989. A "tracking sheet" from the camp now out-of-power illustrates consolidation of institutional authority in many areas:

SBC Home Mission Board: Just prior to the 8/6/86 meeting, of the SBC Home Mission Board "takeover" trustees met privately and then forced the resignation of 6 of 7 of the HMB presidential search committee. M.A. Winchester of Whitley City, Ky. refused to resign. HMB votes of 40/36 indicated the first "takeover " majority on an SBC board.

Baptist Sunday School Board: At the 8/4/86 meeting of the Baptist Sunday School Board "takeover" trustees attempted to reprimand BSSB president, Lloyd Elder, for an article critical of the takeover party, written by former BSSB president, James L. Sullivan and published in *Facts and Trends*.

Baptist Press: On 9/86 the Southern Baptist Press Association (composed of 37 editors of state Baptist news journals) branded as "absolutely unacceptable" the enormous increase in closed door sessions of SBC agency board meetings. The secret nature of the Peace Committee has allowed the takeover leaders to make war at its meetings while staying safely out of public view.

On February 17, 1987, the "takeover" party narrowly lost an effort to gain control of Baptist Press. The Executive Committee of the SBC elected Alvin C. Shackelford, editor of the Baptist and Reflector of Tennessee, as the new BP director by a vote of 32 to 26. Shackelford, himself an inerrantist has distinguished himself as an objective newsman. Opposition to his candidacy by Rogers and Pressler showed that the control of the SBC structure, not theology, is their true agenda.

SBC Christian Life Commission: On January 15, 1987 Christian Life Commission trustees elected, by a vote of 16 to 13, ethicist Larry Baker as their new executive director. The "takeover" party wants an executive they can control. Baker is not that man. With more "takeover" trustees scheduled to rotate on to the CLC board, the agency is set for a future crisis.

Baptist Joint Committee on Public Affairs: On October 3 and 4, 1986 the fact finding committee met to begin work on a resolution made from the floor of the 1986 Atlanta SBC by takeover activist M.G. Daniels of Alabama. The resolutions' intent is "to defund the Baptist Joint Committee on Public Affairs and establish an exclusive Southern Baptist presence in Washington, D.C."

Peace Prospects: At the July 28, 1986 Peace Committee subcommittee meeting, "takeover" leaders (Rogers/Pressler/Patterson) rejected all moderate peace proposals, advancing no peace proposals of their own. Dr. Adrian Rogers said, He "cannot allow a moderate seminary such as Southern because its graduates are totally unacceptable on the mission field" (Watkins 1987b).

A clearly coercive elite structure, the new power group no longer sought to involve other factions in a cooperative effort at government. The new, dominant group both clarified and "fought" for its position. Efforts to suppress and eliminate rival factions persisted: This was illustrated by the increase in secret meetings, in official sanctions against agency heads sympathetic with the former elite, and in attempts to defund organizational subunits whose leaders and/or policy statements were not in line with current political agenda.

As a new political elite, Stan Coffey admitted in 1986: "If we don't change at the top, we don't have any hope" (Hefley 1987, p. 210). By the end of 1989, the new political elite had the following denominational leaders in place: (1) Larry Lewis, president of Hannibal-LaGrange College in Missouri "a leading figure in the conservative movement" was elected president of the Home Mission Board, (2) William Crews, not a "conservative activist" but having the "full confidence of the leaders in the resurgence movement,"—was elected president of Golden Gate Seminary, (3) Lewis Drummond, a "conservative" who served as the Billy Graham Professor of Evangelism at Southern Seminary, was elected president of Southeastern Seminary (following the resignation of Randall Lolley after the Board reorganized to increase their involvement in hiring practices at Southeastern), (4) Mark Corts, "conservative" North Carolina pastor, was elected chairman of the Foreign Mission Board, and (5) Richard Land, vice president of academic affairs at Criswell College, was elected executive director of the Christian Life Commission (after the resignation of Larry Baker) (Hefley 1990, pp. 33ff). A total elite transformation was occurring. Having solidified control of the Presidency, key Committees and Boards, the new political elite were moving to fill vacancies at the helm of denominational agencies with "like-minded" people. And these "like-minded" people represent a deep tradition in Southern Baptist life: Southwestern, independent, and anti-institutional.

However, as long as the old political elite held significant positions in the Seminaries and other agencies like the Sunday School Board (the admitted "cash cow" of the Convention), the new political elite knew the job was not complete. The escalating scale of the conflict reflected the disunity in the elite structure. Hefley records the summer and fall of 1989 as particularly "stormy" for all concerned (Hefley 1990, pp. 83ff).

The Foreign Mission Board faced widespread criticism over a decision to deny appointment to a prospective missionary couple—both ordained. The Baptist Sunday School Board trustees were also criticized (particularly by Baptist Press) for an attempt to fire the executive director, Lloyd Elder. In addition, the Executive Committee voted to recommend to the larger

Convention that the program assignment of the BJCPA be transferred to the Christian Life Commission. Finally, both Southeastern and Southwestern Seminaries experienced "rocky" Fall trustee meetings: The first dealt with scrutiny by its accrediting agencies for administrative changes regarding faculty hiring and the second witnessed conflict between trustees and President Dilday over his "political statements" against the current regime (Hefley 1990, pp. 116ff).

Although the SBC Presidency (and most of the Boards) was firmly in the hands of the new elite, the segmented nature of the organizational structure made total control difficult to achieve. The old political elite faction became increasingly alarmed at what it considered "blatant" tactics to wrest total ("totalitarian") control of the denomination and reacted accordingly (Sherman 1985, p. 12; Daley 1990, p. 5). Irregular and escalating political actions characterized both sides in the conflict, prolonging the inherent instability of the political order.

> Early in 1990, Alan Neely, former professor at Southeastern Seminary, concluded: Time has virtually run out for the moderates. If they fail again next June in New Orleans to elect their candidate as Convention president, the show will be over (Neely 1990, p. 62).

This sense of urgency over the 1990 SBC Presidential election was also reflected in conservative writing. New Foreign Mission Board Chair, Mark Corts, asserted that "the election of Morris Chapman [the 'conservative' candidate] will bring the revolution in the Southern Baptist Convention" to "necessary maturity." Or, the "election of Dan Vestal [the 'moderate' candidate] would muddle the signals, diminish the consensus, resulting in a protraction of the conflict" (Corts 1990, p. 3). Would the elite structure move toward a unified-coercive position, or would it continue in disunity and instability?

New Elites Prevail: Unity Over Diversity (1990-   )

> A new day is dawning in the Southern Baptist convention. For the first time in many years, many pastors, in our denomination are expressing their hopes that the eleven-year old theological and political struggle within our convention may be coming to an end. Pastors who have previously been unaligned, have in recent weeks taken public stands. The call has gone out for a new coalition of denominational leadership which will broaden the base of our cooperative efforts yet, at the same time, will be unswervingly committed to the Bible as God's perfect word.... ("Summit Conference Statement," 1990).

The critical nature of the 1990 Convention was clear to both camps. Political mobilization began in the Fall of 1989 with Dan Vestal's statement that he would run again for President. As the new year began, Carolyn Weatherford Crumpler declared her "candidacy" for the SBC First Vice-Presidency as

Vestal's "centrist" running mate. Shortly thereafter, four of the five immediate past presidents of the SBC settled on the conservative candidate during a summit cruise in the Caribbean. The prospective nominee was Morris Chapman. Chapman was a Texas pastor of one of the 25 largest SBC churches and is a graduate of Southwestern Seminary.

In March, John Bisagno and Joel Gregory—both conservative pastors of "largest" Texas Baptist churches—issued separate calls to broaden the base of the new political elite. Having seized control of every board and agency (except the flagship Southern Seminary), the new political elite were poised to accept "applications" to fill leadership positions of this vast denominational structure. One thing was needful, however, the successful election of the new political elite candidate: Morris Chapman. In what most of the former elite viewed as a "tactical move," the new conservative strategy was consolidation under a "less-politicized" term: The "perfect Bible." In addition to Bisagno and Gregory, other, very influential, and previously nonaligned pastors, such as Jim Henry from Florida (pastor of one of the 25 largest SBC churches) and Ken Hemphill from Virginia (the conservative, Cambridge-educated pastor of a very large, fast-growing church) joined in the effort to elect Morris Chapman. According to Jim Henry:

> Our leader must be one who will affirm the course of the past 11 years that will keep us off the reefs of denominational destruction, the spiritual oil spill that polluted and practically destroyed every mainline denomination, the environmental hazard that has wasted too many lives and evangelical pursuits to the toxic waste of compromise (Martin 1990, p. 13).

The old political elite were once again backing Daniel Vestal—previously the pastor of a "largest church" in Midland, Texas, now pastor of Dunwoody Baptist in Atlanta—who was a "theological conservative" but not a part of the takeover coalition. Vestal termed himself a "denominational conservative." He described Chapman's nomination as a:

> ... very clear political strategy to "enlarge the tent" of leadership in the central core. The college of cardinals is reaching out to select a group of influential pastors in order to perpetuate control of the past 11 years by enlisting fresh leadership into it. This is part of the problem. The SBC does not need an episcopate, a presbytery, a college of cardinals. We do not need to be a centrally controlled denomination by a centrally controlling group determining who can and who cannot be part of Southern Baptist life (Harwell 1990, p. 1).

A review of the principal "movers and shakers" in the 1990 campaign on behalf of the "moderates" is instructive: Former Woman's Missionary Union President, Carolyn Crumpler; former director of the Baptist Press, W.C. Fields, former head of the Radio and Television Commission, Jimmy Allen; former President of Southeastern Seminary, Randell Lolley; former editor of *Home Missions*, Walker Knight; former editor of the *Christian Index*, Jack Harwell;

and former associate director of the Baptist Joint Committee, Stan Hastey. Indeed, the now-rival faction is a veritable cavalcade of "former" political and denominational elite.

Yet, while "moderates"—the old denominational elite are working for "one more try" at unseating the Pressler-Patterson coalition, the final Seminary falls to the aims of the new political elite. At its full Board meeting in April 1990, Southern Seminary trustees: (1) adopt a resolution asking seminary employees to work for anti-abortion legislation, (2) introduce a measure that would more narrowly define what professors must believe in order to teach at Southern, (3) discuss a report issued by the Reverend Jerry Johnson, a trustee from Aurora, Colorado which claimed President Honeycutt "just does not believe the Bible" and (4) and block the appointments of three trustees recommended by the Board's executive committee to fill vacancies (Wolfe 1990). In addition, the "conservative-dominated" Board "issued resolutions criticizing two prominent professors for their outspoken positions on abortion and the moderate-conservative struggle within the Southern Baptist Convention." Trustee Jerry Johnson reported that the Board's actions were "very reflective of the convention." And "conservative trustee," John Michael concluded that Southern's professors "need to be in harmony with the board of trustees" (Wolfe 1990).

Response from alumni of this long-time nursery of denominational elites was quick and anguished. A state President of Southern Seminary alumni was quoted as saying:

> I feel such deep grief. The only plant in my Southern Baptist garden which still has green leaves on it is being pulled up by its roots. What is left for me in the SBC? (Harwell 1990, p. 8).

The Seminary faculty, itself, did not remain silent in the face of this onslaught. On May 8, 1990, a faculty group called for the "resignation of trustee Jerry Johnson." The statement released by the seminary's "Faculty Club" expressed "moral outrage" at the "malicious attack" on seminary President Roy L. Honeycutt and several moderate professors. The statement was "unanimously approved" at a "meeting attended by 60 of the school's 78 full-time faculty members" (Wolfe 1990, p. A1).

The actions of the Trustees at Southern Seminary confirmed the "purge" mentality of the new political elite and fears that some kind of doctrinal guidelines would be imposed. In fact, John Bisagno, in a pre-Convention article in *The Communicator*, issued the following challenge:

> Let every Southern Baptist Seminary and University Professor promise that he [sic] will teach only in accord with dominant convictions and beliefs held by Southern Baptists at large in the four areas of theological concern cited by the Peace Committee, and the battle is over (Bisagno 1990, p. 9).

The focus in the Convention is uniformity, and the party line is sharply drawn. Further, the new political elite demonstrated that they would move boldly to ensure that the "will of the Convention" is implemented in its agencies and institutions.

On the third morning of the 1990 Southern Baptist Convention meetings, the *Times-Picayune* carried the following headline: "Conservative Baptists solidify takeover." Indeed, Morris Chapman was elected by "one of the largest margins of victory by a conservative candidate since convention infighting began more than a decade ago." Texas Appeals Court Judge, Paul Pressler, concluded: "Our greatest days are ahead of us" (Grissett and Faciane 1990). Not incidentally, Southern Baptists voted at this Convention to take the "job of representing First Amendment issues on Capitol Hill from the hands of its long-time lobbying arm ... [and give] it to a more conservative agency" (Grissett 1990, p. A8).

Having consolidated power, the new political elite made several overt moves to tighten control. At the Convention, Southern Seminary trustees made known their intention to call a "full meeting of the Board" in the Fall. Ordinarily, only the Executive Committee of Southern Seminary's Board met at that time. Further, some "officers" of the Executive Committee of the SBC met with the Executive Secretary, Harold Bennett and persuaded him to offer a "generous" severance package to two Baptist Press heads, Al Shackelford and Dan Martin, if their resignations were tendered immediately. The two newsmen refused and stated later that "no charges were mentioned." The chairman of the committee explained that the officers made the move in order to avoid an awkward "confrontation" in the Executive Committee meeting itself.

In response to Shackelford and Martin's disclosure of the proffered "deal," the Executive Committee scheduled a July 17 meeting to discuss the fate of the two Convention employees. A statement from "Concerned Southern Baptists" was released through Baptist Press shortly after the July meeting where the two men were officially fired (Statement from Concerned Southern Baptists 1990).

The new political elite moved to consolidate ideological unity through the censure of Baptist Press officials viewed as "partisan" toward the rival faction. Characteristic of an ideologically unified elite operating in a coercive mode, any "critics" are viewed negatively. They threaten the basis of unity—and so risk at least, censure and at worst, dismissal from positions of authority. Power is only shared with those who hold to the "party line"; coercive action is used to ensure that power is restricted to those who accept and support the current regime. Elites who disagree, therefore, will not retain power in a unified-coercive regime.

Effectively cut-off from the power structure of the Convention, the older elite faction worked outside the system. Immediately following the firing, a lawyer and member of Woodmont Baptist Church in Nashville announced the formation of "Associated Baptist Press." He noted that the press is "being launched by interested and concerned state Baptist news editors, pastors and laypersons" and is "totally apart from the Southern Baptist Convention Executive Committee." Further, the lawyer announced that "ABP is aligned with no political group—nor will it ever be (Statement Announcing Associated Baptist Press 1990).

In addition, a meeting of "Southern Baptist Convention Moderates" was held August 23-24, 1990. The publicized purpose of the meeting was to "draft an alternate funding plan for Southern Baptists dissatisfied with the way the SBC Executive Committee divides the convention's Cooperative Program unified budget." The meeting was requested by Daniel Vestal—the defeated Presidential candidate. This August meeting was a follow-up to a smaller caucus of moderates which met earlier in Dallas (*Baptist and Reflector* 1990, p. 3).

The firing of Baptist Press officials and the moderate meeting in Atlanta foreshadowed future events in the SBC. In 1991 and 1992 purges in the form of forced retirements of agency and seminary Presidents continued. Each announcement was followed by resignations of other top administrators at the institutions. January 1991 saw the forced resignation of Lloyd Elder from the Sunday School Board. In March 1992, under pressure from trustees, Keith Parks took early retirement several years early from the Foreign Mission Board. And in October 1992, Roy Honeycutt made a similar decision to retire from the presidency of Southern Seminary. Replacements came from the new political elite. Jimmy Draper and Morris Chapman, both key conservative leaders, former SBC Presidents, largest church pastors and graduates of seminaries other than Southern, were named, respectively, to head the Sunday School Board and the Executive Committee. In addition, Paige Patterson, one of the architects of the takeover, was named President of Southeastern Seminary.

The former political elite—no longer able to share power with the elite in the Convention they largely built—had to work outside the system to rebuild their own power bases. They no longer contested Presidential elections, nor sought to replace conservative nominees to boards and agencies. They were not willing to leave the Convention, however. Where did that leave the former political and denominational elite and their followers? Harwell responds:

> It leaves us without notice, influence or recourse within SBC policy-making councils. We have been told in no uncertain terms, "You cannot serve on our boards or committees. You cannot receive our mission funds. You cannot be appointed as our missionaries. You cannot even speak on the convention floor unless you indicate in advance your support of our positions. But, keep sending us your money, by all means!" (Harwell 1990, p. 8).

This untenable situation led to the formation of the Cooperative Baptist Fellowship; the founding and expansion of an "alternative" seminary in Richmond, Virginia; the organization of a parallel foreign mission organization, headed by Keith Parks (former President of the SBC Foreign Mission Board), and the establishment of a new Press to produce Sunday School curriculum and other "moderate" publications. In essence, a "Convention within the Convention" formed which continued to gain financial strength—even as it lost national press coverage.

The primary battle for control now is at the state convention level. In 1990 both Furman and Baylor Universities instituted major changes in the election of trustees to avoid a future takeover by conservatives in South Carolina and Texas. Virginia and several other states conventions redirected Cooperative Program funds in order to support the CBF (Cooperative Baptist Fellowship), the Baptist Joint Committee, Ruschlikon Seminary and other institutions. New divinity schools are planned at Baylor, Mercer, and Gardner-Webb. At the same time, conservatives in all state conventions have organized into political factions in order to repeat their national success at the state level. As yet, they have had only mixed success. And, according to Wayne Allen, past chair of Southern Seminary's trustees,

> Many conservatives are battling in their minds whether the state conventions are worth fighting for. I see the future of the Convention being regional associations that are centered in metropolitan areas. If I could wave my magic wand, I would do away with state conventions…either the state conventions are going to have to change or they're going to have trouble existing. They might get bypassed.

Yet many former members of the old denominational elite have given up the fight at both the national and state level. Howard Cobble, once the chair of the SBC Executive Committee, said in an interview with one of the authors that he is not involved in the Cooperative Baptist Fellowship or anything else political and that he only comes to the convention now because his church wants him to attend. He said he "feels like a man without a country" and "about as useless as a tit on a boar hog." He, and many others, have capitulated to the rule of the new political elite.

The elite transformation in the SBC is now accomplished. The cool, civil "culturalists" of the old South have bent to the fiery, anti-institutional "counterculturalists" with the souls of the old Southwest. After the election of Oklahoman, Morris Chapman, the *Times-Picayune* reported,

> "…the Reverend Bill Sutton, a conservative from McAllen, Texas, applauded the vote" and said "They call this a takeover, but what we're experiencing is the final stage of a take-back. We're going back to where I came from" (Grissett and Faciane 1990, p. A8).

CONCLUSIONS

The revised elite paradigm provides a framework for interpreting and predicting political stability and instability. The approach is applicable to both nation-states and large, non-state polities—particularly national, federated organizations. The Southern Baptist Convention was chosen to illustrate how the model can be employed to interpret political conflict in a non-state organization. In fact, because it is more an appointive oligarchy than a democracy, an analysis of elite dynamics is especially critical for understanding conflict and change in the SBC. Not only have presidential candidates been selected by a small, informal group of elites, but the process through which political appointments are made is extremely centralized. The role of non-elites is minimal, at best.

In essence, elites maintain control over the SBC and its boards and agencies by mobilizing non-elites to show up one day a year for a presidential vote. Despite an illusion of democracy, the margin of victory reflects the ability of one side to mobilize sufficient numbers of messengers to attend the convention and cast their vote for the right nominee. And as has been shown, elites with a compelling ideology—and the energy and resources to spread the word—have the upper hand in this process. By creating and sustaining a social movement, former rival elites were able to "seize the palace" in 1979 and have protected it from attack every year since.

Using the revised elite paradigm, we show that the conflict and current realignment of the SBC political elite structure, if not inevitable, certainly should have been no great surprise. Similarly, the process through which the elite structure moved, from unified-cooperative to unified-coercive, was a theoretically interpretable progression—given the orientation and goals of rival elites.

The next step is prediction. Within the parameters of the elite model, where can we expect the Southern Baptist Convention to move? If the SBC were a nation-state, we might anticipate the beginning of long-term stability as political elites continue their purges of those with potential access to political power who disagree with the "party line." Also, we can expect that new appointments will be made from rising elite in the conservative camp.

Former political elites are attempting to create viable bases of power outside the formal structure of the Southern Baptist Convention. In addition, leaders in some state conventions are mobilizing resources to apply pressure on the current regime by reducing the flow of funds to the denomination. Such efforts are viewed by the new regime, interestingly enough, as uncooperative. All in all, they are likely to have little effect on new political elites in the SBC. Despite talk about cooperation and broadening the tent, only persons who believe in biblical inerrancy—and also hold accepted stances on certain social issues like abortion and homosexuality—will be appointed to the boards of SBC agencies and seminaries. The political elite, however, cannot prevent new bases of power from developing nor can they force opposing elites from the older regime out of the SBC. Purged leaders are still Southern Baptists, of course, even if their national bases of power have been removed.

The next step is difficult to predict. Political elites want to become "cooperative" rather than "coercive," and some movement has been made in that direction. By the spring of 1993, two "prime" positions, the Presidents of Southern Seminary and the Foreign Mission Board, were filled by conservative elite with stronger network connections to the old regime than to the current political elites. The pool of possible recruits for denominational elite status has been expanded to include conservative non-elites and denominational elites who support the actions of the current regime. Nevertheless, we do not believe that a regime structure can move *directly* from a unified-coercive elite structure to a unified-cooperative one.

If the SBC had undergone schism and the "moderates" had left *en masse*, it might have been possible for the Convention to move toward a unified-cooperative stance. Theoretically, since there would be no so-called liberals left, "agreement to disagree" would be possible over less substantive issues. Two kinds of threats persist that should keep the political elite focused on the need for ideological and practical control. First, a large number of moderates and their churches remain within the Convention. There cannot be an agreement to disagree when a considerable segment of potential elites are automatically excluded. Second, even larger numbers of conservatives are at odds on issues including freemasonry and the role of women in ministry. One, fairly clear ideological agenda like biblical inerrancy was an effective unitive concern for a broad segment of SBC conservatives—elites and non-elites alike. However, as the list of what is "orthodox" and what is "unorthodox" grows, conformity· becomes more difficult for political elites in a federated organization both to define and enforce. The likely result? If current political elites continue to define and enforce orthodoxy based on a few relatively straightforward and broadly acceptable conservative tenets, a unified-coercive structure may persist. On the other hand, if simmering factions within the larger SBC or even in the political elite itself—gain the power and the will to challenge the current regime, there is a chance that the unified-coercive elite structure will eventually break down. If so, another period of unconventional political activity and harsh political sanctions will ensue.

Finally, the next step in testing and refining the revised elite paradigm is to apply the theory to past denominational and political schisms, to elite transformations which did not seem to fit the original elite paradigm (such as France and Japan), and to the breakdown of once stable "ideologically unified" elite structures in the former Soviet Union and Eastern Europe. By clarifying the analytical dimensions of the elite paradigm, a useful tool for analyzing political change is now more powerful and its potential applicability is significantly broadened.

NOTES

1. Field and Higley (1978; 1985) identify this factious disunity as the "pure type." They also have identified another variant of the disunified elite, "the imperfectly unified elite" or the elite state of "partial unity." As described, this variant is structurally similar to our disunified cooperative elite (see below).

2. Cammack's (1990) "top-level elites" and Putnam's (1976: 10ff) "proximate decision makers."

3. This type is very similar to Share's (1987) Consensual Regime Leaders (who facilitate democratic transitions from authoritarian regimes).

4. Finally, it should be noted that the coercive nature of a disunified-coercive elite structure refers to actions of the dominant elite faction in the government, and not necessarily to all elite factions in the nation state. Rival elite groups may be calling for cooperation as they are being repressed, while in other situations all elite factions may be in a coercive mode—seeking to rule and to remove power from their rivals.

5. These data were obtained from three sources: associational minutes (1852-1920); various editions of the *SBC Handbook* (1922-1969); and SBC Uniform Church Letter data (1972-1989) from the Sunday School Board.

6. Adrian Rogers is counted twice, since he was President twice in non-consecutive terms.

7. We owe this insight to John Loftis, a Baptist historian who interviewed several of the professors who resigned from Southern Seminary in 1958.

8. "Takeover" terminology is most frequently used by the older political elite faction. See, for example, James (1989) and Watkins (1986).

9. Prior to the 1985 Convention, Roy Honeycutt gave a convocation address at Southern Seminary speaking of "unscrupulous and unethical acts by politicians" who enlisted students to tape lectures for "the Dallas war room..." He called for a "holy war" against "unholy forces" that are "seeking to hijack" the denomination and its agencies (quoted in Hefley 1986, p. 108).

10. In the waning years of the "holy war," one of the authors overheard one SBC messenger say to another: "Who are you voting for this year? Their fundamentalist or ours?

11. The term "elite settlement" was taken from Burton and Higley (1987).

REFERENCES

Ammerman, N. 1990. *Baptist Battles*. New Brunswick, NJ: Rutgers.
Baptist and Reflector. 1990. "Atlanta Meeting to Study SBC Funding." July 18, 3.
————. 1990a. "Virginia Baptists to Have 'Choice' for SBC Funding." July 18, 8.
————. 1990b. "Chapman Encourages CP Giving." July 18, 5.
Barnes, W. W. 1954. *The Southern Baptist Convention, 1845-1953*. Nashville, TN: Broadman Press.
Barnhart, J. E. 1986. *The Southern Baptist Holy War*. Austin, TX: Texas Monthly Press.
Beale, D. 1985. *S.B.C.: House on the Sand?* Greenville, SC: Unusual Publications.
Bisagno, J. 1990. "Let Us Take the High Road." *Southern Baptist Communicator* 1:9.
Burton, M. G. and J. Higley. 1987. "Elite Settlements." *American Sociological Review* 52:295-307.
Cammack, P. 1990. "A Critical Assessment of the New Elite Paradigm." *American Sociological Review* 55:415-420.
Corts, M. 1990. "Let's All Support the Revolution." *Southern Baptist Communicator* 1:3,5.
Daley, C.R. 1990 "Vast Difference Separates Old and New SBCs." *Western Recorder*. July 24, 5.
Elder, N. et al. 1982. *The Consensual Democracies?* Oxford: Martin Robinson.
Encyclopedia of Southern Baptists. 1958. Vol. I-II. Nashville, TN: Broadman Press.
Entzminger, L. n.d. *The J. Frank Norris I Have Known for Thirty-Four Years*. Fort Worth, TX: n.p.
Field, G. L. and J. Higley. 1973. "Elites and Non-Elites: The Possibilities and Their Side Effects." *Warner Modular Publications* 13:1-38.

_____. 1979. "Elites, Insiders, and Outsiders: Will Western Political Regimes Prove Non-viable?" Pp. 141-160 in *Legitimation of Regimes,* edited by B. Dinitch. Beverly Hills, CA: Sage.

_____. 1985. "National Elites and Political Stability." *Research in Politics and Society* 1:1-44.

Givens, L. M. 1988. *A Programmed Piety: Education for Spirituality in Southern Baptist Study Course Literature, 1908-1986.* unpublished Ed.D. dissertation. Louisville, KY: The Southern Baptist Theological Seminary.

Grissett, S. and Valerie F. 1990. "Conservative Baptists Solidify Takeover." *The Times-Picayune.* June 13, A-1, A-8.

Gross, J. 1989. "Social Consequences of War: Preliminaries to the Study of Imposition of Communist Regimes in East Central Europe." *Eastern European Politics and Societies* 3:198-214.

Hadaway, C. K. 1990. *What Can We Do About Church Dropouts?,* Nashville, TN: Abingdon Press.

Hagopian, F. 1990. "'Democracy by Undemocratic Means'? Elites, Political Pacts, and Regime Transition in Brazil." *Comparative Political Studies* 23:147-170.

Harwell, J. 1990a. "'Finality a Reality' for SBC Takeover." *SBC Today* 8 (4):1.

_____. 1990b. "Southern Trials Shock Alumni to SBC Action." *SBC Today* 8 (4):8.

Hawkins, O.S. 1990. "Declining Conversions and Denominational Controversies." *Southern Baptist Communicator* 1:17.

Hefley, J. C. 1986. *The Truth in Crisis: The Controversy in the Southern Baptist Convention.* Dallas: Criterion Publications.

_____. 1987. *The Truth in Crisis: Updating the Controversy.* Hannibal, MO: Hannibal Books.

_____. 1988. *The Truth in Crisis: Conservative Resurgence or Political Takeover?* Hannibal, MO: Hannibal Books.

_____. 1990. *The Truth in Crisis: "The Winning Edge."* Hannibal, MO: Hannibal Books.

Higley, J. and M. G. Burton. 1989. "The Elite Variable in Democratic Transitions and Breakdowns." *American Sociological Review* 54:17-32.

Higley, J. M. G. Burton, and G. L. Field. 1990. "In Defense of Elite Theory." *American Sociological Review* 55:421-426.

James, R. ed. 1989. *The Takeover in the Southern Baptist Convention: A Brief History.* Decatur, GA: SBC Today.

Knight, W. 1987. "Pressler: Politicizing the SBC." *SBC Today* 4:1.

Knox, M. 1990a. "McCarty: Party Perceptions Deceptive." *Western Recorder.* June 26, 1.

_____. 1990b. "Independents' Immigration Presents Challenges," *Western Recorder.* July 17, 4.

Leonard, B. 1990. *God's Last and Only Hope.* Grand Rapids, MI: Eerdmans.

Leftwich, A. 1984. "Politics: People Resources and Power." Pp. 62-84 in *What is Politics?,* edited by A. Leftwich. Oxford: Basil Blackwell.

Martin, D. 1990. New Perfect Bible Coalition Emerges. *Northwest Baptist Witness.* March 20, 13.

Mattingly, T. 1986. "Old Baptists, New Baptists: A Reporter Looks at the Battle to Control the SBC." *Southwestern Journal of Theology* 28:5-11.

McBeth, L. 1987. *The Baptist Heritage.* Nashville, TN: Broadman Press.

McClellan, A. 1975. "The Origin and Development of the SBC Cooperative Program." *Baptist History and Heritage* 10:69-78.

McDonough, P. 1983. "'Let Us Make the Revolution, Before the People Do': Elite-Mass Relations in Brazil." in *Political Elites and Social Change,* edited by M. Crudnowski. DeKalb, IL: Northern Illinois Press.

McSwain, L. L. and T. Wilkerson. 1987. "Negotiating Religous Values: Dilemmas of the SBC 'Peace Committee' in Resolving Denominational Conflict." Louisville, KY: unpublished manuscript.

Moodie, Graeme. 1984. *What is Politics?,* edited by A. Leftwich. Oxford: Basil Blackwell.

Morlino, L. 1987. "Democratic Establishments: A Dimensional Analysis." Pp. 53-78 in *Comparing New Democracies* edited by E. Baloyra. Boulder, CO: Westview Press.

Morris, J. O. 1966. *Elites, Intellectuals, and Consensus: A Study of the Social Question and the Industrial Relations System in Chile.* Ithaca, NY: Cornell University Press.

Neely, A. 1990. "Southern Baptist's Quiet Conflict." *Christianity and Crisis* 50:61-65.

Patterson, P. 1985. "Stalemate." *The Theological Educator.* New Orleans, LA: New Orleans Seminary.

Pressler, P. 1985. "An Interview with Judge Paul Pressler." *The Theological Educator.* New Orleans, LA: New Orleans Seminary.

Putnam, R. 1976. *The Comparative Study of Political Elites.* Englewood Cliffs, NJ: Prentice-Hall.

Rosenberg, E. 1989. *The Southern Baptists: A Subculture in Transition.* Knoxville, TN: University of Tennessee Press.

Routh, P. 1954. "A Period of Expansion, 1946-1953." Pp. 420-433 in *The Southern Baptist Convention, 1845-1953,* edited by W.W. Barnes. Nashville: Broadman Press.

_____. 1976. *Chosen for Leadership.* Nashville: Broadman Press.

Russell, C. A. 1976. *Voices of American Fundamentalism.* Philadelphia: Westminster Press. *SBC Annual.* 1920; 1962; 1987.

Share, D. 1987. "Transitions to Democracy and Transition Through Transaction." *Comparative Political Studies* 19:525-548.

Shurden, W. 1972. *Not a Silent People.* Nashville, TN: Broadman Press.

_____. 1978. "The Problem of Authority in the SBC." *Review and Expositor* 75:220-233.

_____. 1981. "The Southern Baptist Synthesis: Is It Cracking?" *Baptist History and Heritage* 16:2-11.

_____. 1985. "In Defense of the SBC: The Moderate Response to Fundamentalism." *The Theological Educator.* New Orleans, LA: New Orleans Seminary.

Southern Baptist Communicator. 1990. "Summit Conference Endorses Chapman for SBC President." *Southern Baptist Communicator* 1:19.

Spain, R. B. 1967. *At Ease in Zion: Social History of Southern Baptists, 1865-1900.* Nashville, TN: Vanderbilt University Press.

Statement Announcing Associated Baptist Press. 1990. July 17, 1.

Statement from Concerned Southern Baptists. 1990. July 17, 1.

Thompson, J. 1982. *Tried As By Fire: Southern Baptists and the Religious Controversies of the 1920s.* Macon, GA: Mercer University Press.

Torbet, R. 1963. *A History of the Baptists, 3rd ed.* Valley Forge, NY: Judson Press.

Tull, J. 1975. "The Landmark Movement: An Historical and Theological Appraisal." *Baptist History and Heritage* 10:3-18.

Watkins, J. 1986. "Southern Baptists Held Hostage in Fundamentalism Battle." *Dallas Morning News.* June 8, H-2.

_____. 1987a. "Stop the Takeover." Decatur, GA: SBC Mainline Ministries.

_____. 1987b. "Since 86Atlanta 'Takeover' Summary." Decatur, GA: SBC Mainline Ministries.

Western Recorder. 1990. "Moderates to Discuss Alternate Funding Plan." July 24, 2.

Wolfe, B. 1990a. "Seminary Trustee Ouster Called Unlikely." *The Courier Journal.* n.d., B-1, B-6.

_____. 1990b. "Seminary Faculty Seeks Resignation of Critical Trustee." *The Courier Journal.* May 9, A-1, A-8.

_____. 1990c. "Two Outspoken Professors Denounced at Southern Baptist Seminary." *The Courier Journal.* April 26, B-5.

_____. 1990d. "Conservative Trustees Move on Baptist Seminary." *The Courier Journal.* April 25, A-1.

Woodsen, H. 1950. *Giant in the Land.* Nashville, TN: Broadman Press.

Zald, M. N. and M. A. Berger. 1978. "Social Movements in Organizations: Coup d'Etat, Insurgency, and Mass Movements." *American Journal of Sociology* 83:823-861.

CATHOLIC FEMINIST SPIRITUALITY AND SOCIAL JUSTICE ACTIONS

Adair Lummis and Allison Stokes

ABSTRACT

A number of feminist Catholic women theologians and historians argue that Catholic feminist spirituality involves both imaging God as having a female aspect and working for social justice for women and all disempowered. Are Catholic women likely to express a feminist spirituality by being active in social justice causes? Results from this study indicate that the more women espouse a feminist spiritual orientation, the more likely they are to be active in social justice concerns.

Catholic sisters are most likely to be involved in social justice causes among the 3,746 women surveyed in this cross-denominational study. Sisters have support for engaging in social action among groups (feminist or otherwise) in their orders. Being part of a feminist spirituality group is more important for other women in channeling and sustaining their work for social justice and systemic change. But having multiple group memberships and spending time in community outreach to the needy appear to facilitate and increase social activism among all women surveyed.

Feminist spirituality is a very serious challenge to the Catholic Church, according to Sandra Schneiders in her recent book, *Beyond Patching* (1991),

Research in the Social Scientific Study of Religion, Volume 6, pages 103-138.
Copyright © 1994 by JAI Press Inc.
ISBN: 1-55938-762-9

because it directs Catholic women to go beyond attempting to make church leadership structures more inclusive of women to questioning the whole tradition based on the God of Judeo-Christian revelation (109-110). Schneiders defines feminist spirituality as:

> a reclaiming of female power beginning with the likeness of women to the divine, the rehabilitation of the bodily as the very locus of the divine likeness, and the right of women to participate in the shaping of religion and culture.... A final but perhaps the most important characteristic of feminist spirituality is...a commitment to the...relationship between personal growth and transformation and a politics of social justice (pp. 80-81, 88).

Most Catholic women feminist scholars are committed to this vision of feminist spirituality, and indeed credit feminist spirituality as the force which now motivates Catholic women, vowed and non-vowed (hereafter referred to as Sisters and lay Catholic women respectively) to take strong stands in confronting patriarchy in the Church and working for social justice in the world. These scholars include Ashe (1991), Quinonez and Turner (1992), Rader (1989), Riley (1989), and Weaver (1985) as well as Schneiders (1991). Whether feminist spirituality groups and movements which do not incorporate all these elements should be called "quasi-feminist spirituality movements" (to use Robbins and Robertson's term, 1991, p. 328) is a conceptual issue. It would seem at least empirically interesting to ascertain to what extent these facets of a feminist spirituality actually combine in individuals and groups. This paper addresses the question of the relationship between personal feminist spirituality and involvement in social justice activities among Catholic sisters and laywomen in comparison to women in other denominations.

DEVELOPMENT OF A FEMINIST CONSCIOUSNESS WITHIN THE CHURCH

Rapid social change resulting in the expansion of roles open to women, as Chaftez notes (1989, pp. 147-152), is a major impetus for women's pressing for further changes in society. Certainly Vatican II put in motion many changes and raised hopes for further involvement of women in the liturgy and hierarchy (Ebaugh 1991, 1993; Quinonez and Turner 1992; Weaver 1985). But as Catholic feminist scholars cited argue, such changes would not be sufficient for women's pressing for changes unless their self-esteem and individual consciousness is raised. Women need to feel they have the right to confront church patriarchy and can envision themselves doing so. For this to eventuate, these scholars predicate that women must also have: (1) a feminist spirituality emphasizing woman as central to divinity and religion, (2) a supportive group of women, and (3) active involvement in social justice. Each of these can occur separately and certainly has in past centuries. It is the present combination of the three that is newer (Lerner 1993).

1.   A Feminist Spirituality.   Religious patriarchy unlike secular patriarchy is difficult to confront precisely because it is seen by adherents as *divinely* sanctioned. Hence, it takes a feminist *spirituality*, not just a secular feminist orientation, to challenge religious patriarchy effectively. A feminist spirituality embodies some notion of the feminine qualities of an androgenous divinity, and in most pristine form, a goddess or female divinity. It is the belief in a female divinity that studies by Finley (1991), Jacobs (1990), Neitz (1990), and Saussey (1991) show are so important for raising participants' self-esteem in women's spirituality groups. Women's groups which focus exclusively on a female divinity are usually outside of established Christian denominations. However, some emphasis on a female or goddess aspect of God is also deemed important by Catholic scholars Schneiders (1991, pp. 80-91) and Weaver (1985, pp. 181-188) for the development of a feminist spirituality among Catholic women who are trying to remain within their church.

One of the major *feminist* critiques of spiritual feminism, particularly of women's support and worship groups geared to female images of God, is that women's energies are drained off by these groups. With their own satisfying spirituality groups, the argument goes, women may have little interest in changing church structures and even less in working for justice for women and other oppressed groups in society (Finley 1991; Walters 1985).

2.   A Supportive Group.   Women's self-esteem can be raised by participation in women's support groups, as their commitment to work for other goals of the group is also elevated. Women's church-related groups historically have been pivotal in strengthening commitment to denominations and in promoting outreach to the needy (Zikmund 1993). Although women's groups may be very traditional in theology and in their conception of women's place, some of the more traditional women's organizations have changed goals in response to external factors and thus have served as vehicles of further change. A good example of this is the Catholic women's religious orders.

One reason leaders of Catholic women's religious orders have continued to push for changes set in motion by Vatican II, according to Quinonez and Turner (1992), is that they have had close community support. Similarly well-educated Catholic sisters share their view that sisters and all women should have a more pivotal place in the church structures. Sisters are exercising an active and very visible presence in an array of organizations and ministries in the United States. American Catholic sisters are "central figures in the feminist movement" (Ebaugh 1993, p. 148) in the Church if not in society as well. Some sisters administering parishes are being called "pastor," not legitimately yet justifiably, given the fact they are doing the major ministry of any parish priest (Wallace 1992). Neal's (1991) Third Sisters Survey provides evidence that the majority of sisters approve the liberalization of orders since Vatican II and nearly half endorse their orders' "exercising leadership toward full participation of women" in the life and decision-making "at all levels of the Catholic Church."

During the last two or three decades lay women within the Catholic Church, other denominations and religions have also been forming new types of women's groups, which have a decidedly feminist focus (Wuthnow 1989, p. 229). These women's spirituality groups, unlike most traditional church women's groups, promote women's taking greater leadership in church structures and even sometimes challenging the gendered identity of God as male. A feminist spirituality group might be such an exodus community that women members would lose interest in changing institutional structures to achieve greater inclusion of women and all disempowered (see review by Robbins and Bromley 1992).

Feminist spirituality has served as a devastating critique of what Jacobs (1991, pp. 349-350) terms "false universalism", that is, using only men's perspectives to study patriarchal religious institutions; but she also warns feminist scholars not to "universalize" some women's experiences to all women in religion. For example, characteristics of women other than their feminist orientation such as health, age, dependent children, and various life situations, may also promote or retard women's involvement in trying to make changes in church and society.

3.   Involvement in Social Justice Activities.   Trying to effect systemic change in society to improve the situation of the poor and oppressed through better services and more representation on political and institutional levels has been a focus of the Catholic clergy, religious and lay leaders for some time. These objectives are not absent from the mission of other churches and faiths. Still there may be more encouragement within the Catholic Church for demonstrating a "political spirituality," to use Weaver's (1985, pp. 185-190) term for a strong orientation to achieving social justice, than there is in some other denominations. If the area is heavily Catholic, sisters may have a "disproportionate impact" on any social cause they take up. Sisters may be so encouraged by their success and by leaders in the Church and community that they expand their work for social justice (Demerath and Williams 1992, pp. 152-153 *et passim*). Sisters are not as apt to obtain encouragement for engaging in social justice causes in dioceses where bishops strongly disapprove of sisters being politically active; in such dioceses sisters' social activism is likely to be less visible and possibly less extensive.

Members of certain ethnic groups may also be more active in social justice causes than others. Hispanic Catholics, now almost 30 percent of the U.S. Catholic Church (*Origins* 1992, p. 780), are projected to form the majority of American Catholics within twenty years (Sandoval 1990, p. 135). At the same time, Hispanic Catholics are on the periphery of society in socioeconomic status and are similarly excluded from the leadership of the predominantly middle-class Catholic Church (Sandoval 1990, pp. 131-137). This situation results in a sense of defeatism for many Hispanics, but also provides Hispanic leaders with the impetus for strong advocacy of social justice causes. Educated

Hispanic Catholic women are leaders in articulating Hispanic Women's Liberation Theology. From this theological perspective, Hispanic women leaders promote the use of social action, particularly political involvement, to free Hispanics to live fully in a transformed society in which women share equally with men (Isasi-Diaz & Tarango 1988, pp. 3-9,94-96). Many Catholic Hispanic women leaders are members of Las Hermanas, a national organization of Hispanic Catholic women with regional and local chapters. This organization is involved in social justice activities and educational efforts aimed at empowering impoverished Hispanic women.

Local churches of any denomination may promote social justice through sermons, education and programs. Churches that encourage outreach to the area's hungry, homeless and institutionalized people through programs they sponsor, do not necessarily advocate individuals' lobbying city governments to change laws and allocation of resources. Given the emphasis on the separation of church and state, religious bodies prefer to set forth principles and leave specific political involvements and actions to individuals (Wuthnow 1988, p. 65). Yet, those who engage in church-sponsored outreach programs may come to realize in their efforts to feed, house and clothe the community needy that more systemic changes are needed to overcome poverty and racism. This realization may led them to put some energies into working through the political process or by lobbying organizations.

Available time and sufficient energy are other factors which may affect whether individuals are heavily involved in political and human rights causes. Women's resources of time and energy are likely to be affected by their employment, family situation, health and age. Working mothers and all mothers of young children, for example, are apt to have less time than other women to volunteer.

Do in fact Catholic women who espouse a spiritual feminism also tend to be active in social justice concerns? Are Catholic women more likely to combine feminist spirituality with political spirituality to a greater degree than women in other denominations and faiths? How important are other factors mentioned in women's being active in social justice causes?

SAMPLE AND METHODS

Data Collection

Data to address these questions is available from a national study of women's spiritual support groups with some "feminist" focus. Because the focus of the full study is on characteristics of feminist spirituality groups whose members are or once were Christians, a strong effort was made to locate women likely to be in such groups. Accordingly, names and addresses were obtained from mailing lists of centers and journals known to draw women with both spiritual and feminist interests, including WATER, the Women's Theological Center, Women's Institute for Theology, *Daughters of Sarah*, the *Journal of Feminist Studies*, and from notices about the study placed in journals and in newsletters, such as the *Christian Century*. Address lists for particular groupings of women (e.g., denominational organizations, racial/ethnic minorities, etc.) were solicited.[1] In some cases packages of questionnaires were given to group leaders to distribute.

In the first stage of data collection in the spring of 1991, a mailing of about 4,000 surveys went to samples of women on these lists, stratified to insure geographical distribution. A question on the survey asked respondents to list the names and addresses of others who might be interested in filling out the survey. From this snowball sample, a second stage of data collection took place between the fall of 1991 and the spring of 1992. About 3,000 surveys were mailed to a selection of names and addresses sent in by those who returned questionnaires,[2] and about 500 to names on additional lists provided by consultants. Altogether, approximately 7,500 questionnaires were sent with a return rate of about 55 percent without follow-up, a total of 3,758 women and 112 men. (This paper is based only on the responses of the women.)

The third stage of data collection was interviewing a selection of women in spiritual support groups, predominantly the more feminist ones. Approximately 75 percent of respondents indicated on their questionnaire they would like to be interviewed. In-depth telephone and in-person interviews were conducted with about 150 women.

Characteristics of the Sample

The women respondents are predominantly well educated and over thirty. *They are not representative of the majority of women attending churches in these denominations, nor were they intended to be. They are probably more feminist than the majority of women in Catholic and Protestant congregations.* These women respondents, however, may well be representative of the better educated leaders in their congregations and communities. The great majority of this sample are also white Anglos. However, we do have a sample of mainly Hispanic Catholic women, members of Las Hermanas. (About 20 percent of Las Hermanas respondents consider themselves white or mixed in race/ethnicity rather than "Hispanic.") By design Catholic women comprise about a third of this sample. The remaining two-thirds are women representing over thirty Christian denominations, other religions, and no religious affiliations. But most of these, 45 percent of the total sample, are affiliated with one of the mainline liberal Protestant denominations.

Characteristics of Catholic Respondents

The 488 sisters returning surveys are similar in many ways to the general population of Sisters in the United States (Neal 1991, pp. 31,34). Over 80 percent are white and two-thirds are over fifty years of age. Our sample is somewhat better educated than the population of women religious; 86 percent have at least a master's degree, compared to 63 percent among all women religious surveyed by Neal. Sisters surveyed for this study are more likely to be feminist than the majority in their orders.[3] Sisters' responses can be compared to those of 725 Catholic lay women and 2,533 women of other Christian traditions or no religious affiliations. Further, since in the Las Hermanas sample there are about equal numbers of sisters (92) and laywomen (65), additional comparisons of Catholics by ethnicity are possible.

Feminist Attitudes and Attitudes toward the Church

The sisters in this sample espouse most value positions usually considered "feminist" to an extent greater than the other women. The majority take a more "feminist" than "non-feminist" position on all 16 value items in the survey included to measure a feminist perspective; however, the items do not scale well. This is not surprising, given others' observations that there are many varieties of feminism within the Catholic Church (Riley 1989; Schneiders 1992; Weaver 1993; Wittberg 1989), as well as among women belonging to other religious traditions (Briggs 1987). For example, just because most sisters (and other women) advocate using inclusive language in church services does not mean they are very likely to endorse a cultural feminist perspective of believing women have special attributes not as apt to be possessed by men. Nor just because Catholic women in majority would like to see women's greater participation in leadership at all levels of the church, *are* they necessarily secular structural feminists who advocate affirmative action policies favoring women. Sisters surveyed are predominantly strong feminists on most of the measures. Catholic lay (non-vowed) women also tend to be more feminist than those from the other denominations in our study.

1. Perceptions of patriarchy are more acute among these Catholic women, especially sisters, than among women in other denominations. Percentages in Table 1 illustrate differences between Hispanic and non-Hispanic Catholic sisters and laywomen in comparison to all women of other faiths. Almost all of the sisters (98 percent) and lay Catholic women (94 percent) *agree* that "Women have less access than do men to leadership in churches, regional and national offices in my denomination," compared to 74 percent of the women in other denominations. Leadership is one of the opportunities women miss in church, and they believe they should have it. A 90 percent majority of Catholics as well as other women *disagree* with the statement that "Women

Table 1.   Selected Feminist Attitudes

	Catholic		Las Hermanas		
Selected Attitudes	Sisters (396)	Lay Women (660)	Sisters (92)	Lay Women (65)	All Other Women (2533)
1. Women in my denomination have all the opportunities they need for participation in the church.					
a. Agree	1%	4%	5%	15%	20%
b. Not sure/Ambivalent	1%	3%	0%	9%	12%
c. Disagree	98%	92%	94%	75%	68%
	100%	100%	100%	100%	100%
2. There should be more hymns and prayers using female imagery and names for god.					
a. Agree	90%	82%	87%	64%	80%
b. Not sure/Ambivalent	4%	10%	11%	22%	10%
c. Disagree	6%	8%	2%	14%	10%
	100%	100%	100%	100%	100%
3. Women's spiritual growth is best attained through worship experiences shared with men.					
a. Agree	28%	24%	30%	21%	24%
b. Not sure/Ambivalent	32%	39%	30%	38%	39%
c. Disagree	40%	37%	39%	41%	37%
	100%	100%	100%	100%	100%
4. Women leaders tend to learn and use people names more than do men leaders.					
a. Agree	52%	41%	58%	50%	33%
b. Not sure/Ambivalent	40%	44%	36%	35%	50%
c. Disagree	8%	15%	6%	15%	17%
	100%	100%	100%	100%	100%
5. Women leaders tend to share power more than do men leaders.					
a. Agree	71%	64%	74%	62%	62%
b. Not sure/Ambivalent	23%	26%	18%	24%	28%
c. Disagree	6%	10%	8%	14%	10%
	100%	100%	100%	100%	100%

(continued)

Table 1. (Continued)

| Selected Attitudes | Catholic | | Las Hermanas | | |
	Sisters (396)	Lay Women (660)	Sisters (92)	Lay Women (65)	All Other Women (2533)
6. I often feel alienated from the institutional church					
a. Agree	84%	83%	73%	59%	62%
b. Not sure/Ambivalent	4%	5%	7%	13%	9%
c. Disagree	12%	12%	20%	28%	29%
	100%	100%	100%	100%	100%
7. For now—in hiring, job promotion and salary increases—women should be given preference over men with equal abilities.					
a. Agree	34%	32%	46%	41%	31%
b. Not sure/Ambivalent	28%	33%	27%	21%	33%
c. Disagree	38%	35%	27%	38%	36%
	100%	100%	100%	100%	100%

should not be concerned with attaining top leadership positions." Catholic women are more apt than those of other denominations combined to *disagree* that "Women in my denomination have all the opportunities they need for participation in the church." Hispanic Catholic lay women in Las Hermanas are slightly less likely than other Catholic women (including Hispanic sisters) to disagree with this statement, however.

Typically, though not invariably, differences in the espousal of feminist perspectives among Catholic women surveyed are between sisters and laywomen. Sisters are more feminist than laywomen in a variety of areas; Hispanic laywomen are the least feminist among Catholic women in their perceptions of church and God.

2. Women are seen by Catholic women, and particularly by Sisters, as being better leaders than men. Sisters and Catholic laywomen, are more likely than women in other denominations to see women as possessing an important leadership skill: naming. Noted by Wallace (1992, pp. 48-54) in her study of Catholic women "pastors," *naming* is the ability to remember and call individuals to and with whom they minister by name. About half of the sisters agreed that "Women leaders tend to learn and use people's names more than do men leaders," compared to no more than a third of the women belonging to other denominations. Sisters in two-thirds majority agree that women have the further advantage over men in women's greater willingness to share power and express "virtues of empathy, intuition and warmth."

3.   A majority of feminist Catholics want to see the Church ordain women as priests, but many feminists also seem to be somewhat ambivalent about women's ordination. Although Catholics in two-thirds majority believe "More women should seek ordination in my denomination;" about a fourth are ambivalent. Comments written on the questionnaire and made in interviews suggest this is because Catholic women have mixed feelings about whether women should aspire to be ordained into a patriarchal denomination. In answer to a survey question asking whether respondents would like to be ordained, only 12 percent of the sisters said "yes," 35 percent "maybe," and 53 percent "no." Age does affect responses. The younger sisters are more likely to at least consider being ordained in the distant future.

4.   On the endorsement of affirmative action, a more secular feminist measure, there is a substantial disagreement among women. Catholic sisters and lay women are just as likely to be divided as women in other denominations. To a question on whether "For now—in hiring, job promotion and salary increases—women should be given preference over men with equal abilities," about a third of all women respondents "agree," a third agree are "ambivalent," and a third "disagree." The Hispanic Catholic women are more likely than any other group to value affirmative action in achieving equality for women. This more positive response from Hispanic women may tie directly to an original goal of Las Hermanas, that is, to support Hispanic women's gaining education and skills that will enable them to be financially self-sufficient.

5.   Catholic women, like women in other denominations, want inclusive language in worship. Around 90 percent of the sisters and 80 percent of the lay Catholic women and women of other denominations are quite clear they want more hymns and prayers "using female imagery and names for God." Hispanic Catholic laywomen are least likely to want female imagery for God used in worship, yet still three-fifths do. A similarly strong four-fifths majority of Catholic women desire "male and female images for God...balanced in worship." Almost all, including 97 percent of the sisters, disagree that they would find "inclusive language during scripture reading disruptive" and concur that "inclusive language should be used in all church services." These items dealing with inclusive language in worship do scale. By this Church Language Feminism Scale, Catholic sisters remain among the most feminist of all women surveyed.[4]

6.   At least a degree of feminist spirituality is indicated in the female and androgenous images of God preferred by both Catholics and other women. The great majority of women respondents are more likely to have shifting, changing images of God than one or two clear, definite images. They further are likely to see God as Father, Mother and Jesus at least to some extent. If compelled to choose the one image that is most important or pivotal in their conception of God, they would select "encompassing presence." It can be seen that among Catholics, Hispanic laywomen are most apt to endorse the

Table 2.   Selected Images of God

| | Catholic | | | | |
| | Catholic (not Hermanas) | | Las Hermanas | | |
	Sisters (396)	Lay Women (660)	Sisters (92)	Lay Women (65)	All Other Women (2533)
To what extent do you see God as:					
1. Father					
a. Much	21%	28%	32%	54%	29%
b. Some	69%	54%	62%	38%	54%
c. None	10%	18%	6%	8%	17%
	100%	100%	100%	100%	100%
2. Mother					
a. Much	22%	21%	29%	27%	21%
b. Some	70%	62%	67%	55%	62%
c. None	8%	17%	4%	18%	17%
	100%	100%	100%	100%	100%
3. Jesus					
a. Much	54%	50%	70%	64%	46%
b. Some	43%	39%	29%	31%	40%
c. None	3%	10%	1%	5%	14%
	100%	100%	100%	100%	100%
4. Goddess					
a. Much	22%	23%	18%	30%	20%
b. Some	46%	39%	52%	31%	39%
c. None	33%	38%	30%	39%	41%
	100%	100%	100%	100%	100%
5. Wisdom					
a. Much	79%	82%	77%	86%	82%
b. Some	19%	15%	23%	11%	15%
c. None	2%	3%	0%	3%	3%
	100%	100%	100%	100%	100%
6. Master					
a. Much	7%	16%	11%	48%	21%
b. Some	25%	26%	40%	27%	33%
c. None	68%	57%	49%	24%	46%
	100%	100%	100%	100%	100%

(*continued*)

Table 2.   (Continued)

	Catholic				
	Catholic (not Hermanas)		Las Hermanas		
	Sisters (396)	Lay Women (660)	Sisters (92)	Lay Women (65)	All Other Women (2533)
7. Encompassing Presence					
a. Much	86%	80%	90%	69%	75%
b. Some	13%	16%	9%	25%	20%
c. None	1%	3%	1%	6%	5%
	100%	100%	100%	100%	100%

traditional patriarchal images of God as father and master. Ironically perhaps Hispanic laywomen are also slightly more likely than other Catholic women to be "spiritual feminists," in that they perceive God as in part "goddess." Since Hispanic women who most strongly perceive God as a male power or paternal figure are not the same women who have a strong feminist spirituality, this indicates some divergence in theology and spirituality among Hispanic Catholic women.

7.   A majority of Catholic women see God as at least in part "goddess." It is not the androgenous image of God that is most indicative of feminist spirituality, however, but the actual "goddess" image, which for some can be Mary, but more likely a Sophia image or possibly an earth goddess, according to Weaver (1985, pp. 184-186) and also found in our interviews with women in feminist spirituality groups.

Only a third or so of this sample, including Hispanic women, say that "goddess" in no way forms part of their image of God, leaving about two-thirds who do see God, at least to some extent, as "goddess." At the same time no more than 1 percent see "goddess" as the "most important" or "pivotal" image in their conception of the divine. This is a more Christian feminist spirituality, rather than the spiritual feminism of the Goddess movement, but still feminist and it has consequences. Women's holding female images of God and wanting inclusive language in church services, is significantly related to their being disillusioned with the *institutional* church. Further those who most strongly envision the Divine as female are also more likely to *dis*agree that: "Women's spiritual growth is best attained through worship experiences shared with men," and they see themselves as "alienated" from the Church.[5] Actually, even those Catholic women in this study who rarely envision God as female are not particularly happy with the Church.

8.   Sisters and non-Hispanic Catholic laywomen on the whole are more alienated from the institutional church than women in other denominations.

Over four-fifths (84 percent) of both the Anglo majority of sisters and of Catholic laywomen surveyed agree "I often feel alienated from the institutional church." A smaller majority of Hispanic Catholic women expressed alienation, 73 percent of the sisters and 59 percent of the laywomen, compared to three fifths (62 percent) of the women in all other denominations combined. The lesser degree of alienation expressed by Hispanic Catholics may occur because they are more comfortable with traditional images of God as father and master as well as with lack of female imagery in church services than are other Catholic women. It may also occur because as Isasi-Diaz and Tarango (1988, pp. 54-55) suggest, "church" connotes for Hispanic women more a picture of community, a set of programs, rather than an organization, building or hierarchy.

Community and Group Supports for Alienated Sisters and Catholic Lay Women Staying within the Church

Given that Catholic women see themselves as alienated from a Church which provides neither the kind of worship experience nor opportunities they want, one may well ask why are these women still in Catholic parishes? Not all, but still a majority of women in this study, do belong to a parish which they attend with some regularity (including 66 percent of the sisters and 74 percent of the lay Catholic women). Our interviews support Greeley's response to his own question of why *any* Catholics stay in the Church. He answers that they stay from loyalty based on "identity, community, and sacramentality," but they stay on their own terms, rejecting many of the Church's teachings and moral regulations (1990, p. 181). Well-educated feminist Catholic women interviewed, perhaps unlike "the ordinary laity" Greeley discusses (1990, p. 183), also give these reasons for remaining Catholics. These women were born Catholic and want to die Catholic, love the liturgies, and can worship together with family members in parishes. But highly educated feminist Catholic women may need an additional support other than "loyalty" to stay with an institution they view as patriarchal and destructive.

Comments written on the questionnaire and interviews indicate that community provides such a support for Catholic sisters. Living in a community of women with whom one can worship using inclusive language and some female images for God, provides major sustenance for staying with the Church, according to some "alienated" sisters. This can be their living community, where at least among themselves they use inclusive language and female imagery for God. One of the many self-described "alienated" sisters respondents who want more inclusion of women in church structures and inclusive language comments:

> As a Catholic nun, I live with twenty other women. Our discussions and sharing are...always available...Although I am viewed by many as pious and devoted to the Church, as the years go by my ties and devotion, etc. to church are less and less strong and more indifferent. Spirituality is more important than formal church involvement.

As Wittberg (1991) points out, however, group living communities of sisters are fast disappearing in favor of more associational groups where sisters live on their own. What does single housing bode for alienated sisters remaining in the Church? There may well be no problem if such sisters can find supportive groups who share their feminist spirituality, as illustrated in the following quote:

> Being a member of the Roman Catholic Church, I experience much frustration and some anger with the male dominated, patriarchal system. I have found there is value for me in remaining within this Church—but it is not easy. I meet with a group of sisters for support and growth... In our spiritual rituals only female imagery for God is used. I live alone— so participation in this group gives me support, involvement and helps me feel anchored.

Alienated lay Catholic women would seem to need supportive feminist spirituality groups more than sisters, especially since they have less access than sisters on the whole to a supportive community of other women. From interviews we found that some sisters are taking the lead in organizing feminist spirituality groups for lay women in dioceses, although they may eschew the word "feminist" as being unnecessarily divisive. In other instances, lay women have been solely responsible for forming Catholic feminist spirituality groups. Sometimes these groups include sisters, but in several instances lay women leaders report that sisters do not participate. One reason they give is that sisters, though privately supportive, are afraid to become members for fear that the bishop would retaliate by having them fired from church positions or impeding their ministries and activities.

The more feminist Catholic women's groups tend to develop outside a particular parish, though they may well draw the modal number of members from one or two parishes. Some of these groups are either affiliated directly with, or have leaders who are active in, the Women Church Convergence or Women's Ordination Conference, and are thus linked to the larger Women Church Movement (Trebbi 1990). Other Catholic women's feminist spirituality groups appear not only to be totally autonomous, but also more or less unaware of what these national Catholic organizations are doing; they are small, grass-roots, women-church groups (Winter 1989).

The support provided to individual members of these women's groups is the major benefit for many lay Catholic women members, interviews suggest. Sharing personal experiences in their groups can lead to voicing problems that they are having with parish practices or Catholic Church teaching. This sharing usually ends "pluralistic ignorance" that their private misgivings about the

Church are unique. Catholic women's groups can raise and focus anger about the Church, at the same time they help women members commit themselves to working for change within the Church rather than leaving.[6] A Catholic grandmother, who is very active in her parish, comments:

> It is increasingly difficult to convince, encourage, the *young*, intelligent, educated women (our daughters) that they have a future in the Catholic Church. I find myself becoming, being anti-authority and anti-hierarchy. The very evident and dangerous bend of the young clergy to conservative theology and liturgical practices is frightening to me. It is only in my support group (of other Catholic women) that I find the creative spirit that gives me the courage to go on. It is there that I find the encouragement and affirmation and acceptance that engender the hope that some day things may change.

Not all women's spirituality groups are feminist by any definition. Some groups, even if feminist in social outlook, neither value inclusive language in church services nor ever image God as female in group prayers and rituals. In picking out probable feminist spirituality groups from the survey data, we looked at women's answers to a question about the extent "female imagery and names" for God are used in group rituals or discussions.

Women's feminist spirituality groups are operationally defined in this study as those in which female imagery and names for God or the Divine are used "to a great extent" or exclusively (but just 11 percent of the women surveyed are in spirituality groups which use "only female imagery for God"). Using this definition, 37 percent of all women respondents are in feminist spirituality groups, 34 percent do not belong to any women's spiritual/ religious group currently, and 29 percent are members of more traditional women's groups. This demarcation for feminist spirituality groups as compared with more traditional church women's groups is supported by significant correlations with the feminist value items discussed. Even among this fairly feminist sample, those in spiritual feminist groups take a more feminist position on different issues than those who do not belong to any women's group with a spiritual focus. Those who are not part of a women's spirituality group are concomitantly more feminist on various positions concerning women in church and society than those in more traditional church women's groups.[7]

Sisters, regardless of ethnicity, are more likely to be in feminist spirituality groups than Catholic laywomen or women in other denominations and faiths, as can be seen in Table 3. One reason why about three-fifths of the sisters compared to two-fifths or less of lay Catholic and other women, are in feminist spirituality groups is probably that sisters are already in a connective system with other women and can more easily find others to meet with who share their feminist spirituality. The fact that those sisters in feminist spirituality groups are predominantly in ones composed only of women associated with religious orders (Table 4) gives credence to this interpretation.

Table 3.   Types of Women's Spirituality Groups

	Catholic Women Not Hermanas		Non-Catholic Women Hermanas		All Other Women
	Sisters	*Lay*	*Sisters*	*Lay*	
A. *Group Orientation*					
Feminist Spirituality Group	65%	39%	58%	33%	32%
No Group	11%	39%	11%	33%	37%
Traditional Group	27%	22%	31%	34%	31%
	100%	100%	100%	100%	100%
(N =)	(396)	(660)	(92)	(65)	(2533)
B. *Feminist Spirituality Group Membership From:*					
Within one parish	5%	15%	8%	26%	17%
One denomination, different parishes	16%	26%	25%	48%	28%
Religious order(s) (including non-vowed associates)	63%	5%	51%	5%	2%
Mixed in faith	16%	54%	16%	21%	53%
	100%	100%	100%	100%	100%
(N =)	(250)	(320)	(51)	(19)	(735)

Generally, feminist spirituality groups with their radical theological thrust are outside of one local church. Sometimes Catholic lay women angry with the Church and wanting more feminist liturgies are more likely to come together from several parishes in an area for a womenchurch group or a Catholic action group. Hispanic Catholic lay women surveyed who belong to feminist spirituality groups are most likely to be in ones composed of women from different Catholic parishes, usually a Las Hermanas local, regional or national group. However, most Catholic lay women are in feminist spirituality groups composed of women from different faith perspectives. Feminist interpretations of the church, as Russell (1993) describes, transcend denominational boundaries.

INVOLVEMENT IN ACTIONS FOR SYSTEMIC CHANGE IN THE AREA OF SOCIAL JUSTICE

Involvement in Community Outreach

Church women's groups have historically been active in bringing food and clothing to the needy, visiting shut-ins at homes and in institutions, and trying to better the lives of destitute women and children in their communities. Therefore, it is understandable why feminist women surveyed are no more likely than non-feminist women to be active in community outreach.

Women surveyed were asked how much time in the last year (1990) they had given to each of the following activities: (1) donating time and money to helping the poor in the community through food banks, clothing, and funds for those crises, (2) fund raising drives to benefit the needy, (3) serving in soup kitchens or shelters for the homeless, (4) helping disadvantaged children, or (5) aiding women who have been abused, raped, or battered. These five kinds of community service are summed in Scale of Involvement in Community Outreach (Alpha =.65). Sisters and clergywomen are somewhat more likely than lay women of any denomination to be highly involved in community outreach. This is probably because they are more likely to be coordinating these efforts than lay women. For all women community outreach can be an avenue to raising feminist consciousness about the place of women in the Church.

Hispanic women give particularly cogent reflections on how their work in community outreach led to their involvement in trying to change Church and social structures. An Hispanic Catholic laywoman who was the leader of an area group devoted to raising funds and planning educational programs to benefit impoverished Hispanic women describes how women in this group came to realize that the Church was part of the problem:

> In our group we learn and grow from each other in planning our programs, studying and sharing. One of the things I have come to see is that there is a huge deficiency of real support by the Roman Catholic Church for women as heads of households...or minority women. It is sad to know the heads of our church are narrow-minded old men, especially here in...

For Catholic Hispanic women leaders, meeting with other women in spiritual support groups which are also typically action groups provides the needed peer encouragement to continue trying to make the Church more responsive to Hispanics. Groups help these women overcome frustration:

> I am president of a Catholic woman's group that tries to help with the needs of the Hispanic community in this deprived area. I find the women to be courageous but lacking in involvement, not easily motivated, and too worried about insignificant things, withdrawn. I love to help people who help themselves. Our woman's group is also a support to us when we get frustrated with trying to make changes....

Involvement in community outreach can also lead women to realize that more lasting changes are needed in secular social and political institutions. The more heavily involved women are in community outreach activities, the more time they also give to achieving systemic change in the area of social justice ($r = .46, p = .0001$).

Table 4. Involvement in Social Justice

	Catholic Women		Hermanas		All Other
	Sisters (396)	Lay (660)	Sisters (92)	Lay (65)	Women (2533)

A. Items in Social Justice Index. Question stem: About how much time in a typical month last year (1990) did you give to each of the following?

a. Supporting political candidates

1. No time	39%	44%	41%	38%	45%
2. Very little time	32%	31%	25%	24%	31%
3. Some time	27%	23%	29%	29%	22%
4. Much time	2%	2%	5%	9%	2%
	100%	100%	100%	100%	100%

b. Changing laws or public policies to benefit needy

1. No time	19%	37%	21%	42%	40%
2. Very little time	26%	24%	29%	24%	28%
3. Some time	45%	32%	41%	25%	27%
4. Much time	10%	6%	9%	9%	5%
	100%	100%	100%	100%	100%

c. Peace or anti-war efforts

1. No time	12%	32%	17%	50%	31%
2. Very little time	21%	20%	25%	26%	24%
3. Some time	55%	37%	45%	20%	36%
4. Much time	12%	11%	13%	4%	9%
	100%	100%	100%	100%	100%

d. Obtaining rights for racial and ethnic minorities

1. No time	29%	43%	22%	28%	42%
2. Very little time	27%	28%	14%	23%	27%
3. Some time	32%	22%	43%	28%	24%
4. Much time	11%	6%	11%	1%	7%
	100%	100%	100%	100%	100%

e. Obtaining rights for gays and lesbians

1. No Time	43%	54%	46%	64%	48%
2. Very little time	32%	22%	37%	19%	23%
3. Some time	22%	19%	15%	14%	23%
4. Much time	3%	5%	2%	3%	6%
	100%	100%	100%	100%	100%

(continued)

Table 4. (Continued)

	Catholic Women		Hermanas		All Other
	Sisters (396)	Lay (660)	Sisters (92)	Lay (65)	Women (2533)
f. Getting better opportunities and working conditions for women					
1. No time	40%	57%	31%	43%	54%
2. Very little time	30%	20%	23%	18%	25%
3. Some time	23%	18%	32%	26%	17%
4. Much time	7%	5%	14%	13%	4%
	100%	100%	100%	100%	100%

B. *Social Justice Activity Index.* The above items are put in an index, with a scale alpha of between .77 and .79 for all of the above groups. Scale items scoring is *reversed* for the index so that *low* scores indicate *high* involvement in social justice. The sample mean is 18.3

Involvement in Social Justice Causes For Systemic Change

A Social Justice Action scale was formed from survey items asking how much time respondents spent in various activities. The activities are: supporting political candidates, changing laws or public policies to benefit needy; working for peace or anti-war causes; obtaining rights for racial and ethnic minorities, and for gays and lesbians; and getting better employment opportunities and conditions for women. Although there is a range in how much time individual women give to each of these activities as can be seen in Table 4, sisters, regardless of ethnicity, are more likely to put a lot of time in social justice activities than Catholic lay women or women belonging to other denominations.

Feminist Values and Involvement in Social Justice

A personal feminist spirituality promotes involvement in social justice activities for the total sample of women responding. Feminist perspectives on women in church and society are significantly related to high involvement in social justice causes also, some perspectives more than others. But the degree to which Catholic and non-Catholic women insist on a "goddess" aspect of God (i.e. are spiritual feminists), is the strongest overall value predictor of how involved they will be in social action. This is true regardless of women's ethnicity or whether they are sisters or lay women, although the latter statuses continue to influence social justice activity (Table 5).

Women across denominations who want inclusive language used in church services including female imagery for God in hymns and prayers, also tend

Table 5.   Social Justice and Feminist Values for Major Populations Groups

| | CATHOLIC | | | | |
| | Non-Hispanic | | Hermanas | | All Other |
	Sisters (396)	Lay (660)	Sisters (92)	Lay (65)	Women (2533)
1. Church Language Feminism Scale (low = want inclus. lang., high = don't)	n.s.	.18	−.13	.07	.18
2. Spiritual Feminism (see God as goddess: much, some, none)	.17	.21	.22	.27	.18
3. Secular Feminism: want affirmative action	.11	.20	.09	n.s.	.17
4. Cultural Feminism item: Women leaders use peoples names more than men	.17	.13	−.09	.28	.08
5.In a Feminist Spirituality Group: yes, no group, trad. women's group.	.12	.23	.08	.24	.26

Note: Correlations with Involvement in *Social Justice Activities Scales* (high to low involvement). All correlations significant at .01 or less.

to be fairly active in working for systemic social change. Sisters, however, want inclusive language in church services in such great majority that the Scale of Church Language Feminism cannot discriminate for them well, especially for Hispanic sisters (who may even decrease their social justice activity if they are strong advocates of inclusive language). But the more that lay Catholic women, particularly those who are Anglo, are advocates of using inclusive language throughout the church, the more apt they are to also be active in social justice causes.

The stronger the endorsement women in the total sample give to the more secular feminist position of affirmative action on behalf of women, the somewhat greater their involvement in working for systemic change in the area of social justice. This is particularly true for Catholic lay women who are Anglos. The value placed by Hispanic Catholic lay women on the use of affirmative action is, however, unrelated to the amount of time they give to achieving social justice.

Believing women possess qualities and abilities not as prevalent in men, is less strongly related in the total sample to involvement in social justice causes. Of the items in this survey dealing with attributes or abilities special to women (which do not scale well), the most predictive of social justice involvement is the degree to which women leaders are perceived as using people's names more than men. Catholic women are particularly likely to be heavily involved in social justice if they believe women are superior to men in this regard, unless they are Hispanic sisters. In fact, sisters who are members of Las Hermanas are somewhat more likely to be active in social justice causes if they see no consistent behavioral differences between women and men.

Membership in a Women's Spirituality
Group and Involvement in Social Justice

Belonging to a feminist spirituality group for women in all denominations appears to generally promote their involvement in social justice activities. Feminist spirituality *group* membership for all Catholic women, but especially for lay women regardless of ethnicity, appears to support and encourage their involvement in social justice causes. Interviews indicate that the manner in which these groups operate to increase members' involvement in social justice, however, differs. Some groups are involved in social action as a collectivity. Most groups encourage members to be involved as individuals in their preferred social justice activities.

A small group of women, and most of these groups are under 15 members, does not have the financial or personnel resources to do much as a group in addressing social issues. This is especially true if it is a grass-roots group, not part of a larger national organization. At the same time, small spirituality groups can support or discourage their members being individually involved in social justice concerns. Reuther (1985, p. 94) in reflecting on the "the ecclesiology of women-church" noted that women who are heavily involved in social action may also "join a feminist study group that is not made up of the same people as the social ministry, but that serves as a forum for reflection on this and other struggles for change." Feminist spirituality groups, in short, · can promote members involvement in social justice causes even if the *group* is "only" a spiritual support group. At least half of the women in spiritual feminist groups interviewed for our study indicate that they receive support from other women in their groups for their individual outreach to needy persons in the community or for their lobbying actions to obtain justice for societal victims of bigotry.

The other statuses of women in the group can also impact the effect the group can have. Small groups of sisters, interviews suggest, can accomplish more in impacting social justice concerns than similar sized or substantially larger groups of Catholic women, not exclusively made up of sisters. There are two reasons. First, sisters are typically better trained for group leadership, more knowledgeable about how to lobby church, social or political organizations effectively, and have more clout than laywomen. Second, sisters who have formed their own action group tend to have developed common goals and established objectives to meet these goals.

Lay women are far less likely than sisters to share a common vision of what social causes they should pursue as a group or how best to proceed. Sometimes a group of women comes together initially to perform a community service or achieve certain goals affecting the denomination or surrounding community. However, the task becomes more difficult than they had imagined and they become more of a support group for each other's personal development. Even so, our survey results indicate that if women are members of a feminist spirituality group they will be more actively involved in social justice causes than if they are in no women's group or in a traditional church women's group. [8]

It is evident that of these predictors of involvement in social justice discussed, feminist spiritual beliefs and being in a feminist spirituality group are the most important. Which is more crucial for women's involvement in social justice causes?

THE RELATIVE IMPACT OF FEMINIST SPIRITUALITY AND GROUPS

The consequences of a personal feminist spirituality and of membership in a feminist spirituality group on Catholic women's participation in activities promoting social justice appear to be somewhat different depending on women's ethnicity and vowed status. Catholic sisters (as seen in Table 6) are apt to be involved in social justice causes no matter what their image of God or the kind of women's group to which they belong. But the likelihood that sisters will be social activists is increased if they have a strong feminist spirituality and are in a woman's spirituality group, especially if it is feminist in theology. Not being in *any* women's spirituality group, however, seems more a depressant to sisters' social justice involvement than their being in a more traditional women's spirituality group. The "ungrouped" sisters include those who are very busy in other activities and those who are not physically well. This category also includes at least a few sisters, comments on surveys and interviews indicate, who are withdrawing from all groups and causes while they rethink their vows.

Catholic lay women are not quite as likely as sisters to be involved in social justice causes, but like sisters, they are more active in social justice if they have a strong feminist spirituality. For Catholic lay women without a strong feminist spirituality, being a member of a feminist spirituality group is an important bolster for their spending time in social justice causes. Catholic lay women's involvement in social justice activities appears most diminished if they have a traditional image of God (i.e., are not spiritual feminists) and are members of a traditional church women's group.

The patterns for Hispanic Catholic women generally follow those just reported for non-Hispanic Catholic sisters and laywomen, but with wider fluctuations. For both vowed and non-vowed Hispanic women a personal

Table 6. The Effects of Feminist Spirituality and Membership in Types of Spiritual Support Groups on Women's Involvement in Social Justice

		WOMEN'S GROUP		
See GOD as GODDESS		*Spiritual Feminist Group*	*NO Group*	*Non-Feminist Spiritual Group*
I. ROMAN CATHOLIC				
A. Not Hermanas				
1. Sisters/Nuns				
av. sc. =16.9				
N = 396	Much	15.7	18.0	16.2
	Some	16.4	16.9	18.2
	None	17.5	19.1	17.4
2. Lay women (non-vowed)				
av. sc. = 18.3				
N = 660	Much	16.9	17.9	16.8
	Some	17.3	18.2	18.6
	None	18.3	19.5	20.2
B. Hermanas				
1. Sisters/Nuns				
av. sc. = 16.5				
N = 92	Much	15.0	16.0	16.4
	Some	16.6	18.6	16.3
	None	16.5	22.7	17.0
2. Lay women				
av. sc = 18.1				
N = 65	Much	14.7	19.3	17.6
	Some	14.0	17.9	17.8
	None	19.2	19.8	19.8
II. NON-CATHOLIC TRADITIONS				
A. Clergywomen				
av. sc. = 17.6				
N = 698	Much	16.6	18.0	17.8
	Some	16.7	17.6	17.3
	None	17.7	18.2	18.9
B. Liberal Protestant and Unchurched Churchwomen				
av. sc. = 18.5				
N = 1453	Much	17.0	17.5	19.7
	Some	17.7	18.9	18.7
	None	17.7	19.7	19.4
C. Laywomen in Conservative churches				
av. sc. = 20.1				
N = 382	Much	16.3	18.0	20.8
	Some	19.1	19.6	20.7
	None	18.8	20.3	20.5

Note: SOCIAL JUSTICE ACTION INDEX: (Scores on individual scale items reversed, scale scores range from 6 to 26 (high to low) involvement.)

feminist spirituality and belonging to a feminist spirituality group have a strong *additive* impact on their involvement in social justice causes. In fact, Hispanic women who are spiritual feminists *and* in spiritual feminist groups are more likely to have higher Social Justice Action index scores than any other grouping in this study. Not all Hispanic women are activists. Hispanic sisters and laywomen are apt to be uninvolved in social justice causes if they are neither spiritual feminists nor in any type of women's spiritual support group.

Sorting the women in other denominations into whether they are clergy[9] or lay women, and among the latter whether they are in more liberal or conservative churches,[10] gives more depth to understanding the relationship between feminist spirituality, membership in a feminist spirituality group and involvement in social justice. These comparisons may also have implications for women in more liberal or conservative Catholic parishes.

Protestant clergywomen are more apt to be active in social justice causes than Protestant lay women, just as sisters are more active than Catholic lay women. Similarly, as found for sisters, clergywomen's having a strong feminist spirituality and having the support of a feminist spirituality group have a clear additive effect on the amount of time clergywomen spend in social justice causes. Among Protestant lay women those in liberal churches are more likely to be involved in social activism than women in conservative churches. Part of this difference may be due to a more favorable climate supporting social activism aimed at systemic change in liberal compared to conservative churches.[11] Part of it may also be due to the fact that women surveyed in the liberal Protestant churches are less likely to have children at home than women in the conservative churches, giving them more free time to volunteer for any community or social cause. But neither marital status nor the amount of time women volunteer for church affairs seem to affect how much time lay women give to social justice causes.[12] For lay women in both conservative and liberal Protestant churches, belonging to a feminist spirituality group is more important than having a personal feminist spirituality in predicting whether they will be active in social justice causes. Women in conservative churches appear particularly vulnerable to the kind of support they receive. In conservative churches, women who have a strong personal feminist spirituality are as unlikely as women who have a more traditional spirituality to work for systemic social change if they are in traditional church women's groups. Unless they are in feminist spirituality groups, women in conservative congregations are somewhat unlikely to volunteer time for social justice causes of the kind measured.

MAJOR INFLUENCES ON INVOLVEMENT IN SOCIAL JUSTICE CAUSES

Eleven characteristics of women, other than their denominational affiliation and church employment status, appear to be among the most important in affecting their involvement in social justice causes. Column 12 of Table 7 shows that some demographic characteristics are significantly related to social justice activity for the total sample. Women who are older, have higher education, are employed full-time, and do not have children at home are more likely to be active in working for systemic change than women who are young, have less education, are not employed outside the home, and are caring for a number of children. Being a member of a local church is slightly related to relative inactivity in the area of social justice.

More important overall than these kinds of characteristics in predicting involvement in social justice causes, correlations in Table 7 indicate, are the kinds of feminist attitudes women hold and whether they are in a feminist spirituality group, as described. But there are two characteristics which appear to be even more strongly related to how active women will be in social justice concerns: The amount of time they give to community outreach and how many groups they belong to in total.

Involvement in Community Outreach and Being a "Joiner"

Women who are active in community outreach are also apt to be volunteering time for social justice causes. It is possible for feminist women to become active in lobbying for social justice and subsequently realize they need to give some immediate individual help to the needy while they are attempting to change structures and policies. However, as indicated in interviews, most women become active first in volunteer efforts to help the community poor, and later realize that the community situation will not change until laws and policies are altered.

Being part of any voluntary group indicates some interest in joining with others for purposes of worship, mutual support, study, or action. Giving time to community outreach usually entails working with a number of individuals and probably groups. Striving to achieve social justice almost requires group action; changing laws or public policy would seem to need group rather than individual activity. Correlations in Table 7 suggest that women involved in community outreach, but particularly those active in working for systemic change in the area of social justice, are "joiners."

Women were asked what kinds of groups they had participated in during the last couple of years, other than spirituality or church-related groups. Overall, 29 percent have been or are in a community action group and 27 percent in a peace or anti-war group. About a fifth each had been involved in a personal growth or encounter group, a consciousness-raising group on gender or racial issues, a 12-step program or other health support group. Additionally, 14 percent have recently been in a political campaign or party support group, 8 percent have participated in a massage or body-work group (Tai-Chi, yoga), and 5 percent have been involved in a dream analysis group.

Table 7. Pearson Correlations on Total Sample of Women for Selected Variables (N = 3468)

	VARIABLES											
	1	2	3	4	5	6	7	8	9	10	11	12
1. Age (young to old)	1.0	n.s	.22	−.20	−.06	n.s.	n.s.	n.s.	.08	−.06	n.s.	−.12
2. Education (low to high)		1.0	−.23	−.07	n.s.	−.22	−.14	n.s.	n.s.	.12	n.s.	−.14
3. Employment (full-time to not)			1.0	n.s.	n.s.	.13	.07	.07	n.s.	.12	.10	.10
4. Children at home (0 to 9)				1.0	−.13	.11	n.s.	n.s.	.08	−.08	n.s	.14
5. Church Member (1. yes; 2. no)					1.0	−.05	−.11	−.13	−.13	.07	.07	−.07
6. Church Language Feminism (scale of desiring inclusive language: low = yes, very much						1.0	.23	.22	.26	−.13	.06	.22
7. Secular Feminism (want affirmative action: 1. yes; 2. mixed; 3. no)							1.0	.18	.17	−.08	n.s.	.17
8. Spiritual Feminism (see God as "goddess" 1. much; 2. some; 3. none)								1.0	.23	−.16	n.s	.17
9. Spiritual Feminist Group (1. yes; 2. no wm. spr. grp.; 3. trad. wm. sp. grp.)									1.0	−.12	n.s.	.19
10. Total Other Kinds of Groups (none to nine)										1.0	−.26	−.44
11. Involvement in Community Outreach Scale (much to little)											1.0	.46
12. Involvement in Social Justice Activities (much to little)												1.0

Signif .001

128

Not surprisingly, women who participate in community action, peace group, political groups, etc. are more likely to be involved in social justice than women who are in groups devoted to body-work, dream analysis, or are 12-Step programs. However, it is also true that the greater number of different kinds of groups women join, the more likely their scores on the Involvement in Social Justice Scale indicate high activity in working for systemic change.

Predicting Involvement in Social Justice: Multivariate Analyses

In the total sample of women, many of the eleven characteristics correlated with time given to working for social justice are also correlated with one another, though not highly. Which characteristics are most important in predicting women's involvement in social justice?

The best fit regression model in Table 8 depicts the flow of influence on women's involvement in social justice. This model portrays women most active in social justice causes as those in their forties and fifties with graduate education, full-time employment (typically in a professional capacity), and no children at home. They are feminists, especially spiritual feminists who image God as having female characteristics.

Local church membership remains a slight depressant on women's involvement in social justice causes. Congregations differ in how supportive they are to social justice concerns; and this is one likely reason that church membership is of minor predictive value. Another reason is that church membership encourages women's involvement in community outreach, which as discussed, can lead to their becoming more active in social justice. Traditionally women have been encouraged in churches to donate time to lay ministries of feeding, educating, and otherwise helping the poor. Women surveyed who are church members are somewhat more likely to be involved in serving the needy in the community. An unanticipated consequence of women's involvement in these good works may be that their outreach activities raise their social consciousness and lead them into becoming social activists!

Being a member of feminist spirituality group definitely helps women with feminist values become involved in social justice causes. Two thirds of the feminist spirituality groups draw members from several local churches if not denominations and faith traditions. In these mixed church and faith groups women may obtain a broadened perspective of what other congregations and denominations do in the way of addressing community outreach and social action. This in turn helps individual women, some interviews indicate, envision possibilities for addressing social problems through political action.

A simpler path model version of the above is depicted in Table 9. This model shows that including the degree to which women affirm various feminist values improves the ability to predict their social justice activity over using their background and situational characteristics alone. Adding the amount and kind

Table 8. Regressions on Involvement in Social Justice Activities (N = 3,367)
Betas for Best Fit Path Model on Total Sample of Women (standard errors in parentheses)

	Dependent Variables						
	Feminist Attitudes			Groups and Activities			
	Sec. Fem.	Church Language Feminism	Feminism	Spiritual Feminism Group	Total Groups (0 to 9)	Involvement in Community Outreach (much to little)	Involvement in Social Justice (much to little)
1. Age (young to old)	.04* (.01)	n.s.	-.04* (.01)	-.04* (.01)	.07 (.02)	n.s.	-.10 (.05)
2. Education (low to high)	-.14 (.01)	-.19 (.02)	-.03* (.01)	-.03* (.01)	n.s.	n.s.	-.06 (.01)
3. Employment (full-time to not)	n.s.	.08 (.02)	.07 (.01)	.07 (.01)	.05 (.02)	-.09 (.04)	.05 (.04)
4. Children at Home (0 to 9)	n.s.	.09 (.03)	n.s.	n.s.	-.05 (.02)	n.s.	.07 (.05)
5. Church Member (1. yes; 2. no)	-.11 (.03)	-.04* (.08)	-.08 (.03)	-.08 (.03)	.04* (.07)	-.08 (.14)	-.04 (.14)
6. Church Language Feminism (scale of desiring inclusive language: low = yes, very much			.18 (.01)	.18 (.01)	-.09 (.01)	-.04 (.08)	.08 (.03)
7. Secular Feminism (want affirmative action: 1. yes; 2. some; 3. no)			.08 (.02)	.08 (.02)	-.04* (.03)	n.s.	.09 (.07)
8. Spiritual Feminism (see God as "goddess" 1. much; 2. some; 3. none)			.16 (.02)	.16 (.02)	-.13 (.04)	-.04* (.08)	.05 (.08)
9. Spiritual Feminist Group (1. yes; 2. no wm. spt. grp.; 3. trad. wm. sp. grp.)							.08 (.07)
10. Total other kinds of Groups (0 to 9)							-.29 (.03)
11. Involvement in Community Outreach Scale (much to little)							.37 (.02)
R	.18	.25	.14	.35	.22	.14	.63
Adj R2	.03	.06	.02	.12	.05	.08	.39

Note: Beta levels are significant (T levels) at .0005 or less, unless followed by * in which case they are significant at .05 to .001. Multiple R's are significant at .0001

Table 9. Paths to Involvement in Social Justice Activities

Background	Attitudes	Groups/Activities	Involvement in Social Justice Activities
AGE young to old (beta = −.10)	SECULAR FEMINISM (Affirmative Action) agree to disagree (beta = . 09)	SPIRITUAL FEMINIST GROUP 1. yes 2. no group 3. more trad. w. group (beta = .08)	(scale) much to little
EDUCATION Low to high (beta = −.06)	CHURCH LANGUAGE FEMINISM (Inclusive language liking) (beta = .08)	TOTAL OTHER KINDS OF GROUPS	
EMPLOYMENT fully to not (bet = .05)		none to 9 kinds groups (beta = . 29)	
	SPIRITUAL FEMINISM (seeing God as Goddess)		
KIDS AT HOME none to many (beta = .07)	much to none (beta = . 05)	INVOLVEMENT IN COMMUNITY OUTREACH (scale) much to little (beta = . 37)	
CHURCH MEMBER yes, no (beta = .04*)			
R with Social Justice Activity			
R =	.24	.34	.63
	+	+	
R² =	.06	.12	.40

Note: N of cases: 3468
Beta's under variable cases are the relationship to INVOLVEMENT IN SOCIAL JUSTICE INDEX
Beta levels are significant at .001 or less, unless followed by a * indicating significance between .05 and .002.
R's are significant at .0001

of women's group memberships and community good works to their attitudes and background characteristics further improves the ability to predict how active they will be in social justice causes. But the most important predictors of whether women are likely to be social activists, even considering all these other characteristics, are whether these women are "joiners" (total number of different groups to which they belong) and whether they are involved in community outreach. Do these generalizations hold for Catholic sisters and laywomen, for those of Hispanic ethnicity, for Protestant clergywomen, and laywomen in liberal and in more conservative churches? Regressions that run separately for these groups indicate that there are some differences. (See Table 10.)

It is apparent that for *sisters* neither background characteristics, nor whether they are in feminist spirituality groups, nor whether they endorse feminist

Table 10. Regressions on Social Justice Within the Major Groups

Dependent Variable: Involvement in Social Justice Activities
(Standard errors in parentheses)

Independent Variables	Catholic			Other Laywomen	
	Nuns N = (428)	Laywomen N = (668)	Clergy-women N = (688)	Liberals N = (1,336)	Conservative N = (348)
1. AGE (Young to old)	n.s.	n.s.	-.13 (.11)	-.10 (.08)	n.s.
2. EDUCATION (low to high)	n.s.	n.s.	n.s.	-.07 (.06)	-.13 (.09)
3. EMPLOYMENT (full-time to not)	n.s.	.10* (.09)	n.s.	n.s.	n.s.
4. CHILDREN AT HOME (0 to 9)	n.s.	.08* (.10)	n.s.	.08 (.09)	.08* (.08)
5. CHURCH MEMBER (1. yes; 2. no)	n.s.	n.s.	n.s.	-.08 (.22)	n.s.
6. CHURCH LANGUAGE FEMINISM (Scale of desiring inclusive language: low = yes, very much)	n.s.	n.s.	.12 (.09)	.09 (.05)	.10* (.06)
7. SECULAR FEMINISM (want affirmative action: 1. yes; 2. mixed; 3. no)	.10* (.18)	.08* (.15)	.11 (.15)	.10 (.12)	.13 (.19)
8. SPIRITUAL FEMINISM (see God as "goddess:" 1. much; 2. some; 3. none)	n.s.	.07* (.17)	n.s.	n.s.	n.s.
9. SPIRITUAL FEMINIST GROUP (1. yes; 2. no woman spiritual; 3. traditional women spiritual group)	n.s.	.10* (.16)	.09* (.14)	.07 (.12)	.14 (.20)
10. TOTAL OTHER KINDS OF GROUPS (none to nine)	-.29 (.08)	-.32 (.08)	-.39 (.08)	-.26 (.06)	-.34 (.10)
11. INVOLVEMENT IN COMMUNITY Outreach Scale	.39 (.04)	.37 (.04)	.30 (.04)	.40 (.03)	.400 (.04)
R	.05	.61	.60	.61	.73
R^2	.31	.36	.36	.38	.53

Note: Beta levels are significant (T values) at .0005 or less, unless followed by * in which case they are significant at .05 to .001. Multiple R's are significant at .0001.

132

values on church and God, predict their involvement in social justice activities with other factors controlled by regression. Those who hold secular feminist value of using affirmative action, however, continue to be more involved in social activism. Still, the most important predictors of sisters' involvement in social justice causes are the number of groups to which they belong and the time they give to community outreach.

Being a joiner and being active in community outreach are also the key predictors of the degree to which Catholic lay women are involved in social justice causes. For *Catholic lay women* not being tied to the home is also important in having the freedom to volunteer for community and social justice causes. Those who have no or only one child at home and are employed full-time are more active in social justice than full-time housewives and mothers. Catholic laywomen, however, also need the legitimation that feminist values provide for being social activists, and the group support of other women who share these values.

Whether sisters or Catholic laywomen are of Hispanic ethnicity and members of Las Hermanas does *not affect* their social justice scores with other variables controlled by regression. Only three characteristics are significant in determining *Hispanic Catholic* women's involvement in social justice causes: Whether they are active in community outreach (beta = .49), whether they are "joiners" (beta = .29) and whether they are sisters (beta = .18). Within Las Hermanas, sisters are more likely than laywomen to be involved in social justice when other factors are taken into account. (Multiple R = .66, squared .44).

For women in other denominations, the same characteristics remain pivotal in predicting how active they will be in social justice causes: Whether they are "joiners" and whether they are active in community outreach. Among *clergywomen* those who are older and those who endorse affirmative action and inclusive language tend to be somewhat more active in social justice. Whether clergywomen personally adhere to a feminist spirituality does not affect their involvement in social justice with other important variables controlled by regression, but being a member of feminist spirituality group is of some support.

Among *liberal Protestant and unaffiliated lay women,* the older women with higher education and no children at home are also more active in social justice causes, but whether they work outside the home is unrelated. Membership in a local church typically does not support their working for social justice. Desiring inclusive language in church services and affirmative action to place women in jobs are values which reinforce their social activism. Being in a feminist spirituality group, however, is more important than their own degree of feminist spirituality in whether they are active in social justice causes.

Women in more conservative churches are also more involved in social justice if they are "joiners" and if they are active in community outreach. Similar to liberal Protestant lay women, they are more active in social justice causes if they are better educated, have no children at home, and very much want to see their churches use inclusive language and society to support affirmative action for women. But their age, whether they are employed, are church members, or have a strong feminist spirituality do not predict how active they will be in social justice, when other characteristics are controlled by regression. Rather, it is only if women in conservative churches have their feminist spiritual beliefs supported by other women in a feminist spirituality group that they are likely to put time into social justice causes.

SUMMARY AND DISCUSSION

These results support the contention of Catholic feminist theologians and church historians' that *Catholic* feminist spirituality includes a commitment to social justice for all. In fact, feminist spiritual values about the nature of God are likely to be related to Catholic women's involvement in social justice; and for laywomen, being in a feminist spirituality group provides additional support for social activism. Sisters are so generally involved in social justice causes that a particular kind of group does not have much effect on their activity, although involvement with some supportive group of women is helpful. Results for women in other denominations suggest that being in a feminist spirituality group is particularly important if the parishes women attend are conservative theologically and socially.

Getting Catholic women involved in working with others (including men) in a variety of groups and in trying to help needy individuals and families in the community, are major avenues to their becoming active in social justice causes. Interviews with women from different denominations suggest that church-employed feminist women professionals (usually sisters or clergy) are likely to be leaders both in encouraging women to do things for the community destitute and in coming together to effect more systemic change in order to lessen the long term demand for such band-aid operations.

The fact that women leaders involved in organizing social justice work may be similar in some attributes and values does not mean that all those they work with in addressing social justice causes are like them in education, occupation, lifestyle, or all beliefs. The strongest predictors across denominations of women's involvement in social justice are not feminist spiritual values nor membership in feminist spirituality groups, but rather whether women are "joiners," belonging to a variety of groups, and whether they are involved in community outreach to the needy. These results are more suggestive of diversity than similarity among all those committed to working for social justice. Differing backgrounds, life experiences, and outlooks on women in church and society may result in differing perspectives on goal priorities and preferred methods of creating a more just society and peaceful world. This putative diversity may account for the frictions that sometimes arise among those who share a strong commitment to working for systemic social change.[13]

The Hispanic Catholic women leaders especially demonstrate the feminist congruence of belief in a female aspect of God and commitment to social justice. Although they are as likely as other Catholic women to envision God as in part female, they are also more comfortable with male images of God and less alienated from the institutional church than most Anglo Catholic women. Sandoval (1990, p. 133) argues that "Hispanics remain a group apart in the (Catholic) Church, a condition almost certain to increase in the future despite the Church's hope to serve them better." These characteristics of Catholic Hispanic women *leaders* foretell a better future for the inclusion of Hispanics within the Catholic Church than Sandoval predicts. The women of Las Hermanas may well provide the guidance to aide the expanding Hispanic population to integrate within and to become a rejuvenating force throughout the American Catholic Church.

ACKNOWLEDGMENTS

This is a revision of paper prepared for Annual Meeting of the Association for the Sociology of Religion, Pittsburgh, 1992. Miriam Therese Winter, Medical Mission Sister and Professor of Spirituality at Hartford Seminary, is also principal investigator on this Lilly Endowment-funded study, and first author (1994) of a book for the public on its results. Critique and suggestions from Rhys Williams and anonymous *RSSSR* reviewers have substantially contributed to the revisions herein. The authors may be reached at: Hartford Seminary, 79 Sherman Street. Hartford, CT 06105-2260.

NOTES

1. We are indebted to Ada Maria Isasi-Diaz for both supplying address labels for Las Hermanas members *and* writing an introductory letter.

2. Half of the returned questionnaires included at least one name and address, often at least three names. We drew a small sample from the names gathered through this snowball technique.

3. The Sisters who answered this survey may well be among the more radical of women religious. This inference is made from comparisons with Neal's (1991, p. 10) data. Neal found that a minority, although a substantial one (40 percent), want more inclusive language in prayers and services, but no more than 10 percent use feminist prayer styles regularly. The majority (60 percent) of the sisters prefer "traditional modes of prayer and liturgy."

4. Church Language Feminism scale (Alpha .82) consists of the following items: (a) There should be more hymns and prayers using female imagery and names for God, (b) Inclusive language should be used in all church worship, (c) The use of male and female images for God should be balanced in worship, (d) I find (or would find) inclusive language during scripture reading disruptive to my worship (reversed scoring). Low scores indicate a higher degree of feminism. The mean score for all women on this scale is 5.0; for Catholic sisters it is 4.4, clergywomen 4.6, laywomen who are Catholics 4.9, non-Catholic laywomen in liberal churches 5.0 and in conservative churches 6.6.

5. The more emphasis women give to "goddess" in their overall image of God (much, some, none), the more *unlikely* (Spearman correlations significant at the .001 level indicate) they are to believe that "Women's spiritual growth is best attained through worship experiences shared with men" (-.14), and the more likely they are to "often feel alienated from the institutional church" (.26).

6. Interviews and survey results indicate that Catholic women who are so fed up that they have stopped attending parishes altogether, are more likely to be in ecumenical rather Catholic women's groups, if they are in any group at all.

7. In illustration, 92 percent of women in feminist spirituality groups, compared to 76 percent of women in no group, and 67 percent of those in more traditional church women's groups *agree* that: "There should be more hymns and prayers using female imagery and names for God". Similarly, 78 percent of women in feminist spirituality groups, compared to 67% in no group, and to 57 percent in more traditional women's groups *agree* "I often feel alienated from the institutional church." Women in more traditional groups are more likely to disagree (44 percent) that affirmative action favoring women should be used in hiring and salary decisions, compared to those in no group (36 percent) and those in feminist spirituality groups (27 percent).

8. The Social Justice Scale mean scores (low score=high involvement) for all women in feminist spirituality groups is 17.2, for those in *no* women church/spiritual group it is 18.8, and for those in traditional church women's groups it is 19.7. While the linear differences in Social Justice Scale mean scores among women in different types of groups is significant at the .0001 level, so are the deviations from linearity. The standard deviations in social justice scores for all three groups are between 3.7 and 3.9., indicating that other factors besides women's group membership influence women's involvement in social justice.

9. The present denominational affiliations of the 698 clergywomen in this study are Baptist (mainly American) 6 percent, Brethren 3 percent, Episcopal 13 percent, Lutheran 4 percent, Methodist 18 percent, Presbyterian 21 percent, Unitarian 2 percent, UCC and Disciples of Christ combined 20 percent, and 7 percent in an array of other denominations (less than 2 percent each). The remaining 6 percent of the clergywomen did not feel currently identified with any denomination or established church.

10. The division of non-Catholic laywomen into "liberal" and "conservative" churches is based mainly on known characteristics of the churches involved. These 1,453 lay women in the "liberal" church category include Brethren 3 percent, Episcopalians 18 percent, Lutherans 10 percent, Methodists 7 percent, Presbyterians 11 percent, Unitarians 4%, UCC and Disciples of Christ combined 12 percent with the remainder being those who indicated that they have no denominational affiliation presently. The 382 lay women in the "conservative" church category include Baptists 20 percent (mainly Independent and Southern), Mormons 46 percent, and a variety of other conservative churches 34 percent (each less than 5 percent), including AME/CME, Assemblies of God, Church of God, Evangelical, Pentecostal, Salvation Army, and Seventh-day Adventists.

11. Conservative churches are involved in community outreach and even "secular" politics to an extent at least equal to that of liberal churches. But the social activist goal priorities of conservative and liberal churches are likely to differ. Roof and McKinney (1987, pp. 85-94, 202, *et passim*) report that liberal Protestants are significantly more likely than conservative Protestants to support efforts aimed at achieving racial justice and supporting civil liberties for all groups (including women, minorities, homosexuals) through systemic change in public policies and institutions.

12. Women who are regular attenders at conservative churches are slightly more likely to have one and more children still at home than lay women who attend liberal churches (correlation =.17, p. .001). The amount of time volunteered to church activities among women who belong to a local church has, however, no relationship to time spent in social justice causes, regardless of denominational classification.

13. We are indebted to an anonymous reviewer for pointing out the significance of the finding that being a "joiner" and heavily involved in community outreach are more important factors than feminist values or group membership in whether women surveyed are active in social justice causes. The reviewer suggests these findings indicate a probable diversity among all who are active in social justice causes. The reviewer predicates that highly educated women who hold feminist spirituality values and belong to feminist spirituality groups are also likely to have "entered to a wider world of experience unshared by most other people." These women's more cosmopolitan outlook combined with their higher education and feminist values, however, may make it difficult for them to understand and work well with others equally committed to social justice but who are do not have the same backgrounds or perspectives. The reviewer predicates that this source of variance "accounts for the friction in doing social justice action among the dedicated workers with their wide range of perspectives on feminism."

REFERENCES

Ashe, K. 1991. "Women Religious, Feminism and the Future." *Horizon* 16:3-8.

Briggs, S. 1987. "Women in Religion." Pp. 408-441 *Analyzing Gender: A Handbook of Social Science Research,* edited by in B. M. Hess and M. M. Ferree. Newbury Park, CA: Sage Press.

Chafetz, J.S. 1989. "Gender Equality: Toward a Theory of Change." Pp. 135-160 in *Feminism and Sociological Theory,* edited by Ruth A. Wallace. Newbury Park, CA: Sage Press.

Demerath, N.J., III and R.H. Williams. 1992. *A Bridging of Faiths: Religion and Politics in a New England City.* Princeton, NJ: Princeton University Press.

Ebaugh, H.R.F. 1991. "The Revitalization Movement in the Catholic Church: The Institutional Dilemma of Power." *Sociological Analysis* 52:1-12.

_____. 1993. *Women in the Vanishing Cloister: Organizational Decline in Catholic Religious Orders.* New Brunswick, NJ: Rutgers University Press.

Finley, N.J. 1991. "Political Activism and Feminist Spirituality." *Sociological Analysis* 52:349-362.

Greeley, A. 1990. "Why Catholics Stay in the Church". Pp. 177-183 in *In Gods We Trust: New Patterns of Religious Pluralism in America,* Second Edition, edited by T. Robbins and D. Anthony. New Brunswick, NJ: Transaction Books.

Isasi-Diaz, A.M. and Y. Tarango. 1988. *Hispanic Women: Prophetic Voice in the Church.* San Francisco: Harper and Row.

Jacobs, J.L. 1990. "Women-Centered Healing Rites: A Study of Alienation and Reintegration". Pp. 373-384 in *In Gods We Trust: New Patterns of Religious Pluralism in America* (2nd ed.), edited by T. Robbins and D. Anthony. New Brunswick, NJ: Transaction Books.

_____. 1991. "Gender and Power in New Religious Movements: A Feminist Discourse on the Scientific Study of Religion." *Religion* 21:345-356.

Lerner, G. 1993. *The Creation of Feminist Consciousness: From the Middle Ages to Eighteen-Seventy.* New York: Oxford University Press.

Neal, M.A. 1991. *A Report on the National Profile of the Third Sisters' Survey.* Boston: Emmanuel College.

Neitz, M.J. 1990. "In Goddess We Trust." Pp. 353-372 in *In Gods We Trust: New Patterns of Religious Pluralism in America,* Second Edition, edited by T. Robbins and D. Anthony. New Brunswick, NJ: Transaction Books.

Origins. April 21, 1992. (left side column of insert facts) Vol. 21:780.

Quinonez, L. A. and M. D. Turner. 1992. *The Transformation of American Catholic Sisters.* Philadelphia: Temple University Press.

Rader, R. 1989. "Catholic Feminism: Its Impact on U.S. Catholic Women." Pp. 182-197 in *American Catholic Women: A Historical Exploration* edited by K. Kennelly. New York: Macmillan.

Reuther, R. R. 1985. *Women-Church: Theory and Practice.* San Francisco: Harper and Row.

Riley, M. 1989. *Transforming Feminism.* Kansas City: Sheed and Ward.

Robbins, T. and R. Robertson. 1991. "Studying Religion Today: Controversiality and 'Objectivity' in the Sociology of Religion". *Religion* 21:319-337.

Robbins, T., R. Robertson and D. Bromley. 1992. "Social Experimentation and the Significance of American New Religions: A Focused Review Essay." Pp. 1-28 in *Research in the Social Scientific Study of Religion* Vol. 4, edited by M.L. Lynn and D.O. Moberg. Greenwich, CT: JAI Press.

Roof, W. C. and W. McKinney. 1987. *American Mainline Religion: Its Changing Shape and Future.* New Brunswick, NJ: Rutgers University Press.

Russell, L.M. 1993. *Church in the Round: Feminist Interpretation of the Church.* Louisville, KY: Westminster/John Knox.

Sandoval, M. 1990. *On the Move: A History of the Hispanic Church in the United States.* Maryknoll, NY: Orbis Books.

Saussey, C. 1991. *God Images and Self-Esteem.* Louisville, KY: John Knox Press.

Schneiders, S.M. 1991. *Beyond Patching: Faith and Feminism in the Catholic Church.* New York: Paulist Press.

Trebbi, D. 1990. "Women-Church: Catholic Women Produce an Alternative Spirituality." Pp. 347-351 in *In Gods We Trust: New Patterns of Religious Pluralism in America* (2nd ed.), edited by T. Robbins and D. Anthony. New Brunswick, NJ: Transaction Books.

Wallace, R.A. 1992. *They Call Her Pastor.* Albany: State University of New York Press.

Walters, S. D. 1985. "Caught in the Web: A Critique of Spiritual Feminism." *Berkeley Journal of Sociology* 30:15-40.

Weaver, M.J. 1985. *New Catholic Women: A Contemporary Challenge to Traditional Religious Authority.* San Francisco: Harper and Row.

―――――. 1993. *Springs of Water in a Dry Land: Spiritual Survival for Catholic Women Today.* Boston: Beacon Press.

Winter, M.T. A. 1989. "The Women-Church Movement." *The Christian Century* 106 (March 8):258-360.

Winter, M.T., Lummis and A. Stokes. 1994. *Defecting in Place: Women Claiming Responsibility for their own Spiritual Lives.* New York: Crossroad.

Wittberg, P. 1989. "Feminist Consciousness among American Nuns: Patterns of Ideological Diffusion." *Women's Studies International Forum.* 12:529-537.

―――――. 1991. *Creating a Future for Religious Life: A Sociological Perspective.* New York: Paulist Press.

Wuthnow, R. 1989. *The Restructuring of American Religion.* Princeton, NJ: Princeton University Press.

Zikmund, B.B. 1993. "Women's Organization: Denominational Loyalty and Expressions of Christian Unity." Pp. 116-138 in *Beyond Establishment: Protestant Identity in a Post-Protestant Age,* edited by J. Carroll and W.C. Roof. Louisville, KY: Westminster/John Knox.

NON-GLOSSOLALIC CHARISMATICS:
PSYCHOLOGICAL AND RELIGIOUS
CHARACTERISTICS AND THEIR INTERPRETATION

Augustine Meier

ABSTRACT

Non-glossolalic charismatics were compared to two control groups on psychological and religious variables. Performance on psychological variables was assessed by the administration of Eysenck Personality Questionnaire (EPQ), Jackson's Personality Research Form (PRF), Crumbaugh and Maholick's Purpose In Life Test, the Allport-Vernon-Lindzey Study of Values (A-V-L), Schutz's Fundamental Interpersonal Relations Orientation Questionnaire (FIRO-B), and Shostrom's Personal Orientation Inventory (POI). Performance on religious variables was assessed using Hood's Mysticism Scale Research Form D (MS) and Spilka's Religious Orientation Scale (ROS). The data were analyzed using multivariate analysis of variance. Group differences were observed on PRF, MS, ROS, A-V-L, FIRO-B, and POI. The findings were interpreted with reference to strivings toward bonding and toward separating which, it is hypothesized, characterize the charismatic phenomenon.

Research in the Social Scientific Study of Religion, Volume 6, pages 139-165.
Copyright © 1994 by JAI Press Inc.
All rights of reproduction in any form reserved.
ISBN: 1-55938-762-9

Since the "official" beginning of the Catholic Charismatic movement in the 1970's (Bord and Faulkner 1983, p. vii; Greeley 1974, pp. 318; McGuire 1982, p. 4-5; Mills 1986, p. 11), many studies have appeared which described and explained this phenomenon. The early studies described the experiences of those who were charismatics (Bord & Faulkner 1983; Kildahl 1975; McGuire 1982), others explained and interpreted this phenomenon (Castelein 1984; Hine 1965; Hutch 1980; Mayers 1973; Mills 1973; Pothress 1980; Richardson 1973).

The descriptive and interpretative studies were followed by experimental and quasi-experimental studies which are wrought with deficiencies in that terms were not clearly operationalized, comparative groups were either absent or inadequate, sampling procedures were faulty, often the measures used were not appropriate, and/or the conclusions drawn were often inappropriate (Gritzmacher et al. 1988, p. 238-239; Mills 1986, 12-31; Richardson 1973, p. 206).

In a recent review of the psychological characteristics of glossolalic charismatics, Gritzmacher, Bolton, and Dana (1988) stated that it was difficult to "determine from the studies conducted whether psychological commonalities are characteristic of personalities attracted to or developed by involvement in Pentecostalism" (p. 242). They added that the results from psychometric research provided mixed results regarding the degree of psychological adjustment.

Another weakness of the research on charismatics is that the focus has been on glossolalia despite the fact that at the height of this movement about ninety percent of the charismatics did not speak in tongues (Kantzer 1980, p. 8). Several studies used non-glossolalic charismatics as controls (Gonsalvez 1982), however, there is no known research which directly investigated non-glossolalic charismatics. Yet, such research is needed for several reasons. First, research which focuses on the non-glossolalic charismatics is essential to understand this group of persons, and second, this understanding is imperative to the professional who provides services to charismatics, including non-glossolalic charismatics. This notion is echoed by Csordas (1990), one of the contributors in the special issue of *Psychotherapy* on Psychotherapy and Religion in which he compared psychotherapy to charismatic healing.

The goal of the present study is to add to our understanding of the charismatic phenomenon not by testing theory-derived hypotheses but by generating a data based hypothesis. Much of the research on charismatics, thus far, has been based on and/or tested the assumption that glossolalia manifests some form of psychopathology (Cutten 1927; Clark 1949; Gonsalvez 1982; Castelein 1984). An alternate hypothesis, which is based on the data obtained in this study will be proposed.

Although the published research on charismatics has focused on glossolalics and not on non-glossolalic charismatics, yet this body of research will be reviewed in order to provide a broad context for this study. The literature review will be organized around four headings: personal adjustment, personality traits, religious orientation, and mystical experience. The latter two aspects have not been studied previously in relationship to charismatics. This will be followed by a description of the research method, presentation of the research findings, and discussion of their implications.

LITERATURE REVIEW

It should be stated at the outset that any conclusions drawn from the literature regarding glossolalic charismatics must be cautiously applied to non-glossolalic charismatics for two reasons. First, the majority of the studies seldom included non-glossolalic charismatics so there are limited data indicating how the two relate on various variables. Second many of the studies were subjective in nature, and those that were empirical were often deficient in some aspect of the research design. Thus the results of these studies are tentative.

Personal Adjustment

The early psychological studies of glossolalia were driven by the assumption that speaking in tongues was in some way psychopathological. These and other studies have been extensively reviewed by Hine (1969), Malony and Lovekin (1985, pp. 41-244), Mills (1986, pp. 20-28), and Gritsmacher et al. (1988).

One of the more significant and often quoted studies is by Cutten (1927). He assumed that glossolalia was linked to schizophrenia and hysteria because glossolalics seemed to overidentify with their spiritual leaders, thought of themselves as possessing special powers, and were highly suggestible. He stated that the gift of tongues was received by individuals of low mental ability in whom the capacity for rational thought was underdeveloped. This idea was also held by Clark (1949).

In subsequent qualitative studies, the psychopathological hypothesis was put into question. Boisen (1939) found no evidence of mental illness in tongue speakers from his church. Alland (1961) stated that the explanation of glossolalia as schizophrenia or hysteria is no longer acceptable in view of the sociocultural data. Kiev (1964) observed that glossolalia could not be explained as a schizophrenic phenomenon.

Similar conclusions were drawn from empirical studies. Vivier (1960) administered the Cattell Personality Inventory to glossolalics and control groups and found no significant group differences on a measure for general level of neuroticism. Moreover, glossolalics scored low on three factors of the Cattell Personality Inventory which are associated with conversion hysteria and were not significantly different from the control group. Plog (1966) administered a battery of tests, including the California Psychological

Inventory, and observed no particular atypical personality patterns among the glossolalics. He concluded that the glossolalics were very responsible and normally well-controlled individuals. Gerlach and associates (1966) sampled a wide range of glossolalics and concluded that there was no evidence of universal psychopathology among Pentecostal adherents. Although different in some behavior, Pentecostals were not sick, functioned effectively, and coped adequately.

After reviewing a large body of literature, Hine (1969) stated that Pentecostals as a group appear to be normally adjusted and productive members of society (p. 16) and that "available evidence requires that an explanation of glossolalia as pathological must be discarded" (p. 217). In a similar vein McDonnell (1976) concluded that "a good understanding of Pentecostalism is not to be found in the field of abnormal psychology [and] most illuminating psychological research had yet to be done" (1976, p. 234). Spanos and Hewitt (1979) concluded that hypotheses regarding glossolalics as psychopathological are not substantiated (p. 429).

Despite the strong opinion against a psychopathological interpretation of glossolalia, two recent publications viewed glossolalics, at least indirectly, as having personality disorders. In one of these studies, Gonsalvez (1982) administered the Hysteria Scale (Hy) of the Minnesota Multiphasic Personality Inventory (MMPI) to glossolalic charismatics, non-glossolalic charismatics and non-charismatics. She hypothesized that the "psychodynamics and needs of the Pentecostals and glossolalics relate in many ways to the behavioral dynamics and needs of the hysterical personality type" (p. 416). An analysis of variance of group Hy means indicated that glossolalic charismatics scored significantly higher on the Hy scale than did non-glossolalic charismatics and non-charismatics. The author interpreted this to mean that the glossolalic charismatics were more likely to be of the hysterical personality type than the non-glossolalic charismatics and non-charismatics (pp. 419-423). This interpretation, however, can be questioned since the mean scores for the two charismatic groups fell within the first standard deviation of the mean. These scores cannot be interpreted clinically as manifesting hysterical personality disorder.

In the second study, Castelein (1984, p.18) interpreted glossolalics as suffering from a form of narcissistic disorder. According to him, speaking in tongues helps glossolalics to reintegrate their personalities, release their narcissistic rage and shame and develop a sense of their identity. Narcissistic disorders are character or personality disorders and are listed in the DSM-III-R. Even though he might not want to view glossolalics as psychopathological, Castelein did precisely that.

This brief review of the literature identified one study (Gonsalvez 1982) which directly compared glossalic to non-glossolalic charismatics. The results suggest that neither glossolalic charismatics nor non-glossolalic charismatics as a group can be described as pathological. McDonnell's (1976) comment that the "most illuminating psychological research had yet to be done" (p. 234), is appropriate.

Personality Traits

Several studies suggest that glossolalics possess specific personality traits. Vivier (1960), using the Cattell Personality Inventory, found glossolalics, when compared to non-tongue speaking control groups, score higher on "desurgence" and lower on "shrewdness-naivete." Desurgence refers to being renunciative in one's habits. A low score on shrewdness-naivete indicates that a person is less realistic and practical and more concerned with feelings than thought or action. Vivier (1960) described the glossolalics he studied as generally more sensitive, less bound by traditional or orthodox thought processes, less depressed, having less generalized fear, but more in need of emotional catharsis (Hine 1969, pp. 214-215).

Based on interviews of some sixty glossolalics, Morentz (1966) observed several dominant personality patterns. He found that they were hostile toward authority, had a consuming wish to compensate for feelings of inadequacy, rationalized feelings of isolation, and had strong feelings of dependency and suggestibility mixed with strong tendencies to dominate.

Kildahl (1972) administered a number of psychological tests to glossolalics and non-glossolalics. Analysis of the MMPI profiles revealed lower scores for glossolalics on Depression, but no other differences. Analysis of the Thematic Apperception Test showed the glossolalics to be less autonomous and but more dependent than the control groups.

Coulson and Johnson (1977) found glossolalics, when compared to non-glossolalics, to be more external in locus of control, that is, they believed that the events of life are out of one's control and more in the control of the other. One would expect that those who are more suggestible would interpret life events as being in the control of the other (Maloney and Lovekin 1985, p. 73).

Gritzmacher and associates (1988) extensively reviewed the literature and concluded with a list of observations characterizing Pentecostals when compared to the general population. Pentecostals were: (1) neither clearly less well nor better adjusted, (2) less depressed, (3) showed fewer manifestations of hostility, (4) more submissive, (5) had lower self-esteem, (6) just as anxious, and (7) repressed their conflicts (pp. 242-243).

Religious Orientation

In the one reported study on religious orientation of Pentecostals, Rarick (1982) compared 212 neo-Pentecostal college and seminary students to 663 classical Pentecostal college and seminary students. Among the measures administered were Allport and Ross' (1967) Extrinsic-Intrinsic Religious

Orientation Scale and Allen and Spilka's (1967) Committed and Consensual Scales. He observed that the neo-Pentecostals when compared to classical Pentecostals, were more intrinsic and committed and less extrinsic and consensual in their religious orientations.

In an earlier but related study, Malony and associates (1972) observed that those who spoke in tongues were likely to be more intrinsic in their orientation to religion as measured by Allport's Extrinsic-Intrinsic Religious Orientation Scale.

Mystical Experience

Pentecostals, neo-Pentecostals and charismatics, thus far, have not been studied from the point of view of mysticism (mystical experiences) despite the sociological thinking that there is a close relationship between religious revival and mysticism. Troeltsch (1911/1931) for example suggested a three-fold model for understanding religious groups. These were church, sect, and mysticism. Mysticism is based on inward, immediate experience of the transcendent that functioned to legitimize participation in religious institutions. According to Troeltsch, glossolalia belongs to this type of church, that is, to mysticism.

Fichter (1974, pp. 20-21), who was influenced by Troeltsch's description of mysticism, argues that the early stage of the Catholic Pentecostal movement is essentially mystical. Thompson (1977) agrees with Troeltsch's typologies and concludes that Catholic charismatics exemplify this type of religious expression. Malony and Lovekin (1985) contend that glossolalia is more appropriately considered in terms of mysticism rather than under the rubric of sect (p. 259).

Within the domain of the psychological study of religion, it is the work of Stace (1960) that has influenced research in the domain of mysticism. Stace defined the mystical experience as noetic, ineffable, holy, paradoxical, and characterized by positive affect. He distinguished between extroversive and introversive mysticism. In extrovertive mysticism there is a sense of inner subjectivity to all things and the sense of unity in the diversity of things perceived. In introversive mysticism, the experience is timeless, spaceless, that of a void, and there is a sense of the dissolution of the self, and a unity of consciousness devoid of content (Stace 1960, pp. 176-177).

Hood (1975) used the conceptual categories of Stace (1960) to develop a Mysticism Scale described later on in this chapter. Thus far the Mysticism Scale has not been used to study Pentecostals, neo-Pentecostals, and Charismatics.

In summary, this brief review touched on four dimensions of phenomena associated with Pentecostals, neo-Pentecostals, glossolalic charismatics, and non-glossolalic charismatics. First, it seems that Pentecostals and glossolalic charismatics are neither better nor less adjusted than the general population. Second, these groups possess several characteristics including being less depressed, more submissive, with lower self esteem, less hostile, more dependent and suggestible than to controls. As for religious orientation, they tend to be more committed and intrinsically oriented than the general population. Lastly, research has not, thus far, provided any data regarding the prevalence and quality of mystical experience.

Malony and Lovekin (1985), following their review of the literature, concluded that few specific personality traits among glossolalics have been firmly identified although a tendency toward extroversion, intrinsic religious orientation, and suggestibility can be affirmed (pp. 76-77).

The purpose of this study is to extend our understanding of non-glossolalic charismatics by providing objective data using standardized measures of psychological and religious variables. These data were used to generate an alternative to the psychopathological hypothesis. This is the research question: Do non-Glossolalic Charismatics when compared to two comparative non-charismatic groups, (Parish Councilors, Regular Parishioners) score differently on psychological and religious variables? Two studies have investigated this general research question.

STUDY I

The first study compared the performance of non-glossolalic charismatics to two comparative groups on measures of personal adjustment, personality traits, religious orientation, and mysticism. For this study, the general research question was expressed in terms of four specific questions:

1. Do non-glossolalic charismatics, when compared to control groups, obtain similar scores on a measure of personal adjustment?
2. When compared to control groups, do non-glossolalic Charismatics obtain similar scores on a measure of personality traits?
3. When compared to control groups, do non-glossolalic charismatics obtain similar scores on a measure of committed religion and intrinsic religious orientation.
4. Do non-glossolalic charismatics, when compared to control groups, obtain similar scores on a measure of mystical experience.

Research Method

Sample

The sample comprised 90 subjects taken from English-speaking Roman Catholic parishes and from English-speaking Roman Catholic charismatic prayer groups in a large Canadian city. More specifically, 30 subjects were randomly drawn from each of three groups: Parish councilors, non-glossolalic charismatics, and regular parishioners.

Non-glossolalic charismatics were operationally defined as those who had completed the Life in the Spirit seminars (Clark 1973), had been regularly attending the prayer meetings of their group for at least six months, declared themselves to be charismatics, and were non-glossolalics. Priests and members of religious orders and communities were excluded from this group so as to ensure the validity of its comparison to lay members of the church.

Parish councilors were defined as those who served on the parish council and were not members, now nor in the past, of a charismatic group. The regular parishioners comprised those on the parish records who attended church but who were not members of the parish council nor of a charismatic group, presently nor in the past.

The 30 subjects for each of the three comparative groups were matched for age and gender. The three age groups were 30-39, 40-49, and 50-59. Each age group comprised an equal number of males and females. These data are summarized in Table 1.

Gender and age differences have been reported for some of the measurements used in this study and therefore it was imperative that these factors be controlled through matching of subjects. When available, data for these moderating variables will be discussed in conjunction with each measurement.

Measurements

Two psychological tests, namely, the Eysenck Personality Questionnaire (EPQ) and Jackson's Personality Research Form (Form A) (PRF) and two religious measures, that is, Hood's Mysticism Scale, Research Form D (MS) and Spilka's Religious Orientation Scale (ROS) were administered to the subjects.

Eysenck Personality Questionnaire. The EPQ is a factor-analytic derived three dimensional questionnaire designed to measure two basic traits underlying personality, namely, extraversion-introversion and emotional stability-instability. These traits (factors) have been operationalized to form three scales, namely, Psychoticism, Neuroticism, and Extraversion-Introversion (Eysenck and Eysenck 1975, pp. 3-6).

The three scales of the EPQ have been found to have good criterion and predictive validity (Eysenck and Eysenck 1975). As for test-retest reliabilities with one month between testings, Eysenck and Eysenck (1975) report mean scale coefficients which range from .78 for Psychoticism to .89 for Extraversion-Introversion scales across four groups of males and four groups of females (Eysenck and Eysenck 1975, p. 8). Norms for age-by-gender groups, psychiatric groups, and for occupational groups have been established (Eysenck and Eysenck 1975, pp. 9, 13-16).

Table 1. The Sample for Study I Divided According to Age, Gender, and Group

		Group			
Age-Group	Gender	Parish C.	Charismatics	Reg. Parish.	Total
30-39	M	5	5	5	15
	F	5	5	5	15
40-49	M	5	5	5	15
	F	5	5	5	15
50-59	M	5	5	5	15
	F	5	5	5	15
Total:		30	30	30	90

Note: Parish C. = Parish Councilor; Reg. Parish. = Regular Parishioner.

Personality Research Form (Form A) (PRF). The PRF, based on Murray's (1938) personality theory, is designed to yield a set of scores for personality traits relevant to normal functioning in a wide variety of situations. The instrument contains 14 personality variables and one validity scale (infrequency) to detect nonpurposeful and careless responding. The PRF contains 300 items, 20 for each of the 14 scales and the one validity scale. The subject is instructed to respond true or false to each item as to whether the item describes him or her. Five of the PRF scales are aggression, dominance, exhibition, order, and play. All of the PRF dimensions of personality are bipolar (Jackson 1974).

Factor analytic studies provide substantial evidence for the convergent and discriminant validity of the PRF scales (Jackson 1974, p. 25; Jackson and Guthrie 1968; Kusyszyn and Jackson 1967). Test-retest reliability studies with a one week interval between tests produced coefficients which ranged from .77 (autonomy) to .90 (harm avoidance) (Bentler 1964). Norms for males and females and for college students and psychiatric patients are available (Jackson 1974, pp. 29, 42).

Hood's Mysticism Scale (MS). The MS is designed to measure reported mystical experience (Hood 1975). It has 32 items, four for each of eight categories of mysticism initially conceptualized by Stace (1960). A factor analysis of the Mysticism Scale has identified two principal factors, a general mystical experience factor (20 items) and a religious interpretation factor (12 items). Among the categories of mysticism measured by the MS are: Ego Quality, Unifying Quality, Noetic Quality, and Religious Quality. A single score (full scale) can be computed by adding the scores for the eight scales.

Validation studies compared the Mysticism Scale to Hodge's (1972) Intrinsic Religious Motivation Scale, Taft's (1970) Ego Permissiveness Scale and the Minnesota Multiphasic Personality Inventory. The results of these studies demonstrate that the Mysticism Scale has good construct validity and good internal consistency (Hoo 1975, p. 39). No test-retest reliability data, nor age-by-gender norms have found for the MS and its subscales.

Spilka's Religious Orientation Scale (ROS). The ROS, which is an adaptation of Allport and Ross's (1967) Intrinsic and Extrinsic Religious Orientation scale, is designed to measure religious orientation along two dimensions, namely, intrinsic and extrinsic religious orientation and committed and consensual religion.

The ROS is a 54 item questionnaire of which forty items are used. The respondents are asked to indicate, on a six-point scale (1 = disagrees; 6 = strongly agrees) their extent of agreement with each item. Scores for four scales—"Committed Religion," "Consensual Religion," "Intrinsic Orientation," "Extrinsic Orientation"—can be derived from each protocol.

Extrinsic (religious) Orientation is described as being strictly utilitarian (e.g., useful for the self in granting safety, social standing, solace, and endorsement for one's chosen way of life) whereas Intrinsic (religious) Orientation regards faith as a supreme value in its own right, is oriented toward a unification of being, and strives to transcend all self-centered needs (Allport 1966, p. 455). Committed Religion (Faith) is defined as being "candid, open, personally relevant, abstract and relational, discerning, and differentiated" whereas Consensual Religion (Faith) is defined as being "restrictive, detached to the point of irrelevance, concrete, vague, and simplistic (Allen and Spilka, 1967, p. 18).

Research studies have produced either negative or low correlations for the Extrinsic and Intrinsic Religious Orientations Scales, indicating that the two scales measure different aspects of religious orientation (Donahue 1975; Spilka, Hood, and Gorsuch 1985; Gorsuch and McPherson 1989). Age has been found to correlate with religious orientation. Intrinsic orientation is more frequently observed in older persons, whereas, Extrinsic orientation is more frequently observed in younger people (Watson et al. 1988). It is generally agreed that the Extrinsic and Intrinsic Religious Orientation scales are valid and reliable (Donohue 1985). However, the validity and reliability data are sparse and incomplete.

Methodology

Selection of subjects. Pastors of Roman Catholic churches and leaders of Roman Catholic charismatic groups were contacted to explain to them the nature of the research project and solicit their collaboration. A more detailed explanation was provided by letter to those who agreed to collaborate. An information form requesting the name of the potential research subject, gender, date of birth, telephone number, and nature of church participation (parish councilor, charismatic, regular parishioner) was enclosed as well. If a subject participated in more than one group or organization this was to be indicated.

Members of charismatic groups were asked to indicate the charismatic gifts (e.g., tongues, prophesy) that they exercised.

The submitted names were arranged to form eighteen pools organized by group (Parish councilors, Charismatics, regular parishioners), age (30-39, 40-49, 50-59) and gender (male, female). Charismatics who stated that they spoke in tongues were rejected from the pool. From each of the eighteen pools of names, five subjects were randomly drawn and were then contacted by telephone and invited to participate in the research project. The subjects were informed as to the nature of their participation. Those who agreed to participate were invited to attend a testing session the date of which was predetermined. In all there were three testing and three retesting sessions. Each session lasted about two hours. When there was a refusal, another name from the respective pool was drawn. Only five of the research subjects initially contacted, refused to participate in the project.

Administration of tests. The psychological and religious measures were group administered in a large university meeting room. A uniform procedure was followed in the administration of the tests and the standardized procedures for each test were adhered to. The measurements were administered in this order: Eysenck's Personality Questionnaire, Jackson's Personality Research Form, Hood's Mysticism Scale, and Spilka's Religious Orientation Scale.

Prior to the testing session itself, the subjects were asked to complete an information form and to sign a consent form. Each subject was given a code number which he/she was asked to enter on all completed questionnaires. They were informed that they were free to withdraw from the research at any time they so wished.

The tests were repeated one week later and administered in the same order and in the same place as in the initial testing. Out of the 90 subjects, eighteen returned for the re-testing. The test-retest reliabilities for the EPQ ranged from .31 for Neuroticism to .82 for Extraversion. These were lower than those reported by Eysenck and Eysenck (1975, p. 8). For the PRF the test-retest reliabilities ranged from .56 for Aggression to .98 for Dominance. Only three of test-retest reliabilities were below .82. These correlations are slightly lower than those reported by Jackson (1974) and Bentler (1964). The ROS produced test-retest reliabilities which ranged from .76 for Intrinsic Orientation to .83 for Committed Religion. For the MS, the test-retest reliabilities ranged from .45 (Ego Quality) to .94 (Unifying Quality).

Gender differences were observed on Eysenck's Personality Questionnaire, Jackson's Personality Research Form, and Spilka's Religious Orientation Scale. Age differences were observed on Eysenck's Personality Questionnaire and on Jackson's Personality Research Form. These data are summarized in Tables 2 and 3, respectively. Although the findings on age and gender are interesting, they are not part of this study. They are mentioned to justify the age and gender matching.

Table 2. Mean Scores, Standard Deviations, Univariate
F-Values and Level of Significance for the Study I Sample
divided according to Age on EPQ and PRF Subscales

| Variable | Age Group | | | | | | | |
| | 30-39 | | 49-49 | | 59-59 | | | |
	M	S.D.	M	S.D.	M	S.D.	F	p
EPQ Scales (d.f. = 2,72)								
Extraversion	13.43	5.08	12.00	4.53	10.03	3.88	4.15	.010
Lie	7.20	2.93	9.43	3.99	10.63	4.75	5.70	.005
PRF Scales (d.f. = 2,72)								
Aggression	5.93	2.91	6.43	2.40	5.20	2.77	3.45	.030
Dominance	9.57	4.90	9.33	5.13	6.97	3.87	3.48	.030
Endurance	12.37	4.03	12.56	4.06	10.17	3.62	3.92	.030
Exhibition	8.30	3.50	7.60	4.19	5.67	3.06	5.07	.008
Harmvoidance	12.57	3.92	13.00	4.77	14.87	3.41	3.90	.020
Impulsivity	8.63	2.72	6.80	3.59	6.83	3.18	3.00	.050

Note: EPQ = Eysenck Personality Questionnaire; PRF = Personality Record Form; Harmvoidance = Harmavoidance.

Table 3. Mean Scores, Standard Deviations, Univariate
F-Values, and Level of Significance for the Study I Sample
Divided According to Gender on EPQ, PRF, and ROS Subscales

| Variable | Male | | Female | | | |
	M	S.D.	M	S.D.	F	p
EPQ Scales (d.f. = 1,72)						
Neuroticism	8.02	5.01	10.71	4.68	6.17	.010
PRF Scales (d.f. = 1,72)						
Autonomy	6.42	2.98	5.29	2.33	4.50	.030
Dominance	9.77	4.76	7.47	4.54	6.74	.010
Endurance	12.69	3.64	10.71	4.34	5.99	.010
Exhibition	8.33	3.57	6.04	3.59	10.70	.001
Harmavoidance	11.76	4.09	15.20	3.49	23.23	.000
ROS Scales (d.f. = 1,72)						
Committed	88.36	9.74	93.60	10.27	6.67	.010
Intrinsic	35.36	4.45	37.58	4.15	6.67	.010

Note: EPQ = Eysenck Personality Questionnaire; PRF = Personality Record Form; ROS = Spilka's Religious Orientation Scale; Committed = Committed Religious Orientation; Intrinsic = Intrinsic Religious Orientation.

Analysis of Data. The subjects' scores for each of the instruments and their respective scales were computed. The data from the psychological and religious measures were separately rearranged to form three groups, namely, Charismatics, Regular Parishioners, and Parish Councillors.

The data were analyzed using a Multivariate Analysis of Variance. The Duncan Multiple Range Test (Kirk 1968, pp. 93-94) was used for all post hoc procedures because its assumption of equal sample size could be met and because it is relatively powerful when all pairs of experimental groups are compared.

Results

The presentation of the results are organized around the four research questions. The first question states: Do non-glossolalic charismatics, when compared to control groups, obtain similar scores on a measure of personal adjustment? To answer this question, the data for the Eysenck Personality Questionnaire, a measure of adjustment, were arranged to form three groups and a multivariate analysis of variance (MANOVA) was applied to the data. The analysis failed to find significant group differences [$F(8,138)=1.13$; p.$=.34$]. This means that the non-glossolalic charismatics are no more and no less maladjusted than are the Parish Councilors and the Regular Parishioners. The means for all three comparative groups were considerably lower than those reported by Eysenck and Eysenck (1975, p. 15) for psychiatric groups including Psychotics, Neurotics, Personality Disorders.

The second research question states: When compared to control groups, do non-glossolalic Charismatics obtain similar scores on a measure of personality traits? To answer it a MANOVA was applied to the subject's scores on Jackson's Personality Research Form (PRF) scales which are measures of personality traits. The analysis produced a significant multivariate F-value [$F(30,116)=2.37$; p.$=.0006$]. The univariate F's for five of the scales were significant. The mean scores, standard deviations, degrees of freedom, univariate F-values and level of significance are summarized in Table 4.

The application of Duncan's post hoc procedure (Kirk, 1968) produced the following significant results: (1) The non-glossolalic Charismatics scored lower on Order and Play than the Regular Parishioners but the former did not differ from the Parish Councilors, (2) The non-glossolalic Charismatics scored lower on Aggression than the Parish Councilors, (3) The non-glossolalic Charismatics and Regular Parishioners scored lower than the Parish Councilors on Dominance but the non-glossolalic Charismatics and the Regular Parishioners did not differ from each other, and (4) The Parish Councilors scored higher than the Regular Parishioners on Exhibition.

Jackson (1974, pp. 6-7) provides the following descriptions for high scorers on the five PRF scales: *Aggression*—combative, argumentative, and easily

Table 4.   Mean Scores, Standard Deviations, Univariate
F-Values and Level of Significance for the Study I Sample
Divided According to Group on PRF, ROS, and MS Subscales

Variable	Councilors M	Councilors S.D.	Charismatic M	Charismatic S.D.	Reg. Parish. M	Reg. Parish. S.D.	F	p
PRF Scales (d.f. = 2,72)								
Aggression	4.67	2.50	2.90	1.64	3.70	2.40	5.31	.007
Dominance	10.83	4.77	7.73	4.70	7.30	4.15	6.25	.003
Exhibition	8.37	4.51	7.00	3.41	6.20	2.91	3.27	.044
Order	11.23	4.81	11.13	3.86	14.00	3.34	5.30	.007
Play	8.67	2.75	7.45	2.57	9.50	2.98	4.26	.018
ROS Scales (d.f. = 2,72)								
Committed	88.23	9.06	96.10	9.34	88.60	10.74	6.38	.002
Intrinsic	34.83	3.97	38.97	3.07	35.60	4.99	8.72	.000
MS Scales (d.f. = 2,72)								
EQ	10.40	4.06	13.20	3.70	9.00	3.52	9.50	.000
RQ	16.70	4.18	18.83	1.70	15.40	4.34	6.55	.003
FS	98.93	22.16	110.43	22.37	92.00	28.49	4.02	.020

Note: Reg. Parishioners = Regular Parishioners
PRF = Personality Research Form
MS = Hood's Mysticism Scale Research Form D
ROS = Spilka's Religious Orientation Scale
Committed = Committed Religion
Intrinsic = Intrinsic Religious Orientation
EQ = Ego Quality
RQ = Religious Quality
FS = Full Scale.

annoyed, *Dominance*—person attempts to control his/her environment and influence others, *Exhibition*—person wants to be the center of attention and have an audience, *Order*—one who is concerned with keeping personal effects and surroundings neat and organized, and *Play*—person does many things "just for fun," spends a good deal of time participating in games, sports, social activities, and other amusements.

The third research question states: When compared to control groups, do non-glossolalic charismatics obtain similar scores on a measure of committed religion and intrinsic religious orientation? This question was studied by grouping the subjects' scores on Spilka's Religious Orientation Scale into the three comparative groups and applying a MANOVA that indicated significant group differences [$F(8,138) = 2.48$; p. = .01].

A univariate analysis produced significant differences on Committed Religion [$F(2,72) = 6.38$; p. =. 002] and on Intrinsic Orientation [$F(2,72) =$

8.72; p. = .0005]. These data are summarized in Table 4. In post hoc analysis, the non-glossolalic Charismatics were found to score higher than the two comparative groups on Committed Religion and on Intrinsic Orientation.

The fourth research question asks whether non-glossolalic charismatics, when compared to control groups, obtain similar scores on a measure of mystical experience. This question was studied by applying a MANOVA to the subject's scores on Hood's Mysticism Scale. Significant group differences [F(8,138) = 1.92; p. = 01] were found. The results of univariate analysis produced significant group differences on Ego Quality [F(2,72) = 9.50; p. = .0002], Religious Quality [F(2,72) = 6.55; p. = .003] and Full Mysticism Score [F(2,72) = 4.02; p. = .020]. These data are summarized in Table 4. In a post hoc analysis, the non-glossolalic Charismatics were shown to have scored significantly higher than both the Parish Councilors and the Regular Parishioners on Ego Quality, Religious Quality, and on Full Scale Mysticism score.

Hood (1975) defines Ego Quality as "the experience of a loss of sense of self while consciousness is nevertheless maintained. The loss of self is commonly experienced as an absorption into something greater than the mere empirical ego" (p. 31). The author defines Religious Quality as the "intrinsic sacredness of the experience. This includes feelings of mystery, awe, and reverence that may nevertheless be expressed independently of traditional religious language" (Hood 1975, p. 32).

STUDY II

The second study compared the performance of non-glossolalic charismatics to two comparative groups on measures of purpose in life, values, interpersonal needs, and self actualization. The general research question, for this project, was expressed in terms of four specific questions:

1. Do non-glossolalic charismatics, when compared to control groups, obtain similar scores on a measure of purpose in life?
2. When compared to control groups, do non-glossolalic Charismatics obtain similar scores on a measure of values?
3. When compared to control groups, do non-glossolalic charismatics obtain similar scores on a measure of interpersonal needs?
4. Do non-glossolalic charismatics, when compared to control groups, obtain similar scores on a measure of self actualization?

Research Method

The research method for the second study parallels that of the first study. The major differences consist in the use a new sample and new measurements and in the method of analysis.

Sample

The criteria used to select the sample for this project, the composition of the experimental and the control groups, and the operational definitions of these groups are identical to those of Study I. The sample comprised 99 subjects taken from English-speaking Roman Catholic parishes and from English-speaking Roman Catholic charismatic prayer groups in a large Canadian city. The sample divided according to comparative groups, age, and gender is summarized in Table 5.

Gender and age differences have been reported for some of the measurements used in this study and therefore it was imperative that these factors be controlled through matching of subjects. When available, the data regarding these moderating variables will be discussed in conjunction with each measurement.

Measurements

The subjects were administered four psychological tests, namely: Crumbaugh and Maholick's Purpose in Life Test (PIL), Shostrom's Personality Orientation Inventory (POI), Allport, Vernon and Lindzey's Study of Values (A-V-L), and Schutz's Fundamental Interpersonal Relations Orientation-Behavior Questionnaire (FIRO-B).

Purpose in Life Test (PIL). The PIL is an attitude scale designed to measure the extent to which persons have meaningful goals around which to orient their lives. Crumbaugh and Maholick (1964) devised the PIL as an attempt to quantify Frankl's (1963, 1966) concept of "meaning in life." It consists of 20 statements, each to be responded to by indicating personal agreement or disagreement on a 7-point scale. One single score is computed for the test by adding the responses to each of the items. Scores of 113 or above indicate clear meaning and purpose in life (Crumbaugh and Maholick 1969, p. 3). Age differences have been reported on PIL scores with adolescents scoring lower than older age groups (Meier and Edwards 1973). The PIL has produced high split-half reliabilities and has demonstrated good criterion validity (Crumbaugh and Maholick 1968, 1969).

Study of Values (A-V-L). The A-V-L, designed to measure values common to men and women, consists of two parts (Allport et al. 1960). The first part has 30 items each of which offers two alternative responses which are given values between 0 and 3 with the combined value for the two choices equaling 3. In the second part, each of the 15 items has four choices which are rank ordered. The A-V-L comprises six value scales, namely, theoretical, economic, aesthetic, social, political, and religious. The A-V-L has demonstrated good construct validity (Allport et al. 1960, pp. 14-15) and good predictive validity (Allport 1968, pp. 52-54). Split-half and test-retest reliability studies have provided high correlation coefficients which are in the .80 or higher range

Table 5.   The Sample for Study II Divided According to Age, Gender, and Group

Age-Group	Gender	Group			
		Parish C.	Charismatics Reg.	Parish.	Total
30-39	M	5	9	5	19
	F	5	5	6	16
40-49	M	6	6	4	16
	F	4	5	5	14
50-59	M	6	6	5	17
	F	5	7	5	17
Total:		31	38	30	99

Note: Parish C. = Parish Councilor; Reg. Parish. = Regular Parishioner.

(Allport et al. 1960, Allport 1968). The six value scales are interdependent with social-religious, economic-political, and theoretical-aesthetic measures producing positive but low correlations. Allport suggests that the low correlations do not warrant the derivation of a smaller number of more basic types (Allport et al. 1960, p. 10). Gender differences have been reported on the A-V-L (Allport et al. 1960, pp. 11-12).

The FIRO-B Questionnaire.   This questionnaire is designed to measure the fundamental dimensions of Schutz's (1958, 1967a, 1967b, pp. 131-210, 1978) theory of interpersonal interactions. He postulates three dimensions, namely, inclusion, control, and affection, all of which can be considered from an expressed or a wanted mode. The FIRO-B comprises 54 items, nine items for each scale, which are rated on a six-point scale with 1 = usually (or most people) and 6 = never (or nobody), depending on the specific item. Six scores can be derived from the FIRO-B, namely, Inclusion-Expressed, Inclusion-Wanted, Control-Expressed, and so on.

The FIRO-B reportedly is a valid (Schutz 1967a, pp. 6-8, 1978, pp. 9-10; Kramer 1967, pp. 80-81; Lindahl 1975, pp. 5-11) and a reliable instrument (Schutz 1976a, pp. 5-6; 1978, pp. 8-9; Lindahl 1975). Most of the FIRO-B scales have been found to be relatively independent with the exception of Wanted- and Expressed-Inclusion, and Wanted-and Expressed-Affection, which produce moderately high correlations (Schutz 1958, 1967b, 1978; Ullman et al. 1964). Gender differences have been found on Expressed Control with males scoring higher than females (Schutz 1966, p. 74).

Personal Orientation Inventory (POI)

The POI is a psychological instrument purported to measure values, attitudes, and behavior relevant to the development of self-actualization (Shostrom 1974). Its theoretical basis is found in the works of psychologists such as Maslow (1954, 1970, 1971). The POI consists of 150 two-choice comparative value and behavior judgments (Shostrom 1966). The items are scored twice, first for the two basic scales of personal orientation, namely, Inner Direction (I) and Time Competence (TC), and second, for each of the ten subscales which measures a conceptually important element of self-actualization. Included among the subscales are self-actualizing value, existentiality, self regard, synergy, and capacity for intimate contact. Shostrom (1966) reported studies that support the predictive, concurrent and congruent validity of the POI (pp. 25-32). Test-retest reliability coefficients obtained for the POI scales are commensurate with other personality inventories (Shostrom 1966, p. 32).

Methodology

The selection of subjects, administration of the psychological measures, and the analysis of the data followed the same procedures as in Study I with the following exceptions.

Psychological measures were administered in the following order: Purpose in Life Test, Study of Values, Fundamental Interpersonal Relations Orientation, and Personal Orientation Inventory. The tests were repeated one week later and administered in the same order and in the same place as in the initial testing. Twelve of the 99 subjects returned for the retesting session. The test-retest reliability for the PIL was .90 (p. < .01) computed by the Pearson r formula. The test-retest correlation coefficients for the A-V-L subscales ranged from .69 (Theoretical) to .88 (Aesthetic). The FIRO-B subscales produced correlation coefficients ranging from .80 (Wanted Inclusion) to .94 (Expressed Affection). Lastly, the POI subscales, Time Competence and Inner Directed, produced correlation coefficients of .79 and .90, respectively.

Gender differences were observed on Allport-Vernon-Lindzey Study of Values (A-V-L), Schutz's Fundamental Interpersonal Relations Orientation (FIRO-B) Questionnaire, and on Shostrom's Personal Orientation Inventory (POI). Age differences were observed on A-V-L and on POI subscales. The gender and age differences are summarized in Tables 6 and 7, respectively. The age and gender differences are reported to justify matching for these variables.

The subjects' scores for each of the instruments and their respective scales were computed. The data from the psychological measures were rearranged to form three groups, namely, Charismatics, Regular Parishioners, and Parish Councilors. The data were analyzed using a Multivariate Analysis of Variance which tested for group differences across all of the variables. Significant group differences were found [$F(2,58)=2.30$; p.$=.0002$]. The Tukey Test (Guilford 1956) was used for all post hoc procedures because it does not assume equal comparative group size and because it is relatively powerful when all pairs of experimental groups are compared.

Table 6. Mean Scores, Standard Deviations, Univariate F-Values and Level of Significance for the Study II Sample Divided According to Age on A-V-L and POI Subscales

Variable	Age Group						F	p
	30-39		49-49		59-59			
	M	S.D.	M	S.D.	M	S.D.		
A-V-L Scales (d.f. = 2,81)								
Theoretical	35.49	6.41	31.66	6.59	33.71	5.42	4.33	.016
Religious	50.83	9.29	50.76	8.91	54.74	7.46	3.02	.050
POI Scales (d.f.=2,81)								
TI/TC	36.26	21.25	49.60	32.30	31.44	18.99	4.80	.010
TI	5.71	2.61	6.93	3.14	5.06	2.17	4.37	.015
TC	17.17	2.53	15.83	3.50	17.53	2.55	3.57	.032
FR	15.26	2.49	13.90	3.01	13.53	3.04	3.67	.029
C	18.11	2.92	15.87	3.33	16.59	3.44	5.29	.007

Note: A-V-L = Allport-Vernon-Lindzey Study of Values
POI = Shostrom's Personal Orientation Inventory
TI = Time Incompetence
TC = Time Competence
FR = Feeling Reactivity
C = Capacity for Intimate Contact

Table 7. Mean Scores, Standard Deviations, Univariate F-Values, and Level of Significance for the Study II Sample Divided According to Gender on the A-V-L, FIRO-B, and POI Subscales

Variable	Male		Female		F	p
	M	S.D.	M	S.D.		
A-V-L Scales (d.f. = 1,81)						
Theoretical	36.59	5.58	30.64	5.50	19.75	.000
Economic	37.63	8.48	33.70	5.96	6.33	.014
Aesthetic	31.57	6.54	35.30	6.43	7.18	.009
Religious	51.08	9.17	53.34	8.08	4.82	.031
FIRO-B Scale (d.f. = 1,81)						
CE	4.04	2.62	2.30	2.36	12.07	.000
POI Scale (d.f.-1,81)						
SR	11.06	2.39	11.99	2.15	4.55	.036

Note: A-V-L = Allport-Vernon-Lindzey Study of Values
FIRO-B = Schutz's Fundamental Interpersonal Relations Orientation Scale: Behavior
POI = Shostrom's Personal Orientation Inventory; CE = Control Expressed
SR = Self Regard

Results

The presentation of the results are organized around the four research questions. The first question states: Do non-glossolalic charismatics, when compared to control groups, obtain similar scores on a measure of purpose in life? The univariate F obtained for this analysis indicates that there are no group differences [F(2,81)=2.44; p.=.09]. This means that non-glossolalic charismatics have no more and no less meaningful goals around which to orient their lives than do the regular parishioners and councilors. The means for all three groups is around 113 which statistically means that all three groups have definite purpose and meaning in life (Crumbaugh and Maholick 1969, p.3).

The second research question states: When compared to control groups, do non-glossolalic Charismatics obtain similar scores on a measure of values? The univariate F values on the Allport-Vernon-Lindzey Study of Values were assessed for significance. Two of the A-V-L subscales, namely Economic [F(2,81)=7.94; p.=.000] and Religious [F(2,81)=8.43; p.=.000], produced significant group differences. These data are summarized in Table 8. Post hoc analysis showed that the Charismatics alone scored significantly lower than the other two groups on Economic and that the Charismatics alone scored significantly higher than the two comparative groups on Religious (Value). A low score on the Economic Scale indicates a lack of interest in what is useful; the practical affairs of the business world; the production, marketing and consumption of goods; and the accumulation of tangible wealth. A high score on the Religious Scale indicates a high value for *unity* and a permanent mental orientation directed toward the creation of the highest and absolute satisfying value experience (Spranger 1928, p. 195).

The third research question was: When compared to control groups, do non-glossolalic charismatics obtain similar scores on a measure of interpersonal needs? The FIRO-B questionnaire was used as a measure of interpersonal needs. Data analysis produced significant univariate F values only for Inclusion Expressed [F(2,81)=5.28; p.=.007] and for Affection Wanted [F(2,81)=4.05; p.=.021] (See Table 8). These data are summarized in Table 8. The application of the Tukey test as a post hoc procedure produced significant difference for the Councilors-Parishioners and for the Charismatics-Parishioners comparisons on Inclusion Expressed. In both cases the Parishioners scored lower. Significant differences were also found for the Charismatics-Parishioners on Affection Wanted with the Charismatics scoring higher. High scores on Inclusion Expressed are descriptive of persons who make efforts to include others in their activities, to try to belong, to join groups, and to be with people as much as possible. As for Affection Wanted, high scores indicate that the person wants others to express friendly and affectionate feelings to him/her and try to become close to him/her (Schutz 1967a, p. 5).

Table 8.   Mean Scores, Standard Deviations, Univariate
F-Values and Level of Significance for the Study II Sample
divided according to Group on A-V-L, FIRO-B and POI Subscales

Variable	Group						F	p
	Councilors		Charismatic		Reg. Parish.			
	M	S.D.	M	S.D.	M	S.D.		
A-V-L Scales (d.f. = 2,81)								
Economic	36.97	7.28	32.16	6.33	39.07	7.70	7.94	.000
Religious	51.63	8.29	56.29	6.29	47.47	9.39	8.43	.000
FIRO-B Scale (d.f. = 2,81)								
IE	5.10	1.85	4.61	1.67	3.67	2.25	5.28	.007
AW	5.26	1.81	5.92	1.95	4.47	2.05	4.05	.021
POI Scale (d.f. = 2,81)								
C	16.58	3.04	17.89	2.83	16.00	3.95	4.33	.017

Note: Reg. Parishioners = Regular Parishioners
A-V-L = Allport-Vernon-Lindzey Study of Values
FIRO-B = Schutz's Fundamental Interpersonal Relations Orientation Scale: Behavior
POI = Shostrom's Personal Orientation Inventory
IE = Inclusion Expressed
AW = Affection Wanted
C = Capacity for Intimate Contact

To fourth research question states: Do non-glossolalic charismatics, when compared to control groups, obtain similar scores on a measure of self actualization? To test this question, self-actualization was operationalized as the subjects' scores on the Personal Orientation Inventory. The application of Multivariate analysis of variance produced one significant univariate F value which was for Capacity for Intimate Contact [F(2,81) = 4.33; p. = .017]. Table 8 summarizes these data. The results from the application of the Tukey test to the group means indicate that the Charismatics scored significantly higher than both the Councilors and the Parishioners, however, the means for all three groups were slightly higher than those of the college students used to establish normative data (Shostrom 1966, p. 14). No other differences were observed on this variable which measures the ability to develop contactful intimate relationships with other persons unencumbered by expectations and obligations (Shostrom 1966, p. 6).

DISCUSSION

The results from the two studies can be summarized thus: When compared to Parish Councilors and Regular Parishioners, Charismatics: (1) are as well adjusted emotionally, (2) have as meaningful goals around which to orient their lives, (3) show less interest in what is useful (Economic Value), (4) manifest a heightened interest in religious values (e.g., unity), (5) shy away from including others in their activities (low EI Score), (6) desire the affection of others and crave to be close to them (high WA score), (7) are able to develop contactful meaningful relationships with other persons without being encumbered by expectations and obligations (high C score), (8) tend not to be aggressive, orderly, and domineering (low scores on these PRF scales), (9) tend not to do things "just for fun" (low score on PRF Play scale), (10) manifest an intrinsic religious orientation and place value on unification of being and strive to transcend all self-centered needs, (11) demonstrate a religious commitment which is candid, open, personally relevant, abstract and relational, discerning, and differentiated, (12) are able to let go and enter into a religious experience (something greater than themselves) without losing consciousness (high score on the EQ Mysticism subscale), and (13) sense the religious experience to be intrinsically sacred (high score on the RQ Mysticism subscale.

When these traits and qualities are examined more closely, a pattern begins to form which has to do with "being one with" and "being separate from" others. There seems to be a preoccupation about being one with another and a disinterest in being fully individuated and separated.

Many of the findings from the two studies support the notion that the non-glossolalic charismatics yearn and strive for closeness and oneness. For example non-glossolalic charismatics crave religious (spiritual) unity, are able to let go of self and enter into an intense religious experience, crave affection from others, and develop contactful meaningful relationships. It seems that the meaningful goals around which they orient their lives are relationships, be it with God and with other people.

In the same manner there is evidence to support the notion that non-glossolalic charismatics shy away from achieving personal separateness and individuation. For example, they tend not to be aggressive and domineering, are not inclined to include others in their activities, and show less interest in what is useful (e.g., material things, financial security). Energy attached to being aggressive, assertive, domineering, and worldly-wise leads to separateness and individuation. It seems that the charismatics typically invest energy in relationships, friendships, and being one with others and they shy away from investing energy in activities that would lead to separation.

The hypothesis that charismatics are concerned with oneness rather than with achieving separateness is supported by many of the studies reviewed in the first part of this paper. Vivier (1960) found charismatics to be renunciative in their habits (desurgence), less realistic and practical and more concerned with feelings, are more sensitive, and in need of emotional catharsis (pp. 214-215). Morentz (1966) observed that charismatics, among other traits, have strong feelings of dependency and suggestibility. On the other hand, Kildahl (1972) found charismatics to be less autonomous but dependent. According to Coulson (1977) glossolalics tend to believe that the events of their lives are out of their control and are more in the control of others. Gritzmacher and associates (1988) describe pentecostals showing fewer manifestations of hostility, being more submissive, and having lower self esteem. The observation by Gonsalvez (1982) that glossolalic charismatics scored higher on the Hy scale of the MMPI can be interpreted to mean that they are clinging, dependent, other-oriented, and find their meaning by living through others rather than by living their own lives (Angyal, 1965, pp. 135-155). Rarick (1982) and Malony and associates (1972) observed that glossolalics tended to be more intrinsic in their religious orientation. It is difficult to interpret the meaning of this finding since highly prejudiced persons have also shown themselves to be intrinsically oriented (Allen et al. 1967).

Emerging from the data on charismatics, are two interweaving themes namely, that of a striving (or craving) for bonding and a resistance to achieving personal separateness and individuation.

This leads directly to a broader theoretical consideration. Two theorists have made the concepts of bonding and separation essential aspects of their theoretical formulation. Angyal (1965) speaks about "trend towards homonomy" and "trend towards autonomy" as two universal strivings which are in constant tension as a person lives out his or her life. The "trend towards homonomy" is defined as a striving to surrender oneself and to become an organic part of something that is conceived to be greater than oneself (Angyal 1965, p. 15). In a sense, it is a striving to be connected or bonded with that from which one took one's existence. The "trend towards autonomy" refers to the push or drive toward separation from parent, to mastery, independency, freedom, and self-expansion (Angyal 1965, pp. 3-7). Mahler and associates (1975) refer to these phenomena by the concepts of symbiosis and separation. Symbiosis means fusion of the child with the significant parental figure wherein there is no differentiation of the "I" and the "not-I" (Mahler et al. 1975, p. 41). Separation refers to the process of hatching out of and growing away from the symbiotic relationship and eventually achieving a sense of autonomy, mastery and self-identity (Mahler et al. 1975, pp. 52-120). According to both Angyal and Mahler, it is normal for a person to deal with bonding (attachment) and separation (detachment) issues throughout one's entire life. However, for some, this phase of growth is not adequately negotiated at an early age (before the age of three years) and therefore will remain an issue for most or for all of the person's life. When this issue is unresolved, it is often experienced as an insatiable yearning for intimacy or as a resistance to closeness.

Based on the data from this study as well as an interpretation of the results of the studies reviewed in the first part of this paper, it seems that the hypothesis of bonding and separation explains, in large part, the charismatic phenomenon. Thus it seems reasonable to complement or replace the psychopathological hypothesis by a developmental hypothesis which emphasizes the normal process of bonding and separating as essential for individuation and for the achievement of one's own identity and personhood. When something goes wrong with this normal process of separating, the person is left with an intense striving for or a resistance to closeness, bonding, and connectedness.

The findings of this study have implications for theory, practice, and research. From a theoretical perspective, the question still remains as to how glossolalia is part of the charismatics' personality portrait. It is possible that glossolalia is related to the capacity of a person to experience bonding, that is, to a person's ability to let go of self and be fused with the other. Associated with this intense bonding, is a relinquishing and/or breakdown of ego boundaries that allows the person to lose the sense of his/her identity and take on the identity of the other.

It must be kept in mind that the bonding-separating hypothesis is based on the available data. Studies which focus directly on the bonding-separating issue as it relates to glossolalic and non-glossolalic charismatics are needed. If these studies support the hypothesis, then the door has been opened to raising and answering a multitude of questions concerning the charismatic phenomenon, glossolalia, bonding, separating, suggestibility, and relinquishing one's identity and taking on the identity of the other.

The bonding-separating hypothesis has implications for practice. Viewing the charismatic phenomenon from this perspective provides a developmental focus. Rather than viewing a charismatic client as emotionally disturbed, the counselor, psychotherapist, chaplain and pastoral counselor appreciates that the client is working through a developmental issue which is to reconcile or integrate bonding with separateness and separateness with bonding. The helping professional is able to set his or her sights on the client's developmental issues, work from where the client is at developmentally, and help the client move forward and achieve an integration of bonding and separateness.

As for research, it seems that future studies regarding charismatics would be well served if attention is given to such developmental issues as bonding and separating and the consequent tensions. In this way the understanding of the charismatic phenomenon would be lifted out of the psychopathological frame of reference and placed in a normal developmental perspective. It would be interesting to test out the hypothesis using a variety of samples including Pentecostals, Catholic and non-Catholic Christian charismatics (both glossolalic and non-glossolalic), non-active but self-designated Catholics and Protestants, atheists and agnostics.

ACKNOWLEDGMENTS

The author wishes to acknowledge the contributions of the following graduate students from St. Paul University, Ottawa, Canada, without whom the project would not have been possible. Sincere thanks and appreciation are expressed to: Claudette Gallant, Yvette Hebert, Hilary Jebanesan, Casimir J. Krystkowiak, Alice Long, Wanda Manos, Stanley Muldoon, Methodius Ndyamukama, Barbara Smith, Lucille Smith, Selwyn L. Vanterpool, Katherine Wallace, and Charles Weckend.

REFERENCES

Alland, A. 1961. "Possession in a Revivalist Negro Church." *Journal for the Scientific Study of Religion* 1(2):204-213.

Allen, R.O. and B. Spilka. 1967. "Committed and Consensual Religion: A Specification of Religion-Prejudice Relationships." *Journal for the Scientific Study of Religion* 6:191-206.

Allport, G.W. 1966. "The Religious Context of Prejudice." *Journal for the Scientific Study of Religion* 5:447-557.

_____. 1968. *The Person in Psychology*. Boston: Beacon.

Allport, G.W. and M.J Ross. 1967. "Personal Religious Orientation and Prejudice." *Journal of Personality and Social Psychology* 5:432-443.

Allport-Vernon-Lindzey. 1960. *Manual: Study of Values*. Boston: Houghton Mifflin.

Angyal, A. 1965. *Neurosis and Treatment: A Holistic Theory*. New York: The Viking Press.

Bentler, P.M. 1964. *Response Variability: Fact or Artifact*. Unpublished doctoral dissertation, Stanford University.

Boisen, A. 1939. "Economic Distress and Religious Experience A Study of the Holy Rollers." *Psychiatry* 2:185-194.

Bord, R.J. and J.E. Faulkner. 1983. *The Catholic Charismatics: The Anatomy of a Modern Religious Movement*. University Park, PA: Pennsylvania State University Press.

Castelein, J.D. 1984. "Glossolalia and the Psychology of Self and Narcissism." *Journal of Religion And Health*, 23:47-62.

Clark, E.T. 1949. *The Small Sects In America*. New York: Abingdon-Cokesbury.

Clark, S.B. 1973. *Life in the Spirit Seminars: Team Manual*. South Bend, IN: Charismatic Renewal Services.

Coulson, J.E., and R.W. Johnson 1977. "Glossolalia and Internal-external Locus of Control." *Journal of Psychology and Theology* 5:312-317.

Crumbaugh, J.C. and L.T. Maholick. 1964. "An Experimental Study in Existentialism: The Psychometric Approach To Frankl's Noogenic Neurosis." *Journal of Clinical Psychology* 20:200-207.

_____. 1968. "Cross-Validation of Purpose-in-Life Test based on Frankl's Concepts." *Journal of Individual Psychology* 24:74-81.

_____. 1969. *The Manual of Instructions for the Purpose in Life Test*. Chicago Plaza, Brookport, IL: Psychometric Affiliates.

Csordas, T.J. 1990. "The Psychotherapy Analogy and Charismatic Healing." *Psychotherapy* 27:79-90.

Cutten, G.B. 1927. *Speaking with Tongues: Historically and Psychologically Considered*. New Haven, CT: Yale University Press.

Donahue, M.J. 1985. "Intrinsic and Extrinsic Religiousness: The Empirical Research". *Journal for the Scientific Study of Religion* 24:418-423.

Eysenck, H.J. and S.B.G. Eysenck. 1975. *Eysenck Personality Questionnaire* (Manual). San Diego, CA: Educational and Industrial Testing Service.

Fichter, J.H. 1975. *The Catholic Cult of the Paraclete*. New York: Sheed and Ward.

Frankl, V. 1963. *Man's Search for Meaning: An Introduction to Logotherapy*. New York: Washington Square Press.

————. 1966. *The Doctor and the Soul.* New York: Knopf.

Gerlach, L.P. and V.H. Hine. 1966. *The Charismatic Revival: Process, Recruitment, Conversion, and Behavioral Change in Modern Religious Movement.* University of Minnesota. Unpublished paper.

Gonsalvez, E.J. 1982. "A Psychological Interpretation of The Religious Behavior of Pentecostals and Charismatics." *Journal of Dharma* 7:408-429.

Gorsuch, R. L. and S.E. McPherson. 1989. "Intrinsic—Extrinsic Measurement: I/E—Revised and Single-item Scales." *Journal for the Scientific Study of Religion* 28:348-354.

Greeley, M.E. 1974. "Charismatics and Noncharismatics, a Comparison." *Review for Religious,* 33:315-335.

Gritzmacher, S.A., B.Boltan, and R.H. Dana. 1988. "Psychological Characteristics of Pentecostals: A Literature Review and Psychodynamic Synthesis." *Journal of Psychology and Theology* 16:233-245.

Guilford, J.P. 1956. *Fundamental Statistics in Psychology and Education.* Toronto: McGraw-Hill.

Hine, V.H. 1969. "Pentecostal Glossolalia: Toward a Functional Interpretation." *Journal for the Scientific Study of Religion* 8:211-216.

Hodge, D.R. (1972). "A validated Intrinsic Religious Motivation Scale. *Journal for the Scientific Study of Religion, 11*: 369-377.

Hood, R.W. 1975. "The Construction and Preliminary Validation of a Measure of Reported Mystical Experience." *Journal for the Scientific Study of Religion* 14:29-41.

Hunt, R.A. and M. King 1971. "The Intrinsic-Extrinsic Concept: A Review and Evaluation." *Journal for the Scientific Study of Religion* 10:339-356.

Hutch, R.A. 1980. "The Personal Ritual of Glossolalia." *Journal for the Scientific Study of Religion* 19:255-266.

Jackson, D.N. 1965. *Personality Research Form, Form A.* New York: Research Psychologists Press.

Jackson, D.N. 1974. *Personality Research Form Manual.* Goshen, NY: Research Psychologists Press.

Jackson, D.N. and G.M. Guthrie 1968. "A Multitrait-Multimethod Evaluation of the Personality Research Form." *Proceedings of the 76th Annual Convention of the American Psychological Association* 177-178.

Kantzer, K.S. 1980. "The Charismatics Among Us: Gallup Poll Identifies Who They Are and What They Believe". *Christianity Today* (245)25-(249)29.

Kiev, A. 1964. "Study of Folk Psychiatry". Pp. 3-35 in *Magic, Faith and Healing: Studies in Primitive Psychiatry.* Glencoe: Free Press.

Kildahl, J.P. 1972. *The Psychology of Speaking in Tongues.* New York: Harper & Row.

Kildahl, J.P. 1975. "Psychological Observations". *Charismatic Movement* 124-142.

Kirk, R. E. 1968. *Experimental Design: Procedures for the Behavioral Sciences.* Belmont, CA: Brooks/Cole.

Kramer, E. 1967. "A Contribution toward the Validation of the FIRO-B Questionnaire". *Journal of Projective Techniques and Personality Assessment* 31:80-81.

Kusyszyn, I. and D.N. Jackson. 1968. "A Multimethod Factor-analytic Appraisal of Endorsement and Judgment Method in Personality Assessment." *Educational and Psychological Measurement* 28:1047-1061.

Lindahl, L. 1975. *FIRO-B and the FIRO-B Theory. Some Evidence for Validity II.* Uppsala, Sweden: Uppsala University.

Mahler, M., F. Pine and A. Bergman. 1975. *The Psychological Birth of the Human Infant.* New York: Basic Books.

Malony, H.N. and Lovekin, A.A. 1985. *Glossolalia: Behavioral Sciences Perspectives on Speaking in Tongues.* New York: Oxford University Press.

Malony, H.N., N. Zwaanstra, and J.W. Ramsey. 1972. *Personal and Situational Determinants of Glossolalia: A Literature Review and Report of Ongoing Research.* Paper presented at the International Congress of Religious Studies, Los Angeles (September 1-5).

Mayers, M.K. 1973. "The Behavior of Tongues". Pp. 112-127 in *Speaking in Tongues: Let's Talk About it* edited by W.E. Mills. Word Books, 112-127.

Maslow, A.H. 1954. *Motivation and Personality.* New York: Harper.

——. 1970. *Religious, Values, and Peak-Experiences.* New York: Viking.

——. 1971. *The Farther Reaches of Human Nature.* New York: Viking.

McDonnell, K. 1976. *Charismatic Renewal and the Churches.* New York: Seabury.

McGuire, M.B. 1982. *Pentecostal Catholics: Power, Charisma and Order in a Religious Movement.* Philadelphia: Temple University Press.

Meier, A., H. Edwards 1973. "Purpose-In-Life Test: Age and Sex Differences". *Journal of Clinical Psychology* 384-386.

Mills, W.E. (Ed.) 1985. *Speaking in Tongues: A Guide to Research on Glossolalia.* Grand Rapids, MI: W.B. Eerdmans.

Morentz, P. 1966. *Lecture on Glossolalia.* Los Angeles: University of Southern California. Unpublished paper.

Murray, H.A. 1938. *Explorations in Personality.* New York: Oxford Press.

Plog, S. 1966. *Preliminary Analysis of Group Questionnaires on Glossolalia.* Los Angeles: University of Southern California. Unpublished paper.

Rarick, W.J. 1982. *The Socio-cultural Context of Glossolalia: A Comparison of Pentecostal and Neo-Pentecostal Religious Attitudes and Behavior.* Fuller Theological Seminary. Unpublished Doctoral Dissertation.

Richardson, J.T. 1973. "Psychological Interpretations of Glossolalia: A Reexamination of Research". *Journal for the Scientific Study of Religion* 12:199-207.

Shostrom, E.L. 1966. *Manual for the Personal Orientation Inventory.* San Diego, CA: Educational and Industrial Testing Service.

Schutz, W. 1958. *The Interpersonal Underworld–FIRO.* Palo Alto, CA: Science and Behavior Books.

——. 1967a. *The FIRO Scales:* Palo Alto, Calif.: Consulting Psychologists Press.

——. 1967b. *Joy, Expanding Human Awareness.* New York: Grove Press.

——. 1978. *FIRO Awareness Scales Manual.* Palo Alto, CA: Consulting Psychologists Press.

Spanos, N.P. and E.C. Hewitt 1979. "Glossolalia: A Test of the 'Trance' and Psychopathology Hypotheses". *Journal of Abnormal Psychology* 88:427-434.

Spilka, B., R.W. Hood, and R.L. Gorsuch 1985. *The Psychology of Religion: An Empirical Approach.* Englewood Cliffs, NJ: Prentice Hall.

Spilka, B., B. Kojetin, and D. McIntosh. 1985. "Forms and Measures of Personal Faith: Questions, Correlates and Distinctions." *Journal for the Scientific Study of Religion* 24:437-442.

Stace, W.T. 1960. *Mysticism and Philosophy.* New York: Macmillan.

Taft, R. 1970. "The Measurement of the Dimensions of Ego Permissiveness". *Personality: An International Journal* 1:163-184.

Thompson, J.R. 1977. *Social Processes Related to Revivifying Religions from within an Institutional Context: A Case Study of Charismatic Renewal Among Roman Catholics in Southern California.* Santa Barbara, CA: University of California. Unpublished doctoral dissertation.

Troeltsch, E. 1911/1931. *The Social Teachings of the Christian Churches.* New York: Macmillan (Originally published in 1911. Translated by O. Wyon).

Ullman, L.P., L. Krasner, and S.H. Troffer 1964. "A Contribution to FIRO-B Norms". *Journal of Clinical Psychology* 20:240-242.

Vivier, L. 1960. *Glossolalia.* University of Witwatersrand, Department. of Psychiatry. Unpublished thesis.

Watson, P.J., R. Howard, R.W. Hood, and R.J. Morris. 1988. "Age and Religious Orientation." *Review of Religious Research* 29:271-280.

RELIGIOUS IDENTIFICATION AND FAMILY ATTITUDES:

AN INTERNATIONAL COMPARISON

Bernadette C. Hayes and Michael P. Hornsby-Smith

ABSTRACT

Using recent cross-national survey data, this study examines the impact of religious identification on attitudes towards the family in seven western societies: the United States, Great Britain, West Germany, the Netherlands, Austria, Italy and Ireland. The results show a marked variation in patterns of religious identification across these countries and significant effects of religious identification on family attitudes. Religious independents are significantly less supportive of marriage, more likely to approve of divorce, and express a less child-centred attitude than both Catholic and Protestant religious affiliates. Thus, for these seven western countries at least, religious identification is a salient predictor of family attitudes.

Research in the Social Scientific Study of Religion, Volume 6, pages 167-186.
Copyright © 1994 by JAI Press Inc.
All rights of reproduction in any form reserved.
ISBN: 1-55938-762-9

167

INTRODUCTION

In recent years there has been increasing international research activity in the interstices between the Sociology of Religion and the Sociology of the Family (see Clark and Worthington 1987; Erickson 1992; Hayes and Pittelkow 1993; Hayes 1991; Thomas and Cornwall 1990). However, almost all this previous work has concentrated on the determinants of current religious participation and in particular, on the processes of religious transmission or the influence of parental religiosity and primary socialization experiences (Clark and Worthington 1987; Cornwall 1988; Hayes and Pittelkow 1993; Thomas and Cornwall 1990; Wadsworth and Freeman 1983). Thus, as recently argued by Thomas and Cornwall (1990), there still remains a clear need for multidimensional approaches designed to illuminate the interrelationships between religion and the family. Research on religious socialization alone is not enough. Equally important is the undertaking of complementary research on the social or psychological consequences of religious identification for family life. It is with this latter need in mind that the present study addresses not the processes of religious transmission but rather the influence of current religious identification on a range of attitudes towards the family and related matters such as marriage, divorce, and the perceived benefits or costs of children.

As in previous research, however, we wish to locate our study in the context of debates about the supposed secularizing tendencies associated with modernization in advanced industrial societies (Beckford 1981; Martin 1978; Wilson 1982). One indicator of secularizing tendencies in modern societies is the increased research interest in individuals reporting no religious preference ("religious independents"). For example, since the late 1970s, a number of studies of apostasy, disaffiliation, and religious "independents" have appeared in the literature (Bock and Radelet 1988; Brinkerhoff and Burke 1980; Brinkerhoff and Mackie 1993; Condran and Tamney 1985; Glenn 1987; Glock and Wuthnow 1979; Greeley 1981; Hayes 1991; Hogan 1979; Hunsberger 1980, 1983; Hunsberger and Brown 1984; McAllister 1988; McCallum 1987; McCutcheon 1988; Nelson 1981; Roof 1981; Roozen 1980; Sandomirsky and Wilson 1990). This interest must be considered an important development in the sociology of religion, especially in view of the almost complete lack of related research in the past (Brinkerhoff and Burke 1980; Vernon 1968; Welch 1978). Despite this attention, however, a number of limitations still remain.

First, although a number of recent studies have specifically focused on religious independents, many of these studies have either investigated this group in isolation from religious affiliates (Jehenson 1969; Richardson 1975), or have provided a rather crude comparison between religious independents and religious affiliates by simply lumping together all individuals who profess a religious identification into a single category (Bock and Radelet 1988; Hadaway and Roof 1979; Roozen 1980; Welch 1978). Second, much of this research has remained exclusively at the descriptive or bivariate level, focusing at best on a rather narrow range of distinguishing demographic characteristics such as gender, age, education, or occupation (Caplovitz and Sherrow 1977; Greeley 1972; Hogan 1979; McCallum 1987; Roozen 1980; Welch 1978). Third, even when a number of characteristics distinguishing between religious independents and religious affiliates are outlined, the combined consequences of these differences in terms of a range of social behaviour and attitudes has rarely been investigated. Finally, with few exceptions (Hogan 1979; Hunsberger 1983; Hunsberger and Brown 1984; McAllister 1988; McCallum 1987) these studies have largely focused on American respondents (Bock and Radelet 1988; Condran and Tamney 1985; Glenn 1987; Hadaway and Roof 1979; Perry et al. 1980; Roozen 1980; Sandomirsky and Wilson 1990; Welch 1978), among whom college students have traditionally predominated (Brinkerhoff and Mackie 1993; Caplovitz and Sherrow 1977; Greeley 1972; Hunsberger 1980, 1983; Hunsberger and Brown 1984). Thus, little research attention has been paid either to the national representativeness or cross-national applicability of these findings.

Mindful of these limitations and in contrast to previous research, this present study distinguishes between both Catholic and Protestant religious affiliates as well as religious independents. Second, the consequences of religious identification in relation to a wide range of family attitudes are investigated. Finally, to provide a more comprehensive and cross-national test of our findings we examine data from seven western societies.

AN ANALYTIC FRAMEWORK AND HYPOTHESES

Speculation about attitudinal and behavioral differences between religious independents and religious affiliates has increased in recent years. Although it has been pointed out that in many ways religious independents may be considered a highly pluralistic group (Perry et al. 1980, p. 403), past research does suggest a composite picture of these nonaffiliates. First, in terms of sociodemographic characteristics, previous studies suggest that in addition to the obvious differences in religious participation, nonaffiliates tend to be predominantly young, male, well-educated, and of higher social class backgrounds than their religious affiliates. They are also less likely to marry, and if they do marry are more likely to be divorced, separated, or involved in a remarriage. More importantly, however, they have consistently been depicted as marginal or nonconventional individuals who are liberal, both politically and morally, at odds with not only religious but other institutions, and hold values different from the majority in society (see Bock and Radelet 1988; Brinkerhoff and Burke 1980; Condran and Tamney 1985; Hadaway and

Roof 1979; Hogan 1979; Nelson 1981; Perry et al. 1980; Roozen 1978; Welch 1978).

For example, Bock and Radelet (1988) in a recent account of marital integration among religious independents (individuals who reported no current religious denomination), not only found that independents were more likely to be single and younger than their affiliated colleagues, but they were also notably disenchanted with the clergy, and expressed lower feelings of personal and marital well being. Furthermore, they were much more likely to give liberal responses to moral and political questions and refrain from identification with any political party. Not only were religious independents significantly more liberal in relation to abortion than the affiliates, but this was true for both genders and for both the married and unmarried. Although males were more likely than females and the unmarried more likely than the married to support the right to an abortion, religious affiliation was clearly the strongest predictor of this attitude, with three-quarters of independents favoring this position, as opposed to just over two-fifths of the affiliates. Similarly, whereas about a third of religious affiliates denoted their political identification as independent of any political party, the equivalent figure for religious independents was just under three-fifths.

A similar result is echoed in relation to stable independents, those who were raised in no religious group identification and continued to maintain their lack of religious identification. For example, both Hadaway and Roof (1979) and Roozen (1978) in a comparison of stable independents and those who had converted to a religious identification not only found that religious independents were notably more liberal in terms of their political, moral and general social values, but they also appeared to be outside the cultural mainstream, both in terms of attitudes and behavior. More specifically, whereas stable independents were more likely to approve of premarital sex, they were also far more likely than their converted colleagues to express a favorable view in relation to communism, attend x-rated movies, and frequent bars or public taverns (Hadaway and Roof 1979).

Recent Australian research supports these findings (Hogan 1979; Hunsberger and Brown 1984). For example, Hogan (1979) in a comprehensive study of Australian secularists (individuals who claimed no current religious denominational allegiance or the religious "nones") again found that secularists were more likely to be young, male, and significantly better educated than the general population. Furthermore, they were also more supportive of a liberal stance in relation to a range of political and moral issues. More specifically, not only were Australian secularists more likely to be aware of environmental issues, they were also less socially conservative, more supportive of government intervention in the economy, more cosmopolitan and less nationalistic in outlook, and more cynical about politics and propaganda than the Australian population as a whole. Furthermore, on almost every measure, the differences between male and female secularists were minor, with secular women being closer in values to secular men than to the majority of Australian women.

In conclusion, religious independents may be considered what Inglehart (1977, 1990), terms "postmaterialists." They are the more educated, cosmopolitan, and sophisticated members of society, who are more likely to endorse quality of life issues such as the environment and equal opportunity for minorities, adopt a left-wing position on economic issues such as the redistribution of wealth, and take a more liberal position on moral issues such as abortion or premarital sex. To what extent, however, are these differences also reflected in family attitudes? In other words, as is presently the case in relation to a range of economic, social, or moral issues, are religious independents also more likely to reject traditional family values or conventional family living arrangements than their religious affiliates? Our review of the literature suggests they are. For example, not only do the moral and ideological underpinnings of the traditional family stand in direct antithesis to the previously demonstrated liberal philosophy of independents, but this is also the case when the conventional trappings of family life such as marriage, childcare, and collectivized responsibility for marital partners and offspring are considered. In fact, it could be argued that it is the very conventionality of the traditional family in terms of its perceived cultural dominance, exclusivity of sexual license, idealized permanency, and collectivized responsibilities, that sets the opinions of religious independent apart from their religious affiliates in relation to this issue. It is with these differing ideological expectations in mind that we suggest the following two expectations and ` hypotheses in relation to family attitudes:

1. Religious identification exerts an independent impact on family attitudes.
2. Religious independents are less socially conservative than both Catholic and Protestant religious affiliates in relation to family attitudes.

DATA AND METHODS

The data used here are from the International Social Survey Program's (ISSP) Family and Changing Sex Role survey, conducted in 1988.[1] The ISSP collects data annually on a varying set of topics such as politics, attitudes towards income inequality, and social networks. It aims to collect directly comparable data which reveal similarities and differences between countries on social attitudes, values and politics. Although nine countries participated in this particular survey, both Hungary and Australia have been excluded from the analysis because of missing data on key variables. Our data therefore come from the remaining seven western countries. The respective sample sizes from the largely Catholic countries were 972 for Austria, 1028 for Italy, and 1005 for Ireland. From the largely Protestant countries they were 1414 for the United States and 1307 for Great Britain. In the religiously "balanced" regimes they were 2994 for West Germany and 1737 for the Netherlands. As in earlier ISSP surveys, the data represent randomly selected samples of citizens aged 18 and over, that are representative of their parent populations (see Davis and Jowell 1989). The use of cross-national data enables us to test the generalizability of relationships between religious identification and family attitudes across a wide range of national religious regimes where the proportion of Catholics varies from eleven percent to ninety-four percent, the proportion of Protestants from one percent to 65 percent, and the proportion of independents from one percent to 44 per cent.

The analysis proceeds in three stages. First, national differences in religious identification are briefly presented. Examining each country separately, we then proceed to investigate the extent to which these differences in religious identification are associated with a range of family issues, such as attitudes towards marriage and divorce, as well as the perceived benefits or costs of children. This analysis is simply the reported attitudes of Catholic, Protestant and religiously independent respondents in relation to these family attitudes (expressed as means), followed in each case by a t-test assessing whether the observed differences are statistically significant. Finally, using multivariate regression analysis, the extent to which religious differences in family attitudes exist net of other important sociodemographic characteristics is also examined.

Throughout this investigation, religious identification has been defined in terms of current religious self-identification, and operationalized in terms of the following three mutually exclusive groups: (1) Catholic, (2) Protestant, and (3) independent (the reference category).[2] The three categories were chosen to reflect the dominant religious groupings among each of our seven western industrialized nations.[3] Only individuals who explicitly and voluntarily stated their current religious identification as "no religion" have been included as independents. Each of these categories demonstrated a distinctive pattern in relation to religious practice. As expected, whereas independents demonstrated negligible church attendance rates in all seven countries, Catholics were generally the most frequent church-goers, with Protestants occupying a midway position between independents and Catholics (see Table 1).

A number of general family issues, the dependent variables in our analyses, are investigated in this paper. These include attitudes toward marriage and divorce, as well as the perceived benefits of children, and the costs of children. Attitudes towards these general family issues were assessed by ten questions. More specifically, respondents were asked to indicate their opinion in relation to the following ten statements:

Table 1. Church Attendance and Religious Identification by Country

Religious Identification	Church Attendance[a]						
	United States	Great Britain	West Germany	Nether lands	Austria	Italy	Ireland
Catholic	56.9	56.7	40.2	44.7	43.8	50.5	87.0
Protestant	55.0	25.5	15.0	56.8	25.0	30.8	66.7
Independent	3.6	2.2	—	1.1	1.2	0.0	0.0
N of Cases	1380	1185	2711	1691	969	1028	1000

Note: a Church attendance is measured exclusively in terms of weekly or monthly church attendance rates.

Source: Family and Changing Sex Role Survey, International Social Survey Programme, 1988.

A. When a marriage is troubled or unhappy, it is generally better for the wife if the couple stays together or gets divorced? Response categories are: much better to divorce, better to divorce, worse to divorce, much worst to divorce.

B. When a marriage is troubled or unhappy, it is generally better for the husband if the couple stays together or gets divorced? Answer categories are as above.

C. When a marriage is troubled or unhappy it is generally better for the children if the couple stays together or gets divorced? Answer categories are as above.

D. How easy or difficult do you think the law should make it for couples without young children to get a divorce? Response categories are: very easy, fairly easy, neither easy or difficult, fairly difficult, very difficult/impossible.

E. How easy or difficult do you think the law should make it for couples with young children to get a divorce? Response categories are as above.

F. People who have never had children lead empty lives. Response categories are: strongly agree, agree, neither agree or disagree, disagree, strongly disagree.

G. A marriage without children is not fully complete. Response categories are as above.

H. Children are more trouble than they are worth. Response categories are as above.

I. It is better not to have children as they are such a heavy financial burden. Response categories are as above.

J. Having children interferes too much with the freedom of parents. Response categories are as above.

Factor analyses demonstrates that these ten items form four overall scales, two related to attitudes towards marriage and divorce as well as two measures of general attitudes towards children (see Table 2 for the factor analyses results).

More specifically, whereas items A through E form the marriage and divorce scales (Marriage versus Divorce composed of items A through C and the Cost of Divorce for Young Children, items D through E), items F through J forms the basis of the two attitudes towards children scales (Benefits of Children, items F and G, and the Lack of Cost of Children, items H through J). These scales are unidimensional in nature. That is to say, whereas items A through C load strongly on factor I, they have weak loadings on factors II, III and IV. In contrast, items D and E load strongly on factor II, with weak loadings on all other factors.[4]

Each of these attitudinal variables is a series of multiple-item scales which range from zero to 100, with 100 always indicating the most conservative position. More specifically, the four summary scales were constructed by recoding each component item so that the most pro-marriage, anti-divorce, or pro-children response got a score of 100, and the least supportive response got a score of zero. The scores were then summated and divided by the number of component items to obtain a scale ranging from 0 to 100.[5]

Table 2.   Varimax Rotated Factor Loadings
Showing Dimensions of Family Attitudes

Scales and Items	Factor Loadings			
	I	*II*	*III*	*IV*
1. Attitudes Towards Marriage and Divorce:				
A) Marriage vs Divorce				
a) Bad marriage better than a divorce for women	**.92**	.13	.02	.04
b) Bad marriage better than a divorce for men	**.92**	.13	.01	.04
c) Bad marriage better than a divorce for children	**.79**	.16	.10	.01
B) Cost of Divorce for Young Kids				
d) Divorce difficult even if no children	.14	**.87**	−.07	.06
e) Divorce difficult if young children	.22	**.78**	.23	.02
2. Attitudes Towards Children:				
A) Benefits of Children				
f) Without children life empty	.01	.04	**.87**	−.06
g) Necessary for a complete marriage	.10	.07	**.85**	.08
B) Lack of Cost of Children				
h) Non-source of trouble	−.01	−.00	.07	**.77**
i) Lack of a financial burden	−.00	.03	.02	**.75**
j) Non-interference with parental freedom	.09	.05	−.08	**.73**

Source: Family and Changing Sex Role Survey, International Social Survey Programme, 1988.

FINDINGS

National Differences in Religious Identification

Table 3 reports variations in religious identification and the levels of religious independence in each of the seven western societies. As previously noted, three of the countries surveyed (Austria, Italy and Ireland) show a clear Catholic majority. For example, over 90 per cent of Italian and Irish respondents stated their religious identification as Catholic with under five percent Protestants. A predominantly Protestant affiliation is reported for the United States and Great Britain. In contrast to Britain, however, there is a sizeable Catholic minority (over a quarter of all respondents) in the United States. Finally, West Germany and the Netherlands may best be described as having a "mixed" pattern or as "duopolies" (Martin 1978, p. 19, 168-208), with an almost identical proportion of respondents claiming either a Catholic or Protestant religious affiliation.

The proportion of religious independents is least in countries with a near Catholic monopoly and in the pluralistic United States. Non-affiliation or religious independence is most prevalent in Great Britain and the Netherlands. The proportion of those expressing religious independence is highest among the Dutch (forty-four percent) where it exceeds the proportions expressing adherence to either Catholicism or Protestantism. These high levels of non-affiliation in the Netherlands reflect the collapse of Catholic power in the period after the Second Vatican Council (Bakvis 1981; Coleman 1978). More generally, religious independence has been linked to a marked decline in religious practice and the emergence of new forms of religious consciousness (Thung et al. 1985) most notably in urban areas such as Amsterdam and London.

In summary, marked variations exist in the nature of religious identification within these seven western nations. Whereas Austria, Italy, and Ireland all demonstrate clear Catholic majorities, Protestants predominate in both the United States and Great Britain. Religious independence is highest in the Netherlands and Great Britain and lowest in Ireland.

The Consequences of Religious Identification for Family Attitudes

To what extent do family attitudes reflect religious identification? Table 4 investigates this question by comparing the attitudes of independents (the reference category) and religious affiliates (both Catholics and Protestants) in relation to marriage, divorce, and the perceived benefits or costs of children. As previously explained, each of these attitudinal variables are a series of multiple-item scales which range from zero (least conservative) to 100 (most conservative). In Table 4 we simply report the mean attitudes of independent,

Table 3.   Religious Identification by Country

Religious Identification	Country						
	United States	Great Britain	West Germany	Nether lands	Austria	Italy	Ireland
Catholic	26.7	11.1	46.5	29.0	86.7	93.8	94.2
Protestant	65.3	53.3	45.8	27.3	4.5	1.3	4.5
Independent	8.0	35.6	7.7	43.7	8.7	5.0	1.3
N of Cases	1382	1282	2945	1713	972	1028	1004

Source.   Family and Changing Sex Role Survey, International Social Survey Programme, 1988.

Catholic, and Protestant individuals in relation to these issues. In each case a t-test assesses whether the observed differences between the religious affiliates and religious independents are statistically significant.

In confirmation of our hypotheses, the results in Table 4 do suggest significant differences between religious independents and affiliates in relation to family attitudes. Regardless of the attitudinal measure considered, independents are more likely to express a more liberal opinion in relation to these family issues than either their Catholic or Protestant compatriots. Furthermore, this pattern of association holds in all seven countries.

For example, independents are less supportive of marriage in the event of an unhappy marriage in all countries. Furthermore, not only are independents more likely to favor a divorce under these circumstances than their religious colleagues, but this association remains regardless of whether Catholics or Protestants are considered.

A similar result is echoed in relation to the perceived costs of divorce for young children. Not only are religious independents significantly more likely to favor divorce even in the event of young children than either their Catholic or Protestant counterparts, but this relationship holds in all countries, lacking statistical significance only among the small number of Protestants in Austria.

Finally, in relation to the perceived benefits or costs of children, regardless of country of origin, religious independents may be considered less child-orientated than their religious colleagues. Not only are independents less likely to believe in the necessity of children either for personal or marital fulfilment, but they are also more likely to perceive children as an unnecessary burden than either their Catholic or Protestant counterparts in four of the seven countries. Except in Austria, Ireland, and Italy, these relationships generally hold regardless of whether Catholics or Protestant affiliates are considered.

In summary, religious identification and family attitudes are associated in all seven countries. Regardless of country of origin, independents are significantly more likely to approve of divorce under a variety of circumstances, and express a less child-centred attitude than their religious affiliates. Furthermore, this relationship holds regardless of whether Catholic or

Table 4. Means for Family Attitudes by Religious Identification and Country

Variable	Religious Identification					
	Independent	Catholic	Protestant	Independent	Catholic	Protestant
	United States			*Great Britain*		
Marriage vs Divorce	29.42	35.16	38.31*	29.87	37.97*	33.54*
Divorce Costs for Children	42.68	55.22*	56.48*	48.38	56.39*	53.39*
Benefits of Children	45.13	46.74	50.15*	44.01	49.62*	49.08*
Lack of Cost of Children	74.17	77.45	78.82*	74.13	77.29*	77.12*
	West Germany			*Netherlands*		
Marriage vs Divorce	21.84	29.93*	26.88*	27.52	32.51*	36.26*
Divorce Costs for Children	42.98	55.74*	52.50*	46.67	52.72*	58.84*
Benefits of Children	42.27	52.11*	53.34*	36.65	44.29*	42.71*
Lack of Cost of Children	70.08	72.96*	71.52	73.37	75.83*	77.84*
	Austria			*Italy*		
Marriage vs Divorce	24.96	28.90	30.28	20.88	38.14*	37.24*
Divorce Costs for Children	44.41	56.78*	49.69	36.27	51.32*	52.08*
Benefits of Children	57.09	62.09	60.89	36.17	63.68*	51.14
Lack of Cost of Children	68.48	69.43	68.50	77.45	75.31	75.00
	Ireland					
Marriage vs Divorce	14.03	43.31*	34.18*			
Divorce Costs for Children	42.31	65.02*	65.85*			
Benefits of Children	33.33	48.46*	48.84*			
Lack of Cost of Children	84.03	79.46	80.30			

Note: * Significantly different from the independents at p < 0.05, two-tailed.
Source: Family and Changing Sex Role Survey, International Social Survey Programme, 1988.

Protestant affiliates are considered. Thus, it is religious independence, or the lack of a religious identity, that constitutes the key differentiating factor in distinguishing family attitudes.

A Multivariate Analysis

As previously explained religious preferences and attitudes do not exist in isolation; they are determined in interaction with a number of sociodemographic factors such as gender, age, marital status, education and occupation. For example, in addition to religious practices, studies have consistently shown that younger, male, or single individuals are significantly more likely to eschew a religious affiliation than their older, female, or married colleagues (Bock and Radelet 1988; McCallum 1987; Roozen 1980; Welch 1978). A similar result is echoed in relation to socioeconomic status. Not only have past studies found a clear inverse relationship between education and religious affiliation, but this is also the case in relation to other measures of socioeconomic status, such as occupation, and employment status (Condran and Tamney 1985; Hogan 1979; Welch 1978).

To assess the contribution of religious identification net of these factors on family attitudes, a number of sociodemographic background variables as well as religious identification are included in a pooled regression model of all seven countries. The sociodemographic variables are as follows: gender (coded 1 for males and 0 for females), current marital status (coded 1 for married and 0 for other), prior marital status (coded 1 for previously divorced versus 0 for other),[6] age (measured in number of years), church attendance (a five point scale ranging from 0 for never, to 1 for weekly), education (measured in number of years), occupation (coded 1 for nonmanual and 0 for manual), and work status (coded 1 for labor active and 0 for other). Country differences are captured by a set of dummy variables, one for each country with the United States the reference (omitted) category. Preliminary analyses on each country separately, which allowed all possible interactions between country and the variables in the model, suggested that the results are similar in all seven countries. We have therefore preferred the simpler and more robust model with country dummy variables. This analysis is based on ordinary least squares methods, and missing data are treated by the pairwise deletion method (Hertel 1976). Alternative analyses using listwise deletion lead to identical substantive conclusions.

Turning now to the results, inspection of Table 5 again confirms our hypotheses of the independent effect of religious identification on family attitudes. That is to say, even with the inclusion of other sociodemographic characteristics, religious identification continues to exert an independent and statistically significant effect on family attitudes. Furthermore, this relationship holds regardless of whether attitudes toward marriage, divorce, or the perceived benefits or costs of children are considered. More importantly, however, as suggested by our second hypothesis, in all cases, these effects are in agreement with each other and in the direction expected: Both Catholics and Protestants are significantly more likely to adopt a conservative stance in relation to their issues than their currently independent colleagues.

For example, the results in column one of Table 5 again demonstrate that religious identification is an important differential predictor of family attitudes. Here, both Catholics and Protestants are significantly more likely to hold a positive attitude towards marriage even in the event of an unhappy marriage than their independent colleagues. For these two groups at least, not only is their current religious identification a primary predictor of this issue, but this relationship is statistically significant at the 0.001 level. Thus, in confirmation of our earlier bivariate analysis, even with a substantial set of control variables, Catholic and Protestant individuals remain significantly more likely to approve of marriage even under these difficult circumstances than their currently independent religious colleagues.

Table 5. Pooled Cross-National Unstandardized Regression Analyses
for the Effects of Religious Identification on Family Attitudes (n = 6,268)

Variables	Marriage vs Divorce	Divorce Costs for Children	Benefits of Children	Lack of Cost of Children
Socio-Demographic Controls:				
Male	5.71***	2.97***	3.27***	−1.01*
Married	1.05	−0.03	4.52***	3.25***
Divorced	−5.47***	−6.32***	0.85	−1.58*
Age (years)	0.12***	0.12***	0.26***	−0.01
Education (years)	−0.32***	−0.32***	−0.99***	−0.44***
Nonmanual	−0.83	−1.08	−3.95***	0.29
Employed	−0.58	−1.75**	−1.99**	−0.55
Country:				
United States[a]	—	—	—	—
Great Britain	−1.86	−0.64	−1.86	−1.08
West Germany	−9.11***	−2.18*	1.09	−4.77***
Netherlands	−2.91**	−0.38	−7.08***	−1.63*
Austria	−9.09***	−0.62	11.88***	−7.88***
Italy	−1.17	−7.05***	12.23***	−2.53**
Ireland	0.95	3.98***	−2.42	0.10
Religion Effects:				
Identification				
Independent[a]	—	—	—	—
Catholic	4.29***	4.81***	3.90***	1.31*
Protestant	4.19***	5.41***	4.55***	1.86**
Church Attendance	7.51***	11.15***	3.04***	3.28***
Constant	26.47***	45.51***	43.15***	69.51***
R-Squared	0.119	0.114	0.162	0.057

Notes: [a] Omitted category of comparison.
*** Significant at the 0.001 level;
** Significant at the 0.01 level;
* Significant at the 0.05 level.

Source: Family and Changing Sex Role Survey, International Social Survey Programme, 1988.

This is not to suggest, however, that religious identification is the only factor in predicting attitudes. For example, church attendance, gender and age all have a positive influence on attitudes. Frequent church attenders, males, or older individuals are also significantly more likely to support marriage than either their less religiously devout, female or younger colleagues. Several of the other variables used as controls are also significant. For example, whereas education and prior marital status (divorced) both have a depressing effect on marriage attitudes, this is also the case in West Germany, the Netherlands and Austria. That is to say, West German, Dutch, and Austrian respondents are notably less likely to approve of marriage under these circumstances than their United States counterparts (the omitted category of reference).[7] Finally, the fit of the model is much the same as in previous research; the proportion of variance explained by these characteristics is 12 percent.

Turning now to the perceived costs of divorce for children (column two in Table 5), again the main finding of this investigation is the independent effect of religious identification on family attitudes. All such effects are in agreement with each other and in the direction expected: both Catholics and Protestants are significantly more likely to stress the costs of divorce in the case of children than their religiously independent counterparts. Thus, not only is religious identification an important predictor of attitudes, but in both cases, this relationship is again statistically significant at the 0.001 level.

As in our earlier analysis, however, religious identification is only one of a number of factors determining attitudes. Gender, prior marital status (divorced), age, education, employment status and country of origin also demonstrate a noteworthy impact. For example, in contrast to gender, age, and church attendance which all have a positive influence on attitudes, prior marital status, education, and employment status demonstrate significant negative effects. Country of origin also shows some significant negative effects in Italy and West Germany, but a positive effect in Ireland. Finally, when the fit of the model is considered, the explanatory power of this model is almost identical to our previous analysis (the r-squared value is 0.114).

Columns three and four in Table 5 present the results for attitudes towards children. Again, the major finding of these analyses is the highly significant effect of religious identification on family attitudes. Regardless of whether the perceived benefits or costs of children are considered, religious identification emerges as a significant differential predictor of attitudes. These effects are consistently in the hypothesized direction and exist net of other plausible determinants of attitudes, such as gender, marital status, age, education, and employment status. For example, whereas independents are significantly less likely to stress the benefits of children than either their Catholic or Protestant counterparts, an identical but converse pattern emerges in relation to the perceived financial or personal costs of children. Thus, at least at far as attitudes towards children are concerned, independents may be considered less child-centred than either their Catholic or Protestant colleagues.

As in all previous analyses, however, religious identification is not the only predictor of family attitudes in this instance. Other notable influences include: gender, marital status, education, and church attendance. For example, whereas males are significantly more likely to simultaneously espouse both the benefits and costs of children than females, married individuals are notably more likely to stress their overall virtues. Thus, not only are males significantly more likely to combine an awareness of the perceived benefits of children with their possible costs in terms of financial or personal freedom constraints than females, but this is also the case when compared to married individuals who consistently stress their overall benefits.

A similar pattern is echoed in relation to church attendants and the better educated. In contrast to the better educated who are notably more likely to stress both the lack of benefits and costs of children, the religiously devout hold a consistently positive view. Thus, in contrast to the religiously devout who demonstrate a consistently child-centerd attitude, attitudes among the better educated are generally negative.

Other significant factors include prior marital status, age, occupation, employment status and country of origin. More specifically, whereas nonmanual and labor active persons are considerably less likely to espouse the benefits of children, both older individuals and two of our predominantly Catholic countries (Austria and Italy, but not Ireland) are more likely to stress their advantages. It is interesting to note, however, these positive (Catholic) country effects also coexist with a negative estimation of the burdens of children. In other words, as is also the case with previously divorced persons, Austrians and Italians (as well as West Germans and the Dutch) are significantly more likely to stress the costs of children than their American colleagues. While these findings may appear somewhat contradictory at first glance, as is also the case with males generally, they probably reflect nothing more than a realistic appraisal of the consequences of their more child-centerd preference in attitudes. Finally, when the fit of the models is considered, in contrast to our child-cost measure which is rather poorly predicted by our background variables (only six percent of the variance is explained), attitudes toward the perceived benefits of children is reasonably well predicted by this analysis (the r-squared value is 0.162).

In summary, the results of Table 5 are unequivocal. Regardless of whether attitudes towards marriage, divorce, or the perceived benefits or costs of children is investigated, religious identification is a significant differential predictor of these family attitudes. Furthermore, these effects are consistently in the expected directions and exist net of other plausible determinants of attitudes, such as gender, marital status, education, employment status and even church attendance. Even with the inclusion of other sociodemographic characteristics, independents are significantly less supportive of marriage, more likely to approve of divorce, and express a less child-centerd view than either their Catholic or Protestant religious affiliates.

SUMMARY AND CONCLUSIONS

This paper has endeavored to respond to pleas for more research on the interrelationships between religion and the family. While much previous work has focused on the processes of religious transmission and the influence of families in religious socialization, this paper has investigated the relationship between religious identification (trichotomized as Catholic, Protestant, and independent) and a wide range of attitudes relating to family matters. It breaks new ground in utilizing representative samples from seven western societies that differ widely in their religious composition and so provides the opportunity to test the generalizability of relationships cross-nationally.

Returning now to the expectations posed at the beginning of this paper, we draw two main inferences from our research on the influence of religious identification on family attitudes. First, religious identification is a significant predictor of family attitudes. Second, in terms of these family orientations, independents and religious affiliates do differ in expected ways.

Our investigation clearly shows that religious identification is a differential predictor of family attitudes among western nations. In all seven western countries included in this analysis, independents are relatively less inclined to support the institution of marriage, disapprove of divorce, and hold a child-centerd attitude than their religious affiliates. Furthermore, this relationship holds regardless of whether Catholics or Protestants are considered. Thus, it is religious independence, or the lack of a religious identification, that constitutes the primary distinguishing factor in determining family attitudes in this instance.

Multivariate analyses support this conclusion. Regardless of the issue considered, religious identification remains a differential predictor of family attitudes. Not only are all the effects in the direction expected, but they exist net of a number of sociodemographic controls, most notably church attendance, socioeconomic status, age, and gender. Thus, even with the inclusion of other sociodemographic characteristics, independents are significantly less supportive of marriage, more likely to approve of divorce, and express a consistently less child-centerd view than either their Catholic or Protestant counterparts.

This is not to suggest, however, that religious identification is the sole predictor of attitudes. Other notable determinants include: gender, age, education, and especially church attendance. For example, in all but one exception (the lack of cost of children), whereas gender (male) had a significant positive effect on attitudes in relation to these general family issues, the impact of education was consistently negative. In other words, it is both the better educated and females who are more likely to espouse a more liberal view in relation to these attitudes. More specifically, as is also the case with religious independents, females and the better educated are also consistently more likely to support the need for divorce under a number of circumstances, and concentrate on the perceived disadvantages of children generally.

A converse pattern emerges in relation to older persons and church attenders. Not only are regular church attenders consistently more likely to reject divorce even under difficult circumstances and espouse a more child-centerd view generally, but this is also the case as far as older individuals are concerned. Thus, as is also found among both Catholic and Protestant religious affiliates, a more conservative stance in relation to family attitudes is also prominent among church-going population and the elderly.

In conclusion, then, religious identification is a differential predictor of family attitudes. Regardless of the Euro-American country of origin, not only are independents significantly more likely to hold a more liberal opinion in relation to a range of family attitudes than their religious affiliates, but this relationship holds irrespective of whether Catholics or Protestants are considered. Given that there is widespread evidence of a weakening of both Catholic and Protestant affiliations in western societies and an increase in the proportions of independents or religious "nones," these results point to a significant potential weakening of conservative family attitudes with considerable social consequences.

It is important to note, however, that the causal origins of the relationship between religious identification and family attitudes remains unclear. Additional research needs to determine whether current differences between independents and their religious affiliates lead to these different attitudes, or whether divergence in attitudes leads to a subsequent rejection of religious identification. It may be that the current absence of a religious identification is not what is important. Instead, what may be more significant is a past rejection or adoption of a Christian religious belief system and self-identification that is accompanied by attitudes that conserve the conventional family. Unfortunately, given the absence of suitable data, we are unable to test these speculations here. Such an inquiry would undoubtedly be a fruitful avenue for future research. One thing remains certain, however, current religious identification is an important predictor of family attitudes, the origins and consequences of which deserve future international research attention.

ACKNOWLEDGMENT

A revised version of a paper presented at the Association for the Sociology of Religion, Miami, Florida, August 11-13 1993.

NOTES

1. The ISSP was begun in the mid-1980s by established academic survey organizations in a number of countries with the aim of conducting high quality and directly comparable cross-national surveys of the mass public on selected topics of importance in the social sciences. The membership has grown to over a dozen countries and its expansion is continuing. Each year a drafting committee produces a fifteen minute questionnaire which each member country appends to its next national survey. The ISSP is always conducted as a self-completion questionnaire, additional to each organization's regular social survey (usually by mail or as a "leave behind" supplement). Modules fielded so far include the Role of Government (1985), Social Networks and Social Support (1986), Inequality (1987), Family and Changing Sex Roles (1988), and Work and Leisure (1989). The

questionnaires are drafted in English, and translated, if necessary, by the national group, with particular attention paid to the direct comparability of questions. In other words, exactly the same questions are asked in all countries, and identical coding procedures are used. The data, which are publicly available, were supplied by the Zentralarchiv für Empirische Sozialforschung, University of Cologne, Germany. In all countries analyzed, the sample response rates achieved were greater than seventy percent. For further details on the ISSP see Davis and Jowell (1989).

2. More specifically, religious identification was assessed by the following country-specific, though culturally equivalent, questions: To which religious group do you belong? (West Germany and Austria); Do you regard yourself as belonging to any particular religion? If yes, which? (Great Britain); Do you regard yourself as belonging to a church community? If yes, which one? (Netherlands); What is your religious preference? Is it Protestant, Catholic, Jewish, some other or no religion? If Protestant, what specific denomination is that? (the United States); and What is your religion? (Ireland and Italy). Although mindful of the limitations of the use, as well as the slight cross-national variation in wording, of just one question to investigate this complex issue, a number of arguments can be made in its defence. First, regardless of nationality, the question did not directly ask about religious membership. Second, with the one exception of the United States, religious preference was not mentioned. Rather, for the majority of countries, religious self-identification was by far the most important factor in determining current religious identification. Thus, as argued elsewhere by Brinkerhoff and Mackie (1993, p. 239), not only may the use of this question as opposed to measures of religious membership be considered a more valid measure of current religious identification in this instance, but its greater predictability in terms of attitudinal measures is an additional advantage. Second, throughout the ISSP particular attention has been paid to the direct comparability of questions. In other words, where possible, exactly the same questions are asked in all countries, and identical coding procedures are used. Thus, this slight variation in question-wording in relation to the measurement of religious identification reflects a genuine effort to obtain both a cross-national as well as a nationally-specific equivalence in meaning rather than a cross-national distortion in measurement.

3. Note, however, irrespective of country of origin, this restriction of our samples to members of a Christian religious faith resulted in less than two per cent of the original sample being excluded from the analyses. For example whereas only 1.9 per cent of American respondents claimed to belong to a non-Christian church, the equivalent figures for Great Britain, West Germany and the Netherlands, were 1.7, 0.2 and 0.1, respectively. No respondents in either Austria, Italy, or Ireland claimed a non-Christian affiliation.

4. Note, however, with the two partial exceptions of Italy and Ireland where both the marriage and divorce items loaded on just one factor (results available on request), this relationship held regardless of whether each country was examined separately or as in the combined analyses presented in Table 2.

5. Using the dependent variable of the Cost of Divorce for Young Children by way of example, each of the two items (d-e) were scored as follows: $0 =$ very easy; $25 =$ fairly easy; $50 =$ neither easy or difficult; $75 =$ fairly difficult; and $100 =$ very difficult/impossible. The scores were then summated and divided by two (the number of component items) to obtain a scale ranging from 0 (least conservative) to 100 (most conservative). An alternative procedure would have been to use factor score coefficients. The summation procedure was used because factor score coefficients tend to make comparisons between regression coefficients difficult due to factor weightings. In practice, the difference between the two procedures is small (Kim and Mueller 1978, pp. 69-72).

6. As the purpose of this variable was to control for the possible effect of having previously experienced a divorce in relation to these family attitudes, prior marital status was operationalized in terms of the following two mutually exclusive categories: (a) all respondents who stated that they "had previously been divorced," which was coded one, and (b) a residual category coded zero, which was composed of all the non-previously divorced regardless of their current marital status.

7. It is important to note, however, that although these regression coefficients may be interpreted in terms of the rank order of nations in relation to their support for this particular issue, they control for cross-national differences in social structure and religious identification.

REFERENCES

Bakvis, H. 1981. *Catholic Power in the Netherlands.* Kingston and Montreal: McGill-Queen's University Press.

Beckford, J.A. 1981. *Religion and Advanced Industrial Society.* London: Unwin Hyman.

Bock, E. W. and M. L. Radelet. 1988. "The Marital Integration of Religious Independents: A Reevaluation of its Significance." *Review of Religious Research* 29:228-241.

Brinkerhoff, M. B. and K. L. Burke. 1980. "Disaffiliation: Some Notes On Falling From the Faith." *Sociological Analysis* 41:41-54.

Brinkerhoff, M. B. and M. M. Mackie. 1993. "Casting Off the Bonds of Organized Religion: A Religious-Careers Approach to the Study of Apostasy." *Review of Religious Research* 34:235-258.

Caplovitz, D. and F. Sherrow. 1977. *The Religious Dropouts: Apostasy Among College Graduates.* Beverly Hills, CA: Sage.

Clark, C. A. and E. L. Worthington. 1987. "Family Variables Affecting the Transmission of Religious Values From Parents to Adolescents: A Review." *Family Perspective* 21:1-21.

Coleman, J. A. 1978. *The Evolution of Dutch Catholicism, 1958-1974.* Berkeley: University of California Press.

Condran, J. G. and J. B. Tamney. 1985. "Religious Nones: 1957 to 1982." *Sociological Analysis* 46:415-423.

Cornwall, M. 1988. "The Influence of Three Agents of Religious Socialization: Family, Church and Peers." Pp. 207-231 in *The Religion and Family Connection: Social Science Perspectives,* edited by D.L. Thomas. Provo, UT: Brigham Young University.

Davis, J. A. and R. Jowell. 1989. "Measuring National Differences: An Introduction to the International Social Survey Programme (ISSP)." Pp. 1-13 in *British Social Attitudes: Special International Report,* edited by R. Jowell, S. Witherspoon, and L. Brook. Aldershot: Gower.

Erickson, J.A. 1992. "Adolescent Religious Development and Commitment: A Structural Equation Model of the Role of Family, Peer Group, and Educational Influences." *Journal for the Scientific Study of Religion* 31: 131-152.

Glenn, N. G. 1987. "The Trend in 'No Religion' Respondents to U.S. National Surveys, Late 1950s to Early 1980s." *Public Opinion Quarterly* 51:293-314.

Glock, C. Y. and R. Wuthnow. 1979. "Departures from Conventional Religion: The Nominally Religious, the Nonreligious, and the Alternatively Religious." Pp. 47-68 in *The Religious Dimension,* edited by R. Wuthnow. New York: Academic Press.

Greeley, A. M. 1972. *The Denominational Society.* Glenview, IL: Scott, Foresman.

_____. 1981. "Religious Musical Chairs." Pp. 101-126 in *In Gods We Trust,* edited by T. Robbins and D. Anthony. New Brunswick, NJ: Transaction.

Hadaway, C. K. and W. C. Roof. 1979. "Those Who Stay Religious Nones and Those Who Don't: A Research Note." *Journal for the Scientific Study of Religion* 18:194-200.

Hayes, B. C. 1991. "Religious Identification and Marriage Patterns in Australia." *Journal for the Scientific Study of Religion* 30:469-478.

Hayes, B. C. and Y. Pittelkow. 1993. "Religious Belief, Transmission, and the Family: An Australian Study." *Journal of Marriage and the Family* 55:755-766.

Hertel, B. R. 1976. "Minimizing Error Variance Introduced by Missing Data Routines in Survey Analysis." *Sociological Methods and Research* 4:459-474.

Hogan, M. 1979. "Australian Secularists: The Disavowal of Denominational Allegiance." *Journal for the Scientific Study of Religion* 18:390-404.

Hunsberger, B. E. 1980. "A Re-examination of the Antecedents of Apostasy." *Review of Religious Research* 21:158-170.

_____. 1983. "Apostasy: A Social Learning Perspective." *Review of Religious Research* 25:21-38.

Hunsberger, B. E. and L.B. Brown. 1984. "Religious Socialization, Apostasy, and the Impact of Family Background." *Journal for the Scientific Study of Religion* 23:239-251.

Inglehart, R. 1977. *The Silent Revolution.* Princeton, NJ: Princeton University Press.

_____. 1990. *Cultural Shift in Advanced Industrial Society.* Princeton, NJ: Princeton University Press.

Jehenson, R. B. 1969. "The Dynamics of Role Leaving: A Role Theoretical Approach to the Leaving of Religious Organizations." *Journal of Applied Behavioural Science* 5:287-308.

Kim, J. and C.W. Mueller. 1978. *Factor Analysis: Statistical Methods and Practical Issues.* London: Sage.

McAllister, I. 1988. "Religious Change and Secularization: The Transmission of Religious Values in Australia." *Sociological Analysis* 49:249-263.

McCallum, J. 1987. "Secularization in Australia between 1966 and 1985: A Research Note." *Australian and New Zealand Journal of Sociology* 3:407-422.

McCutcheon, A. L. 1988. "Denominations and Religious Intermarriage: Trends Among White Americans in the Twentieth Century." *Review of Religious Research* 29:213-227.

Martin, D. 1978. *A General Theory of Secularization.* Oxford: Basil Blackwell.

Nelson, H. M. 1981. "Religious Conformity in an Age of Disbelief: Contextual Effects of Time, Denomination, and Family Processes upon Church Decline and Apostasy." *American Sociological Review* 46:632-40.

Perry, E. L., J.H. Davis, R.T. Doyle, and J.E. Dyble. 1980. "Toward a Typology of Unchurched Protestants". *Review of Religious Research* 21:388-404.

Richardson, J. T. 1975. "New Forms of Deviance in a Fundamentalist Church: A Case Study." *Review of Religious Research* 16:134-142.

Roof, W. C. 1981. "Alienation and Apostasy." Pp. 87-99 in *In Gods We Trust,* edited by T. Robbins and D. Anthony. New Brunswick, NJ: Transaction Books.

Roozen, D. A. 1978. *The Churched and the Unchurched in America.* Washington, DC: Glenmary Research Center.

_____. 1980. "Church Dropouts: Changing Patterns of Disengagement and Re-entry." *Review of Religious Research* 21:427-450.

Sandomirsky, S. and J. Wilson. 1990. "Processes of Disaffiliation: Religious Mobility Among Men and Women." *Social Forces* 68:1211-1229.

Thomas, D. L. and M. Cornwall. 1990. "Religion and Family in the 1980s: Discovery and Development." *Journal of Marriage and the Family* 52:983-992.

Thung, M. A., L. Laeyendecker, G. van Tillo, G. Dekker, Q. J. Munters, A. H. van Otterloo, and P. H. Vrijhof. 1985. *Exploring the New Religious Consciousness.* Amsterdam: Free University Press.

Vernon, G. M. 1968. "The Religious 'Nones': A Neglected Category." *Journal for the Scientific Study of Religion* 7:219-229.

Wadsworth, M. E. J. and S. R. Freeman. 1983. "Generational Differences in Beliefs: A Cohort Study of Stability and Change in Religious Beliefs." *British Journal of Sociology* 34:416-437.

Welch, M. R. 1978. "Religious Non-affiliates and Worldly Success." *Journal for the Scientific Study of Religion* 17:59-61.

Wilson, B. 1982. *Religion in Sociological Perspective.* Oxford: Oxford University Press.

Wuthnow, R. 1976. "Recent Patterns of Secularization: A Problem of Generations?" *American Sociological Review* 41:850-867.

THE CONTEXTUAL EFFECT OF SECULAR NORMS ON RELIGIOSITY AS MODERATOR OF STUDENT ALCOHOL AND OTHER DRUG USE

H. Wesley Perkins

ABSTRACT

Previous studies suggest that religiosity's effect in moderating youthful drug use is salient only because wider secular and peer norms do not already provide clear normative proscriptions. Yet variations in the secular norms surrounding drug use among students have been largely ignored in testing this claim. If the lack of secular controls is what contextually enables religiosity's restrictive impact, then normative secular constraints on drug use in a particular setting through both *actual* and *perceived* peer norms should be important factors limiting the degree of religious influence. This prediction is tested with survey data collected on drug use, attitudes, and perceptions of peer norms for alcohol, marijuana, cocaine, and hallucinogens in an undergraduate population in two distinct time periods (1982, N = 1,514 and 1989-91, N = 1,510). Support for a contextual effect of secular norms on the association between religiosity and drug use/attitudes is found for males but not females. Implications of this gender difference are discussed.

Research in the Social Scientific Study of Religion, Volume 6, pages 187-208.
Copyright © 1994 by JAI Press Inc.
All rights of reproduction in any form reserved.
ISBN: 1-55938-762-9

INTRODUCTION

Religious influences upon alcohol and other drug use have been a persistent topic of theory and research in the literature on drug abuse for several decades. Such influences have frequently been uncovered in research on the attitudes and behaviors of general populations and teenagers. Even among some college populations of late adolescents and young adults from recent decades, where religiosity is traditionally a less prominent aspect of one's life and where peer influences typically overshadow most other personal background characteristics in these peer intensive environments, an impact of religiosity has been occasionally noted (cf. Hanson and Engs 1987; Humphrey, Leslie, and Brittain 1989; Perkins 1985; Turner and Willis 1979; Wechsler and McFadden 1979).

The expectation that religious commitment within the Judeo-Christian traditions should moderate or restrain youthful alcohol and other drug use may be derived from several factors. Traditions that proscribe abstinence provide an obvious potential deterrent to use for their adherents. More broadly, the basic emphasis on the human body as God's creation or as an "earthly temple" in Judeo-Christian perspectives, in general, may encourage an aversion to physically destructive abuse of drugs. Furthermore, the effects of personal religiosity on young persons may be reinforced through multiple intergenerational linkages by the influences of parental religiosity and drug use behavior (Perkins 1987).

It is frequently argued, moreover, that all major religious traditions serve, at least in part, as social control mechanisms that maintain social order by discouraging delinquent or deviant activity (cf. Rohrbaugh and Jessor 1975). Thus, youth who adhere more closely to dominant religious traditions are expected to exhibit greater conformity to the behavioral norms of society. This notion has been challenged, however, by some research revealing little relationship between religiosity and juvenile delinquency (Hirschi and Stark 1969) and a review of the literature on religiosity and deviance has found inconclusive results (Knudten and Knudten 1971). Subsequent research has refined the hypothesis by suggesting that the degree of social control by other institutions and wider cultural norms is a critical intervening factor (Burkett and White 1974; Elifson, Petersen, and Hadaway 1983; Hadaway, Elifson, and Petersen 1984; Linden and Currie 1977; Tittle and Welch 1983). If society in general strongly opposes and punitively responds to certain behaviors, then any additional emphasis of a religious tradition is not likely to be significant. In contrast, religious prescriptions or prohibitions may be more important when society has otherwise relaxed its restrictive controls or provides only ambiguous normative expectations. Thus, religiosity has a distinct ascetic effect and is salient, it is argued, only in contexts where wider secular and peer norms do not already provide relatively strong normative proscriptions.[1]

This theoretical perspective about the contextual limitation of religiosity's effect on deviant behavior and specifically on drug use has not been fully tested with adequate assessments of contextual variation within a youthful population, however. If the lack of secular controls is what contextually enables religiosity to have a restrictive impact on drug use, then the degree of normative secular constraint on drug use in a particular setting should be an important determinant of the degree of religious influence. First, if variation in the permissiveness of secular norms exists for different types of drug use, then the deterring effect of religiosity on use or heavy use might vary directly with the particular type of drug examined.[2] Second, for any specific drug, if the cultural climate of acceptance or restriction becomes more (or less) restrictive over time, then the moderating effect of religiosity should become correspondingly less (or greater). Third, a distinction between the actual and perceived social norms surrounding alcohol and other drug use among students in various contexts may be important. This distinction has been largely ignored in testing the effects of religiosity, even though perceptions of the secular norms will typically not match the actual behaviors and expectations of peers and not all students in the same campus environment will perceive the same degree of permissiveness in secular norms (Perkins 1991; Perkins and Berkowitz 1986). Thus it may be that any contextual limitations on the effect of religiosity are enhanced or diminished through the subjective perceptions of the secular context by the actor.

Lastly, gender may be an additionally important factor to consider. Peek, Lowe, and Williams (1991, p. 1216) point out that "a healthy dose of gender sensitivity seems much needed generally in sociological theories of religion. These theories need to seriously consider the sociological principle that people in different structural locations behave and think differently, and apply this principle to explaining gender variations in the impact of religion, rather than generating explanations that apply across-the-board." Potential differences in religious participation and the salience of religious commitment may suggest at least the need to control for gender in empirical analyses. Certainly gender differences in student alcohol use have been well-documented, although some gender-related differences may be declining (Berkowitz and Perkins 1987; Engs and Hanson 1989; Perkins 1992). If socially acceptable secular norms for alcohol and other drug behavior are not the same for men and women or if men and women tend to perceive different community norms for drug use regardless of the actual norms, then any contextual effects of religiosity may vary by gender.

Thus, three hypotheses about secular context are tested controlling for gender with data collected in campus-wide surveys of an undergraduate population between 1982 and 1991. First, given substantial differences in use and normative support for use of various drugs, the religious impact should be relatively stronger on the more widely used (more socially acceptable and less secularly controlled) drugs. Clearly alcohol is the drug of choice in virtually all college contexts, with marijuana use less prevalent and cocaine and hallucinogens even less prevalent. Variations in legal restrictions and penalties for use of these substances reflect this pattern of use as well. Thus, the greatest moderating effect of religiosity should occur for the use of alcohol, followed by marijuana, in turn, followed by cocaine and hallucinogens.

Second, to the extent that there have been declines in use and social acceptability of some drugs on campus across the last decade, there should be a corresponding decrease in the relative impact of religiosity in controlling the use of these drugs. Increased minimum ages for alcohol consumption, greater campus control of drinking locations and expanding liability and tougher drunken driver laws have all placed greater secular restrictions on drinking through the 1980s. Declines in students' use of marijuana and even greater declines in the use of cocaine have occurred across this period largely associated with growing perceptions of risk involved with use of illicit drugs and increasing personal disapproval (Bachman, Johnston, and O'Malley 1990; Bachman, Johnston, O'Malley, and Humphrey 1988; Johnston, O'Malley, and Bachman 1991). Thus the moderating effect of religiosity should be greater in the more open period of the early 1980s as compared with the secularly more restrictive end of the decade.

Third, if there are differences among students in what they perceive as the socially acceptable secular norm with some perceiving (regardless of accuracy) a more permissive campus environment than others do, then religiosity ought to have a stronger negative effect on use among students who believe the general campus norm is relatively permissive (i.e., perceive less secular constraint) in contrast with students who perceive peers in general as more moderate (i.e. perceive greater secular control).

METHODS

Samples

The data are drawn from three surveys conducted at an undergraduate liberal arts institution of higher education in New York State with a predominantly Northeastern and upper-middle class student body. Almost all of the approximately 1900 students who attend this institution are between the ages of 17 and 23 and most reside in campus housing including residence halls, small cooperative houses, and fraternities.

The surveys were conducted in 1982, 1989 and 1991 during the latter part of the academic year. Each survey concentrated heavily on questions about alcohol and other drug use in relation to well-being on campus. In 1982 all students were surveyed (N of respondents = 1514, 86% response). In 1989, due to more limited research staff time and resources, a stratified (by gender and class year) random sample of half of the student body was selected and surveyed (N of respondents = 584, 61% response). In 1991, all students were again surveyed, but follow-up of nonresponders was more limited (N of respondents = 926, 50% response).

All questionnaires were completed and returned anonymously for each survey. The variation in response rates essentially reflects the difference in time and resources that could be devoted to follow-up procedures for obtaining responses from initial non-responders. In each survey, however, the large resulting sample was highly representative of the student population in terms of demographic characteristics provided by administrative sources such as class year, academic interests, and type of housing. Moreover, in a detailed analysis of data from 1982 (the year when resources permitted the greatest amount of follow-up and thus the highest response rate), no significant differences were found when alcohol and drug use responses for students who initially responded were compared (controlling for gender) with the responses of those who returned the survey only after being contacted and prompted by repeated follow-up requests. Thus it appears unlikely that non-responders reflect a significantly distinct group of students with regard to the interests of this study or that differences in response rates will distort the time comparisons presented here (i.e., the first 50% and 61% of the 1982 data that responded—response rates that would have been equal to the 1991 and 1989 responses—show essentially the same pattern of use as all 86% that responded that year).

In controlling for and comparing historical periods, the relatively recent data from the 1989 and 1991 surveys are combined and contrasted with the earlier 1982 data. The 1989 and 1991 data do not significantly differ on the measures examined in this study and thus combining these data provided a sample size (N = 1510 for 1989-91) matching that of the earlier and distinct time period (N = 1514 for 1982).

Comparing early 1980s data with late 1980s/1990s provides a particularly useful contrast of historical periods in the examination of contextual effects. In addition to the national trends toward more conservative drug policies and actual reductions in illicit drug use from the early to late 1980s as previously noted, significant state and local changes had occurred altering the context of drug use for the college population under study. At the time of the 1982 survey the minimum legal drinking age in New York State had been historically constant for almost half a century. (From the early 1930s until the end of 1982 a minimum age of 18 was the mandate.) In December of 1982 (the middle of the academic year following the first survey) the minimum age was raised to 19. In 1985 the legal age was further raised to 21. Thus the age 21 requirement had been in effect in New York for more than three years at the time of the second survey in this study. Furthermore, spurred by growing concerns about campus drug abuse and by increasing legal risks of institutional liability nationwide, administrators on this campus in the mid-1980s began introducing more controls on campus alcohol consumption (e.g., banning kegs and other large alcohol sources and mandating provisions for alternative refreshments at campus parties, monitoring fraternity alcohol use more closely, and increasing disciplinary responses to abuse).

The percentage of females in the 1989-91 sample (56%) is notably higher than that of the 1982 sample (44%). This difference reflects two factors. First, the institution admitted more women during the latter 1980s in order to create a closer gender balance in the student body. Second, women generally tended to respond more readily to these surveys on health related behaviors. In the later years when less follow-up was possible, a higher response rate from women emerged. Nevertheless, gender is controlled throughout this study with separate analyses for men and women. Thus, the differing proportions of women between time periods does not distort the basic analysis of alcohol and other drug use with religiosity.

Protestants in the sample accounted for 40/38 percent (1982/1989-91),[3] 33/36 percent were Roman Catholic, 17/10 percent were Jewish, 7/11 percent claimed no religious tradition, and 4/6 percent indicated a faith other than Judaism or Christianity. For the purposes of this study about the effects of Judeo-Christian religiosity, the small percentage of respondents who reported a faith outside the Judeo-Christian tradition were excluded from subsequent analyses.

Measures

Religiosity

Respondents were asked to indicate the strength of their religious faith commitment by choosing from a continuum of response categories provided on the questionnaire.[4] Students who responded with "I have no religious faith," "It is not important to me at all," or "It is not very strong" were initially classified as low religiosity for the purposes of this study. Alternatively, respondents who indicated that "It is fairly strong," "It is very strong," or "It is the most important aspect of my life" were subsequently categorized as high religiosity. High religiosity based on this dichotomy was noted by 43 percent of males and 48 percent of females in 1982 and by 30 percent of males and 39 percent of females in 1989-91.

Drug Use

Alcohol consumption. Individuals who indicated that they "never drink alcoholic beverages" comprised a very small percentage (less than 5% of males and females in each time period).[5] Thus, the virtually ubiquitous prevalence of alcohol consumption does not provide a usefully discriminating measure for the purposes of this study. The frequency of alcohol consumption was measured in each survey year by asking students to report how many days during the past two weeks beer, wine, or liquor were consumed. Frequent drinkers were defined as those students drinking on more than seven of the last 14 days. A quantity measure asked respondents to provide a specific estimate of the total number of drinks consumed during the past two weeks (a "drink" was defined in the survey as a beer, a glass of wine, a shot of liquor, or a mixed drink). Heavy drinkers were defined as those students who drank more than two drinks each day on average across the two week period (i.e., reported having more than 28 drinks in the last 14 days). Because the basic patterns of alcohol use and religiosity were essentially the same for the measure of frequent use and the measure of heavy consumption, these measures were combined in the tabular data of this report as a single measure including frequent or heavy drinkers.

Other drug use. The frequencies of marijuana use, cocaine use, and hallucinogen use were measured in the surveys by asking students to report approximately how often they used each drug type with the following seven response categories: 1) never, 2) tried it one or two times, 3) a few times a year, 4) once or twice a month, 5) about once a week, 6) several times a week, and 7) almost every day. If a respondent had never used the drug or had only ever tried it once or twice, she or he was considered a nonuser. Thus respondents who indicated that they used the drug a few times a year or more often were classified as users.

Drug Attitudes and Perceived Norms

Personal attitudes concerning alcohol use were assessed by asking the respondent to select the statement that best represented his or her own opinion about drinking from the following: (1) "drinking is never a good thing to do", (2) "drinking is all right but a student should never get 'smashed'," (3) "an occasional 'drunk' is okay as long as it doesn't interfere with academics or other responsibilities", (4) "an occasional 'drunk' is okay even if it does occasionally interfere with academics or other responsibilities", and (5) a frequent 'drunk' is okay if that's what the individual wants to do." While students expressed personal attitudes ranging across each of these possibilities, the majority of men and women chose item three (the relatively moderate position) as most reflective of their own attitude in each time period with smaller percentages taking a more conservative or more permissive stance.

Respondents were also asked to give their perception of what they thought was the most common attitude of students in general on campus using the same five response categories provided for personal attitudes. A range of perceived campus norms was also expressed with only about one-third accurately perceiving the norm to be the relatively moderate response (item three). Almost all other students perceived the norm to be more permissive than was actually the case (response items four or five) in both time periods. For both personal attitudes and perceived campus norms, respondents' positions were subsequently dichotomized for initial analyses into a conservative to moderate category (response items one through three) and a highly permissive category (response items four and five). The distinction in this dichotomy is between attitudes and perceived norms that involve at least some degree of responsibility in avoiding negative consequences and some moderation in frequency/amount of consumption versus those attitudes and perceived norms involving very little restraint.

Each survey respondent was also asked to indicate his or her own personal attitude and then his or her perception of the most common attitude on campus concerning the use of marijuana, cocaine, and hallucinogens. (Hallucinogens were not included in the questionnaire items on attitudes and perceptions in 1989-91, however). Response choices were: (1) "it is never a good thing to use", (2) "occasional use is okay as long as it doesn't interfere with academic or other responsibilities", (3) "occasional use is okay even if it does interfere with academic or other responsibilities", or (4) "frequent use is okay if that's what the individual wants to do." Most students chose item on or two as their own position, but, similar to the pattern with alcohol, often perceived the campus as more permissive. For initial analyses presented here these responses on both attitudes and perceptions were also dichotomized between indications of at least a degree of moderation (response items one and two) and essentially unrestricted positions (items three and four).

FINDINGS

The data on drug use and attitudes inclusive of all sample years are presented first by the categories of low and high religiosity for male and female students (Table 1). Here the basic claim that high religiosity is associated with less use and more moderate attitudes is given clear empirical support. Use of all drugs is lower among highly religious students and significantly so in each instance except cocaine use among males where the percentage difference in quite small.[6] Likewise, unrestricted attitudes are less prevalent in the high religiosity category in every instance with significant differences in the expected direction for alcohol attitudes among females and for marijuana attitudes across both genders. Examination of the gamma coefficients reveals that the association between religiosity and use/attitudes is notably higher for females than for males in most instances. Comparing the gamma associations across drug categories, there is no consistent pattern in moving from the less restricted and more pervasive drugs to the more tightly controlled and less popular drugs.

Table 1.   Drug Use and Unrestricted Attitude Percentages Among
Male and Female College Students (1982-1991) By Religiosity

	Males			Females		
	Religiosity			Religiosity		
	Low	High	(Gamma)	Low	High	(Gamma)
Use						
Frequent/Heavy Alcohol	54.6	45.7***	(−.18)	29.1	23.0**	(−.16)
Marijuana	69.0	64.3*	(−.10)	59.6	45.5***	(−.28)
Cocaine	31.2	28.3	(−.07)	20.5	13.4***	(−.25)
Hallucinogens	23.9	18.4*	(−.16)	14.2	6.9***	(−.38)
Unrestricted Attitude[a]						
Alcohol	23.3	20.4	(−.09)	13.9	9.6*	(−.20)
Marijuana	23.0	16.3*	(−.21)	12.3	7.1**	(−.30)
Cocaine	12.4	11.5	(−.04)	5.7	4.2	(−.15)
N of cases	884	525		806	607	

Notes: * Percentage is significantly lower than "low religiosity" comparison at p < .05;
      ** p < .01;
      *** p < .001.
      [a] Data on hallucinogen attitudes were not consistently collected in each survey wave and, therefore, do not appear in this table.

Table 2 provides evidence of a change from a more permissive to a more moderate student environment as drug use, attitudes, and perceptions of the norm are broken down by time period (1982 compared to 1989-91) for each gender. For alcohol, marijuana, and cocaine there was a decrease in student use, unrestricted attitudes, and perceptions of an unrestricted norm with a significant decline in each instance except males' perception of the alcohol norm. There was no evidence of any significant difference over time for hallucinogen use. (No available data in 1989-91 precludes any time comparisons of hallucinogen attitudes and perceived norms).

Given the differences between the early 1980's and the end of the decade in actual and perceived norms of use among sampled students (Table 2), we can pursue the question of the effect of religiosity during periods of greater and lesser general acceptability. In Table 3 drug use and attitudes are again presented for low and high religiosity by gender, but also distinguished by time periods. A clearly more marked association is revealed between religiosity and use/attitudes for males during 1982 in comparison with the 1989-91 data for alcohol, marijuana, and cocaine. This finding would be expected from the hypothesis about greater normative ambiguity permitting greater religious influence. That is, while high religiosity among males is significantly associated with less drug use or unrestricted attitudes in every comparison in 1982, only marijuana use/attitudes differed significantly for religiosity categories among

Table 2.   Percentages for Drug Use, Unrestricted Attitudes, and Perceived
Unrestricted Norms Among Male and Female College Students By Time Period

	Males		Females	
	1982	*1989-1991*	*1982*	*1989-1991*
Use				
Frequent/Heavy Alcohol	53.8	47.7*	35.3	19.6***
Marijuana	76.9	54.9***	65.1	45.1***
Cocaine	42.2	14.0***	30.4	8.1***
Hallucinogens	23.1	20.6	11.7	11.1
Unrestricted Attitude				
Alcohol	26.6	16.8***	16.1	8.8***
Marijuana	24.4	15.7***	14.8	6.9***
Cocaine	19.0	3.6***	10.9	.8***
Hallucinogens	7.5	No Data	3.4	No Data
Perceive Unrestricted Norm				
Alcohol	55.5	53.2	75.7	70.9*
Marijuana	58.2	48.7***	72.2	58.6***
Cocaine	41.1	13.1***	47.5	24.9***
Hallucinogens	19.8	No Data	21.9	No Data
N of cases	799	623	626	804

Note: * Percentage is significantly lower in 1989-1991 when compared to 1982 at p $<$ .05;
      ** p $<$ .01;
      *** p $<$ .001

males in 1989-91. In contrast, among females the original association between
religiosity and drug use/attitudes found in Table 1 is essentially replicated in
each time period. Thus, the degree of general permissiveness as reflected in
the different time periods does not appear to have altered the original
religiosity-drug relationship for females.

Next, the question concerning the effect of a relatively permissive perceived
norm was explored. Table 4 breaks down the data on the relationship between
drug use/attitudes and religiosity by the student's own perception of the norm
for each specific drug while controlling for gender and time period. For males
the perception of the norm is also a factor in the drug-religiosity relationship
as predicted. Among men who perceived the particular drug norm to be
relatively unrestricted in the 1982 sample (the year of more permissive actual
norms), drug use and unrestricted attitudes were significantly lower in the high
religiosity group as compared with males indicating low religiosity in seven
of the eight comparisons. Only two of the eight comparisons were significant
in the expected direction, however, for males who perceived a relatively
moderate peer norm in that year. Looking at the gamma correlations for males
in 1982, one finds negative associations between drug use/attitudes and

Table 3. Drug Use and Unrestricted Attitude Percentages Among Male and Female College Students in 1982-1991 by Religiosity

	Males				Females			
	1982 Religiosity		1989-1991 Religiosity		1982 Religiosity		1989-1991 Religiosity	
	Low	High	Low	High	Low	High	Low	High
Use								
Frequent/Heavy Alcohol	59.7	46.8***	49.4	43.6	40.3	30.2**	21.6	16.3***
	(−.25)	[a]	(−.12)		(−.22)		(−.17)	
Marijuana	80.2	72.6**	57.3	49.4*	70.5	59.0**	52.3	33.0***
	(−.21)		(−.16)		(−.25)		(−.38)	
Cocaine	46.3	36.6**	14.4	13.3	36.8	22.7***	9.7	5.5*
	(−.20)		(−.05)		(−.33)		(−.29)	
Hallucinogens	25.3	19.7*	22.5	16.3	14.5	7.7**	14.0	6.2***
	(−.16)		(−.20)		(−.34)		(−.42)	
Unrestricted Attitude								
Alcohol	29.6	22.8*	16.8	16.2	18.3	13.6	10.8	5.7**
	(−.18)		(−.02)		(−.17)		(−.33)	
Marijuana	28.3	19.1**	17.7	11.4*	18.4	9.5***	8.4	4.9*
	(−.25)		(−.25)		(−.36)		(−.28)	
Cocaine	21.9	15.3*	3.0	4.9	12.7	8.4*	—[b]	
	(−.22)		(−.24)		(−.23)		—[b]	
Hallucinogens	9.5	4.7*	No Data		3.2	3.4	No Data	
	(−.36)				(−.04)			
N of cases	448	340	436	185	323	296	483	311

Notes: [a] Gamma correlations for use/attitudes by religiosity are in parentheses.

[b] Observed cases are too small for reliable estimates (expected cell frequencies < 5).

* Percentage is significantly lower than "low religiosity" comparison at $p < .05$; ** $p < .01$; *** $p < .001$.

religiosity in every instance, but the negative association is greater for those men perceiving an unrestricted norm in seven of the eight item comparisons.

Again the contingent effect of perceptions is revealed for male students in the 1989-91 data (the time when actual norms were more restrictive) in Table 4. Among males who perceived an unrestricted norm, drug measure percentages were significantly lower in the higher religiosity category in four of the six items where data were available for comparison. All six gamma correlations were negative as predicted. In contrast, there were no significant differences in drug use or attitudes between high and low religiosity men perceiving a moderated norm. Only two of the five gamma correlations computed were negative here. Thus the negative drug-religiosity association virtually disappears for men who were sampled in a relatively restrictive time

Table 4.   Drug Use and Unrestricted Attitude Percentages
Among Male and Female College Students in 1982 and 1989-1991
by Religiosity Controlling for Drug-Specific Perceived Norm

	Males							
	Perceived Drug Norm—1982 Sample				Perceived Drug Norm—1989-1991 Sample			
	Unrestricted Religiosity		Moderated Religiosity		Unrestricted Religiosity		Moderated Religiosity	
	Low	High	Low	High	Low	High	Low	High
Use								
Frequent/Heavy	54.2	37.0***	71.3	57.6**	45.1	35.0*	55.1	56.8
Alcohol	(−.34)[a]		(−.29)		(−.21)		(−.03)	
Marijuana	78.2	68.5*	85.0	78.7	55.7	45.2*	59.0	54.1
	(−.25)		(−.21)		(−.21)		(−.10)	
Cocaine	49.4	41.4	45.1	36.4*	31.7	13.8*	13.0	13.7
	(−.16)		(−.18)		(−.49)		(−.03)	
Hallucinogens	25.7	6.4**	26.8	23.8	No Data		No Data	
	(−.67)		(−.08)					
Unrestricted Attitude								
Alcohol	31.8	22.3*	28.5	22.5	22.7	17.6	11.1	13.7
	(−.24)		(−.16)		(−.16)		(.12)	
Marijuana	36.6	23.4**	17.2	13.3	26.1	12.5**	10.9	10.2
	(−.31)		(−.15)		(−.42)		(−.03)	
Cocaine	36.0	24.8*	11.3	8.9	13.3	12.5	—[b]	
	(−.26)		(−.13)		(−.04)		—[b]	
Hallucinogens	25.6	5.6**	5.7	4.3	No Data		No Data	
	(−.71)		(−.15)					
	Females							
Use								
Frequent/Heavy	35.0	28.7	56.2	36.2**	21.2	11.8**	19.7	25.6
Alcohol	(−.14)		(−.38)		(−.33)		(−.17)	
Marijuana	70.4	59.0**	73.0	61.2	53.9	33.9***	51.4	32.3***
	(−.25)		(−.26)		(−.39)		(−.38)	
Cocaine	35.9	27.9	38.5	16.7***	10.7	3.2*	8.9	5.9
	(−.18)		(−.52)		(−.56)		(−.22)	
Hallucinogens	—[b]		14.3	8.1*	No Data		No Data	
			(−.31)					
Unrestricted Attitude								
Alcohol	18.6	14.6	16.4	8.8	14.0	7.0**	—[b]	
	(−.14)		(−.34)		(−.37)			
Marijuana	21.9	12.1**	11.8	3.0*	10.1	6.0	5.3	3.1
	(−.34)		(−.62)		(−.28)		(−.27)	
Cocaine	20.4	15.2	7.0	2.9	—[b]		—[b]	
	(−.18)		(−.43)					
Hallucinogens	—[b]		2.2	2.5	No Data		No Data	
			(.07)					

Notes: N of cases within a column category varies according to the specific drug involved.
[a] Gamma correlations for use/attitudes by religiosity are in parentheses.
[b] Observed cases are too small for reliable estimates (i.e., expected cell frequencies < 5).
* Percentage is significantly lower than "low religiosity" comparison at p < .05; ** p < .01; *** p < .001

period and who simultaneously perceive student norms for the particular drug to be relatively moderate.

For women the association between drug measures and religiosity is not specifically affected by controlling for perceived norms in Table 4. A negative gamma association persists in 21 of the 23 drug item comparisons across religiosity levels with significant percentage differences in ten instances. In general, significant associations between drug use/attitudes and religiosity are equally as common overall among the females who perceive a moderated norm as among those who perceive an unrestricted norm for the various drugs examined. In 1982 negative associations were actually more pronounced in the moderated perception group as compared to those with unrestricted perceptions, while in 1989-91 negative associations are somewhat less evident in the moderated versus unrestricted perception categories.

In a final analysis multivariate regression was employed in order to supplement the contingency table tests of the stability, relative strength, and significance of relationships between drug use and religiosity thus far observed. A comprehensive measure of drug use orientation that incorporated the full range of variation in drug use items and a scaled measure of religiosity were used with this analytic technique. An index measuring personal drug use orientation was created as the dependent variable using the full range of variation provided in the original coding of each item concerning alcohol, marijuana, and cocaine. (Hallucinogen data were excluded here because most items were only included in the 1982 time period.) Thus seven items comprised the index: The number of drinking days (0 to 14) and the number of drinks (0 to 100) in the last two weeks, the frequency of marijuana and cocaine use (each originally coded from one for never to seven for almost every day), and one's personal attitude on alcohol, marijuana, and cocaine (each originally coded from one for most restrictive to four or five for most permissive). The index score for each respondent was computed by adding together the standardized z-scores for each of these seven items.[7] Scores on this index of personal drug use orientation ranged from -8.61 (most restrictive) to 17.30 (least restrained) with a mean of -.01 and a standard deviation of 5.15.

Religiosity was entered as an independent variable in the OLS regression with the following coding on strength of faith: 1 (no faith or not important at all), 2 (not very strong), 3 (fairly strong), 4 (very strong), and 5 (most important aspect of one's life). Religious tradition was controlled in the regression analysis by entering dummy variables for Protestant, Catholic and Jewish faiths as independent variables (using those respondents with no tradition as the comparison category). Class year (coded one through four) was also entered in the regression as an independent control variable because strength of faith frequently declines over college years and drug use often increases with age and greater access to drugs among older students in the campus environment.

This regression analysis was conducted with eight sub-samples in order to test the specific effect of religiosity on personal drug orientation for men and women separately during each time period and for those who did and did not perceive normative restraint among their campus peers. In order to categorize students according to their perception about the peer norms for drug use in general, the original scores on the separate items for students' perceptions of the most common campus attitudes about alcohol, marijuana, and cocaine (scored one to four or five) were added together. In the previous analyses response scores of one to three on perceptions of the alcohol norm and response scores of one or two on perceptions of the marijuana and cocaine norms were selected as indications that the individual perceived some moderation or restraint in the environment in the use of the drug. Thus a total score of seven or less was used to determine the category of students perceiving a moderated drug norm overall in the environment with totals greater than seven indicating a perceived lack of restraint.

Table 5 presents the standardized (beta) coefficients from all of the sub-sample regressions of personal drug use orientation on religiosity controlling for faith tradition and class year. In all eight instances (both male and female students in 1982 and in 1989-91 who perceive unrestricted and moderated drug norms on campus) the coefficient is negative indicating greater religiosity being associated with a less permissive personal orientation to drug use. Substantial variation in the strength and significance of religiosity's effect is clearly apparent, however. For males religiosity has a statistically significant impact

Table 5. Standardized (Beta) Regression Coefficients for Religiosity[a] Predicting Personal Drug Use Orientation[b] of College Students in 1982 and 1989-1991 by Gender and Perceived Drug Norm.[c]

	1982 Perceived Drug Norm		1989-1991 Perceived Drug Norm	
	Unrestricted	Moderated	Unrestricted	Moderated
Males	−.22***	−.13	−.12	−.05
(N)	(472)	(188)	(338)	(227)
Females	−.26***	−.30*	−.15*	−.30***
(N)	(473)	(74)	(518)	(178)

Notes: [a] Religiosity scale is scored from 1 (no importance or no faith) to 5 (most important aspect of one's life).
   [b] This index is a total of z-scores for seven items on personal attitudes and frequency/amount of alcohol, marijuana, and cocaine use. Index scores range from −8.61 to +17.30 with higher scores representing more permissive personal attitudes and greater drug use during the academic year.
   [c] The regression equations producing these coefficients for religiosity also include class year and religious tradition (Protestant, Catholic, Jewish entered as dummy variables compared to no faith) as independent control variables.
   * Coefficient is significant at $p < .05$; ** $p < .01$; *** $p < .001$

in the circumstance where the actual (1982) and perceived norms are least restrictive (beta = −.22). In the other three conditions the effect of religiosity for males fails to reach significance. Particularly notable here is the finding that among those men whose more conservative time period of 1989-91 is reinforced by their perceptions of a moderated norm, the predicted effect of religiosity is negligible (beta = -.05). In contrast, the restraining effect of religiosity on women's personal orientations to drug use is statistically significant in every instance. Some variation in the strength of effect exists in the data for women with the effect for those perceiving an unrestricted environment in 1989-91 dipping notably below that of the other three coefficients. There is clearly no pattern here indicating a reduced effect of religiosity for women in the more conservative time period or when the social norm is perceived to be more moderate, however.

DISCUSSION

This study stands within a long tradition of debate and empirical inquiry about the effect of religiosity upon deviance. The focus here is specifically on the controlling or moderating influence of Judeo-Christian religiosity in relation to various forms of drug use. It has been theoretically proposed in prior research that religiosity's potentially constraining effect must be contextualized by the degree of normative ambiguity about the particular behavior that generally prevails in a community. If strong secular controls exist and are reinforced in general community standards, it is argued that the additional restraining contribution of a highly religious orientation upon drug use is likely to be negligible. If, instead, normative ambiguity about a behavior is characteristic of the environment, then religiosity should play an important part as a distinct influence moderating one's attitudes and behaviors. Prior empirical testing of this claim has been quite limited, however, by a dearth of data in which the normative context is examined as it varies over time, for different types of drug use, and across the minds of individuals involved in terms of their perceptions of the norm. Thus, this study employed data from a college student population that allowed for the controlled testing of religiosity's influence in these varying contexts.

Only qualified empirical support emerged for the contextual nature of religious influences. For females in these data, the more basic hypothesis of religiosity's moderating effect on drug attitudes and use was generally supported across types of drugs, time periods, and perceived contexts. Various contextual analyses provided no consistent result altering or refining this basic association. Thus, it appears from these data that for young women in this collegiate environment, religiosity has an important and independent impact on alcohol and other drug use, regardless of secular norms.[8]

Males were similar to female students in that the type of drug (some being more culturally acceptable than others) did not consistently differentiate religiosity's extent of influence. The findings were otherwise quite different for males, however. Although the initial bivariate associations between religiosity and the various drug measures for men in these data were weak, the associations became more prominent when specified under certain contextual conditions. Religiosity was a stronger deterrent during the time period of greater use and more permissive norms (1982) in comparison with the more restricted period (1989-91). Similarly, the male student's personal perception of the norm was an important contingency. The negative association between religiosity and drug use items was more pronounced overall for the men who perceived greater permissiveness or normative ambiguity than for the men who thought that a more moderate norm prevailed in each time period. Ultimately, the strength of religiosity's deterrent effect on drug use for men in the relatively unrestricted time period who simultaneously perceived a permissive environment approximated the effect found among women in general (based on regression analyses). In contrast, religiosity's effect virtually disappeared for men on campus in the time period when greater normative restraint was actually the case if they also perceived that moderation was the norm.

This gender difference in the findings suggesting an independent religious influence on drug use for women and a contextual religious influence for men is unprecedented in empirical research. The lack of similar findings elsewhere may, in part, reflect the paucity of research that adequately introduces actual and perceived variation in norms for otherwise comparable samples. It may also reflect the fact that where gender has been controlled in previous studies, it has been introduced simply as an independent variable along with religiosity predicting drug use/attitudes in a multivariate analysis. Thus, while any spurious religiosity-drug correlation caused by a gender difference in religiosity levels and a simultaneous gender difference in drug use may have been removed, the potentially *interactive* impact of gender across normative contexts in specifying the religiosity-drug association has been ignored. It is also certainly conceivable that any modest differences in negative associations between religion and drug use previously found in differing normative contexts may be the product of large contextual differences for one gender and little difference for the other gender. Of course any generalizations from the present study must be made with caution, given the sampling frame of this particular college population with a northeastern constituency where liberal mainline Protestants, Roman Catholics, and Jews are predominant. Future research will need to conduct separate analyses for men and women or isolate the potential interaction of gender and normative context when examining the influence of religiosity on drug use and possibly on other forms of deviant behavior, and do so in populations where evangelical or fundamentalist Protestants are more common.

There is no clear theoretical perspective at present that can fully explain the gender difference in the empirical findings of this study. It may be that women are guided by their religiosity in a more fundamental way or across broader social situations. Men, in contrast, even with a strong religious commitment may tend to compartmentalize or limit the role of their faith in their secular lives when other normative frameworks are provided by society.

Another more complex approach might explain the gender difference here as a specific product of student culture and personality types. For example, one might consider the nature of conformity or nonconformity in personality dispositions and relate it to drug use and religiosity in a campus context. In times when the norms about drug use on campus are fairly clear and restrictive and when these norms are perceived as such, a nonconformist personality type may be a significant factor raising the likelihood of a student's drug use. If being highly religious for males tends to reflect a nonconformist disposition especially in the student culture of a particular campus, then competing forces may be at work for these highly religious males in times of strong normative secular prohibitions. These collegiate men's religiosity per se may be acting as a deterrent to drug use, but their relatively unconventional dispositions may be simultaneously pulling them in the opposite direction. The net result could make them no different in drug use and attitudes than less religious college males. That is, less religious males may not have the moral deterrent of a particular faith, but being more conventional, may tend to more closely follow the social norms opposing drug use.

When norms about drugs are relatively ambiguous leaving no clear and singular social expectation to follow, however, an individual's conformist or nonconformist disposition may be less relevant to drug use tendencies. Thus, the nonconventional aspect of highly religious college males would not necessarily run counter to the moderating force of their religious beliefs on drug use in this circumstance. That is, a greater negative association between religiosity and drug use for males would be predicted under more ambiguous secular conditions (where conformity dispositions would not be a mitigating factor) and smaller associations would be expected when there was more uniform secular opposition (where unconventional dispositions could compromise the religious deterrence).

In contrast, strong religiosity for female college students may not be associated with conformity or nonconformity overall. That is, traditional religiosity may be linked with a conformist disposition among women in society in general, but this may be counteracted among collegiate women by the dominant religion's lesser popularity in many college contexts. Thus a direct religious influence moderating drug use may predominate for collegiate women regardless of the contexts where conformity dispositions may be more or less salient. While this complex theoretical proposition does provide a possible explanation, it must be acknowledged as mere speculation at this point, of course. More theoretical work as well as empirical research will be needed along these lines.

Finally, there is another branch of theory and research on the contextual nature of religiosity's influence on deviant behavior that deserves comment here. The particular orientation gives attention to the contextual normative conditions of the independent variable, that being the pervasiveness or strength of religiosity in the population under study (Stark 1984; Stark, Kent, and Doyle 1982). It has been argued that a religion's deterrent effect will most likely occur or occur more strongly in contexts where the religion itself is widely affirmed in community standards.[9] Given the notable drop in religiosity in these data between time periods (recall 43% of males were highly religious in 1982 as compared with 30% in 1989-91), this perspective might be suggested as an alternative explanation for the more predominant negative association found between religiosity and drug items for men in 1982 as compared with 1989-91 (Table 3). This interpretation still leaves the gender specific nature of the findings unexplained, however, given similar decline in female religiosity in this collegiate environment over time (48% in 1982 to 39% in 1989-91). Also, this interpretation is ultimately less satisfactory as an explanation of the pattern for men than the argument suggesting that the lack of consistent secular norms permits a specific religious influence. That is because the contextual role of secular norms on the effect of religiosity was clearly demonstrated *within* each time period (when aggregate religiosity levels were constant) by distinguishing between males who perceived secular normative restraint and those who perceived an unrestrained environment (Table 4). Nevertheless, future studies may be able to combine various student populations in a research design that can simultaneously distinguish variation in the actual and perceived secular drug norms and the aggregate levels of religiosity for an even more thorough investigation of contextual effects.

In conclusion, the implications of these findings for practitioners in student culture are worth noting. Campus administrators, counselors, and health educators on college campuses overwhelmingly point to substance abuse as the number one problem on most campuses nationwide. They, along with researchers on the topic, also note that most traditional programs to combat the problem through health education and legal restrictions have produced very little positive effect with peer influence being the predominant factor in student drug use. Amidst such peer influence in the peer intensive environment of a residential college campus, this research points, nonetheless, to the positive effect of religious commitment in moderating alcohol and other drug use. This beneficial effect was persistent across all circumstances for women. It was also at least notable for men in the most problematic peer environmental contexts where actual and perceived norms encouraged greatest usage. Thus administrators and health care professionals as well as religious leaders working on college campuses should recognize the potential contribution of students' religious involvements in controlling the problem of abuse. Just as student involvement in extracurricular activities is often encouraged by college personnel to promote student retention and well-being in general, secular and religious professionals concerned with student development have an additional reason to acknowledge and facilitate the development of student religious life. Obviously, the extent of such facilitation must vary considerably depending upon the role of the college professional and the status of the institution (e.g., public, private, or religiously sponsored). Still it is important for student development professionals to appreciate the support, albeit possibly more limited for men, that religious identification brings to students in resisting drug abuse in the peer environment.

ACKNOWLEDGMENTS

This paper is a revised version of a paper presented at the Annual Meetings of the Society for the Scientific Study of Religion and the Religious Research Association, Pittsburgh, Pennsylvania, November 8-10, 1991. The author gratefully acknowledges the financial assistance of the Christopher D. Smithers Foundation in this research and thanks Alan Berkowitz for his collaboration in the collection of these data. The author may be contacted at the following address: Department of Anthropology and Sociology, Hobart and William Smith Colleges, Geneva, NY 14456.

NOTES

1.   This claim has not received uniform support in research on adolescents, however. Cochran (1988), for example, found a more predominant general impact of religion inhibiting both secular and ascetic deviance among junior and senior high school students.

2.   Cochran's (1991) research on secondary school students did not find significant variation in the negative effect of religiosity on the use of different drugs, however.

3.   Among Protestants there were Episcopalians (38%), Presbyterians (17%), Methodists (9%), United Church of Christ (8%), Baptists (2%), Unitarian-Universalists (3%), small sects (2%) and Protestants claiming no specific tradition (14%) with no significant differences between time periods. Some researchers have called for detailed analyses of denominational backgrounds when studying alcohol and other drug use, pointing to the great diversity within Protestantism as an important factor to consider in addition to any comparisons among major faith groups (Cochran, Beeghley, and Bock 1988; Jensen and Erickson 1979; Nelsen and Rooney 1982). Yet Cochran and Akers' (1989) research on adolescents has suggested that the added predictive value of models specifying the degree of denominational proscriptiveness in examining the effects of religiosity on antiascetic behavior is only slight over the parsimonious claim of a direct effect of religiosity alone. In more detailed analyses on the data of the present study (not provided here), most Protestants in the sample showed a high degree of similarity on drinking and other drug use, and thus, they are not distinguished in this report. The similarity among Protestants on most measures reflects in all likelihood the fact that almost all Protestant respondents in this sample come from mainline traditions and mostly from the relatively liberal Northeast.

4.   Although this measure of religious commitment is based on a single-item indicator, Gorsuch and McFarland's (1972) research with college students provides evidence that single-item measures

of the self-rated importance of religion may be equally satisfactory to a multiple-item counterpart.

5.   This high prevalence rate of alcohol use is similar to that of students at most schools in the Northeast (Wechsler and McFadden 1979).

6.   In more detailed analyses not presented here, the interaction effects of religiosity by specific faiths were not significant in predicting drug use or attitudes. Thus, the data presented here combine all Judeo-Christian traditions in the sample in focusing on the general effect of religiosity rather than on religiosity within particular traditions.

7.   All of the inter-item correlations were positive and statistically significant ($p < .01$) in this sample and the item-total score correlations ranged from .66 to .76, thus indicating sufficient inter-item reliability for this index.

8.   Humphrey, Leslie, and Brittain's (1989) study of southern university women also found that their measure of religious observance is negatively and significantly associated with alcohol and marijuana use. They characterize this finding as evidence of a "contingency model," by arguing that it has occurred in a relatively secular college environment where normative ambiguity about alcohol and other drugs typically exists. Yet they might have found the same negative association between religious observance and drug use for women in a less secular college campus or in the same campus settings at a time when there was less ambiguity about drug norms if they had such comparative data available. Thus their "contingency model" for women is simply an assumption with no comparative empirical support. Their findings equally can be interpreted as another example of a consistent bivariate relationship for collegiate women regardless of context.

9.   Tittle and Welch's (1983) study makes the opposite claim, however, that the salience of individual religiosity is greatest in more secular contexts and Cochran and Akers' (1989) research found no compelling evidence in support of either position.

REFERENCES

Bachman, J.G., L.D. Johnston and P.M. O'Malley. 1990. "Explaining the Recent Decline in Cocaine Use among Young Adults: Further Evidence That Perceived Risks and Disapproval Lead to Reduced Drug Use." *Journal of Health and Social Behavior* 31:173-184.

Bachman, J.G., L.D. Johnston, P.M. O'Malley, and R.H. Humphrey. 1988. "Explaining the Recent Decline in Marijuana Use: Differentiating the Effects of Perceived Risks, Disapproval, and General Lifestyle Factors." *Journal of Health and Social Behavior* 29:92-112.

Berkowitz, A.D. and H.W. Perkins. 1987. "Recent Research on Gender Differences in Collegiate Alcohol Use." *Journal of American College Health* 36:123-129.

Burkett, S.R. and M. White. 1974. "Hellfire and Delinquency: Another Look." *Journal for the Scientific Study of Religion* 13:455-462.

Cochran, J.K. 1988. "The Effect of Religiosity on Secular and Ascetic Deviance." *Sociological Focus* 21:293-306.

————. 1991. "The Effects of Religiosity on Adolescent Self-Reported Frequency of Drug and Alcohol Use." *Journal of Drug Issues* 22:91-104.

Cochran, J.K. and R.L. Akers. 1989. "Beyond Hellfire: An Exploration of the Variable Effects of Religiosity on Adolescent Marijuana and Alcohol Use." *Journal of Research in Crime and Delinquency* 26(3):198-225.

Cochran, J.K., L. Beegley, and E.W. Bock. 1988. "Religiosity and Alcohol Behavior: An Exploration of Reference Group Theory." *Sociological Forum* 3:256-276.

Elifson, K.W., D.M. Petersen, and C. K. Hadaway. 1983. "Religiosity and Delinquency." *Criminology* 21:505-527.

Engs, R.C. and D.J. Hanson. 1989. "Gender Differences in Drinking Patterns and Problems among College Students: A Review of the Literature." *Journal of Alcohol and Drug Education* 35:36-47.

Gorsuch, R.L. and S.G. McFarland. 1972. "Single vs. Multiple-Item Scales for Measuring Religious Values." *Journal for the Scientific Study of Religion* 11:53-64.

Hadaway, C.K., K.W. Elifson, and D.M. Petersen. 1984. "Religious Involvement and Drug Use Among Urban Adolescents." *Journal for the Scientific Study of Religion* 23:109-128.

Hanson, D.J. and R.C. Engs. 1987. "Religion and Collegiate Drinking Problems Over Time." *Psychology: A Quarterly Journal of Human Behavior* 24:10-12.

Hirschi, T. and R. Stark. 1969. "Hellfire and Delinquency." *Social Problems* 17:202-213.

Humphrey, J.A., P. Leslie, and J. Brittain. 1988. "Religious Participation, Southern University Women, and Abstinence." *Deviant Behavior* 10:145-155.

Jensen, G.F. and M.L. Erickson. 1979. "The Religious Factor and Delinquency: Another Look at the Hellfire Hypothesis." Pp. 157-177 in *The Religious Dimension*, edited by R. Wuthnow. New York: Academic Press.

Johnston, L.D., P.M. O'Malley, and J.G. Bachman. 1991. *Drug Use Among American High School Seniors, College Students and Young Adults, 1975-1990. Volume II: College Students and Young Adults*. Rockville, Maryland: National Institute on Drug Abuse.

Knudten, R.D. and M.S. Knudten. 1971. "Juvenile Delinquency, Crime, and Religion." *Review of Religious Research* 12:130-152.

Linden, R. and R. Currie. 1977. "Religiosity and Drug Use: A Test of Social Control Theory." *Canadian Journal of Criminology and Corrections* 19:346-355.

Nelsen, H.M. and J.F. Rooney. 1982. "Fire and Brimstone, Lager and Pot: Religious Involvement and Substance Use." *Sociological Analysis* 43:247-256.

Peek, C.W., G.D. Lowe, and L.S. Williams. 1991. "Gender and God's Word: Another Look at Religious Fundamentalism and Sexism." *Social Forces* 69:1205-1221.

Perkins, H.W. 1985. "Religious Traditions, Parents, and Peers as Determinants of Alcohol and Drug Use among College Students." *Review of Religious Research* 27:15-31.

_____. 1987. "Parental Religion and Alcohol Use Problems as Intergenerational Predictors of Problem Drinking among College Youth." *Journal for the Scientific Study of Religion* 26:340-357.

_____. 1991. "Confronting Misperceptions of Peer Drug Use Norms among College Students: An Alternative Approach for Alcohol and Other Drug Education Programs." Pp. 111-29 in *Peer Prevention Program Resource Manual*, edited by V. Roper. Fort Worth, TX: The Higher Education Leaders/Peers Network, Texas Christian University.

_____. 1992. "Gender Patterns in Consequences of Collegiate Alcohol Abuse: A Ten Year Study of Trends in an Undergraduate Population." *Journal of Studies on Alcohol* 53:458-462.

Perkins, H.W. and A.D. Berkowitz. 1986. "Perceiving the Community Norms of Alcohol Use among Students: Some Research Implications for Campus Alcohol Education Programming." *International Journal of the Addictions* 21:961-976.

Rohrbaugh, J. and R. Jessor. 1975. "Religiosity in Youth: A Personal Control Against Deviant Behavior." *Journal of Personality* 43:136-155.

Stark, R. 1984. "Religion and Conformity: Reaffirming a Sociology of Religion." *Sociological Analysis* 45:273-282.

Stark, R., L. Kent, and D.P. Doyle. 1982. "Religion and Delinquency: The Ecology of a 'Lost' Relationship." *Journal of Research in Crime and Delinquency* 19:4-24.

Tittle, C.R. and M.R. Welch. 1983. "Religiosity and Deviance: Toward a Contingency Theory of Constraining Effects." *Social Forces* 61:653-682.

Turner, C.J. and R.J. Willis. 1979. "The Relationship Between Self-Reported Religiosity and Drug Use by College Students." *Journal of Drug Education* 9:67-78.

Wechsler, H. and M. McFadden. 1979. "Drinking among College Students in New England: Extent, Social Correlates and Consequences of Alcohol Use." *Journal of Studies on Alcohol* 49:969-996.

THE MORALIZATION OF ILLNESS:
THE ROLE OF MORAL VALUES IN THE RELIGIOUS FRAMING OF THE AIDS PROBLEM

John K. Cochran, Jeffry A. Will, and Jill Garner

ABSTRACT

This study explores the role of religion in shaping public support for various AIDS prevention policies. We examine the effects, both direct and indirect, of religious affiliation and religiosity on attitudes toward four intrusive and four non-intrusive AIDS prevention policies. We exploit the unique advantages for such a study provided by the 1988 NORC General Social Survey which included topical modules on both religion and AIDS. Results from logistic regression analyses reveal that the effects of religion are largely indirect, mediated through entrenched political and social-moral values including political conservativism and attitudes toward homosexuality. However, direct inverse effects of religious affiliation (i.e., conservative Protestantism) and religiosity are observed for support of government efforts to promote safe-sex messages. These findings are then discussed as they relate to efforts at educating the public about the spread of AIDS and the likely effectiveness of various AIDS prevention strategies.

Research in the Social Scientific Study of Religion, Volume 6, pages 209-228.
Copyright © 1994 by JAI Press Inc.
All rights of reproduction in any form reserved.
ISBN: 1-55938-762-9

The development of Acquired Immune Deficiency Syndrome (AIDS) as a major issue facing American society represents more than just a medical, biophysiological phenomenon. Indeed, understanding and addressing the moral, legal, social, and political issues and consequences surrounding the disease present challenges which are themselves only marginally less salient than AIDS as a medical phenomenon. Yet, a review of the extant social scientific literature reveals only a limited number of empirical attempts to understand these "other" issues surrounding AIDS and the societal responses which have followed its development.

This lack of social research, of course, is quite understandable. The limited resources which have been made available over the past fifteen years for the study of AIDS have been rightly concentrated on epidemiological and medical research. Nevertheless, the social sciences need to enter into this research arena with greater vigor. To adequately address the medical issues surrounding AIDS and the public health policies to eventually follow, it is essential to understand how the society at large views the phenomenon, those who suffer from the disease, and what potential prevention strategies the public will support.

To be sure, a number of social scientists have been busy examining these issues, particularly those concerning the spread and prevention of the disease (Beckley and Chalfant 1992; Bell 1991); the social construction of AIDS (Albert 1989); public opinion, knowledge, and attitudes about AIDS, its modes of transmission, and its victims (Johnson 1987; Larsen, Serra, and Long 1990; Singer, Rogers, and Corcoran 1987; Stipp and Kerr 1989); and public support for AIDS policies (Greeley 1991; Jelen and Wilcox 1992; Le Poire, Sigelman, Sigelman, and Kenski 1990; Price and Hsu 1992). However, this emerging body of research is quite immature and incomplete.

An attempt to more fully understand public perceptions and concerns about AIDS that guides this research. Specifically, we are interested in the role of religion in shaping the public's support for or against various AIDS prevention policies which have been suggested over the years. As Johnson (1987, p. 106) acknowledges, the challenge before us regarding AIDS prevention is one of "balancing the concerns of people not to expose themselves and their children to the risks of AIDS with the civil rights of AIDS victims." This is a social, moral, legal, and political issue upon which religion is likely to be a salient influence.

RELIGION AND AIDS[1]

The religious framing of the AIDS problem (i.e., the religious meaning and social construction of AIDS) is, like AIDS itself, an emergent phenomenon, which, we argue, is based in large measure upon more entrenched beliefs and values related to sexual promiscuity, homosexuality, drug use, and the appropriate role of government in matters of public health. The arrival of AIDS to the United States in the early 1980s followed several decades of major social changes in the composition of the family, the role of women in society, the extension of rights to minorities, including homosexuals, and the relaxation of sexual norms (Jakobi 1990, p.89). These changes have been virulently opposed by some groups, especially conservatives and fundamentalist Christians who comprise the New Christian Right and the Moral Majority. Religious conservatives have seen these changes as an anathema to their traditional religious values and they have mobilized themselves into political interest groups (Tamney and Johnson 1983; Johnson and Tamney 1984; 1985).

According to Marsden (1977), Christian fundamentalists are characterized by their militant opposition to modernist or liberal theologies, especially "humanistic" theologies, which they see as man-centered rather than God-centered (Jakobi 1990). These fundamentalist beliefs lead their members to dichotomize reality such that God and Satan are the only ultimately significant forces acting on the world (Marsden 1977). The fundamentalist response to the AIDS epidemic is also interpreted under this absolutist (rather than relativistic) dichotomy:

Fundamentalists profess that it is of secondary importance whether one believes that AIDS is caused by HIV or some other pathological agent. Its *cause* is sin; its *origin*, directly or indirectly, is God. AIDS will stop when people once again follow Christian teachings, remaining chaste until marriage and monogamous within marriage, and refraining from illegal drug use (Jakobi 1990, p. 91).

The religious leadership of the fundamentalists have issued a litany of statements suggesting that AIDS is divine retribution for sin, particularly homosexuality (Greeley 1991; Jakobi 1990; Le Poire et al. 1990; Rothenberg and Newport 1984). Similarly, in a *Los Angeles Times* survey, approximately 30 percent of the respondents agreed with a statement that AIDS is a punishment God has given homosexuals for the way they live (AIDS: the Public Facts 1986 cited in Le Poire et al. 1990). Finally, Jakobi (1990) cites several examples of this reductionist etiology issued by fundamentalist physicians. These doctors have "openly proposed a direct relationship between sinful behavior — at both the individual and the national level — and AIDS. While acknowledging the viral etiology of AIDS espoused by the scientific establishment, these physicians attribute the virus's 'birth' to a supernatural, teleological response to sinful practices" (Jakobi 1990, p. 90). This link has been especially established for homosexuality and AIDS, where fundamentalists have invoked Romans 1:26-28 ("... men [committed] shameful acts with men receiving in their own person the due penalty of their error... [and] God gave them up to a base mind and to improper conduct.").

An interesting moral question for fundamentalists involves the problem of "innocent victims" (e.g., persons infected with the AIDS virus through "irty" blood transfusions, children born to HIV+ mothers, etc.). However, the Old Testament offers a solution; here suffering is frequently interpreted as divine punishment for sin. The punishment may be visited upon specific sinners or, more generally, upon a society whose members have sinned (corporate sin). So, for fundamentalists, innocent victims of AIDS are being punished for the sins of others.

In sum, traditional religious values associated with the religious right lay a foundation for disapproval of sexual promiscuity, homosexuality, and drug use, which, in turn, generates antipathy toward persons with AIDS and a willingness to restrict their rights in the name of public health (Le Poire et al. 1990, p. 248). For Jakobi (1990, p. 89) the linking of AIDS to moral values among fundamentalist Christians has created a powerful political coalition which has had a salient impact on the government's response (or lack or response) to the AIDS epidemic during the 12-year reign of the Reagan and Bush administrations.

Traditionally, the role of the government in response to epidemics is to protect the public health without unduly trampling upon the civil liberties of the citizenry, particularly those infected. The way a society chooses to respond to an epidemic often reveals its deepest moral values (Brandt 1988). For those who accept the scientific consensus that the origins of AIDS are biophysiological (i.e., HIV), personal opinions about sexuality and substance use are less relevant in framing the AIDS problem. Such persons are more likely to define AIDS as simply a serious public health issue and tend to support efforts aimed at helping AIDS patients. With regard to AIDS prevention strategies, these persons are more likely to support efforts at educating the public about the transmission of the disease, the teaching of safe-sex practices such as condom use, and clean needle exchange programs.

Highly religious persons, especially those affiliated with evangelical and fundamentalist Protestant faiths, on the other hand, are more likely to attribute the high prevalence and spread of AIDS to what they perceive as ungodly lifestyles (Stevens and Muskin 1987). For these persons, AIDS is the product of moral decay; it is a disease that serves as both a divine warning and punishment for both individual and societal sins (Jakobi 1990, p. 89; see also, Altman 1986 and Beauchamp 1986). By defining AIDS as divine punishment, members of the religious right are less inclined to give aid and comfort to AIDS patients, are vehemently opposed to the teaching of safe sex and to clean needle exchange programs (which they see as a tolerant and permissive response to sinful lifestyle choices), and are more likely to support efforts aimed at preventing the further spread of AIDS by identifying and isolating AIDS victims. The issue before us now is to examine the relationship between religious influences and reactions to the AIDS crises.

DATA AND METHODS

The data for this study come from the 1988 National Opinion Research Center (NORC) General Social Survey (GSS), an independently drawn full probability sample of 1481 English-speaking persons eighteen years of age or older, living in non-institutional arrangements within the United States. The 1988 GSS is appropriate for our purposes for several reasons. First, it represents perhaps the finest collection of survey items regarding public support for prospective AIDS policy initiatives in the United States. Second, the GSS in general, and the 1988 GSS in particular has long been highly regarded for its items on religion and religiosity. In fact, AIDS and religion constitute two topical modules unique to the 1988 GSS. To the best of our knowledge, no other nationally representative data on AIDS and religion of this quality exist. One drawback to these data, however, is the use of a split-half methodology in which the sample was split on the AIDS items. One portion of the sample (n=718) responded to one set of items, while the other portion (n = 763) responded to a different set of items. This technique and other sources of case deletions, resulted in analyses based on greatly reduced sample sizes (584 ≤ n ≤ 665).

Measures

Dependent Variables

For the purpose of this study, eight items regarding public support for various AIDS prevention initiatives were employed as dependent variables. Respondents were asked whether they "support or oppose the following measures to deal with AIDS:" (1) make victims with AIDS eligible for disability benefits (AIDSFARE), (2) have the government pay all of the health care costs of AIDS patients (AIDSHLTH), (3) require the teaching of safe sex practices, such as the use of condoms, in sex education courses in public schools (AIDSSXED), (4) develop a government information program to promote safe sex practices, such as the use of condoms (AIDSADS), (5) permit insurance companies to test applicants for the AIDS virus (AIDSINSR), (6) conduct mandatory testing for the AIDS virus before marriage (AIDSMAR), (7) require people with the AIDS virus to wear identification tags that look like those carried by people with allergies or diabetes (AIDSIDS), and (8) prohibit students with the AIDS virus from attending public school (AIDSSCH). Each item was coded to make a dichotomous distinction between support for and opposition to these prospective policies (0 = oppose; 1 = support). Respondents who gave no reply or who had no opinion were deleted from the analyses.

In our judgment the first four items represent rather innocuous, relatively non-intrusive policy initiatives aimed at helping persons with AIDS, while the last four items appear to be much more invasive, violative of civil liberties, and highly intrusive into the lives of private citizens; their primary purpose appears to be one of identifying persons with AIDS and isolating them from the general population. Hence, we label the first four policies as "non-intrusive" and the last four as "intrusive" (cf., Jelen and Wilcox 1992).

Religion Variables

We also take advantage of the wide variety of religion items available in the 1988 GSS. In fact, we employ twenty separate indicators of religious behavior and beliefs in addition to a measure of religious affiliation. Due to invariation on several of the AIDS items among Jewish respondents, we restricted our analyses to the non-affiliates, Catholics, and Protestants. We follow Smith's (1990) scheme for classifying the Protestant faiths into liberal (typically Epsicopalians and Presbyterians), moderate (typically Lutherans and Methodists), and conservative categories (typically Southern Baptist, fundamentalists, and evangelicals). However, we employ the label "conservative Protestant" over his use of the "fundamentalist" tag due to the fact that many of the Protestant denominations and sects identified as "fundamentalist" by Smith are not fundamentalists (see Kellstedt and Smidt, 1991). Thus, religious affiliation is coded into the following dummy variables: no affiliation, Catholic, liberal Protestant, and moderate Protestant (conservative Protestants serve as the omitted category in the multivariate analyses presented later). Members of other religions (i.e, Islam, Hinduism, etc.) have been excluded from the analysis.

The twenty religiosity items include: (1) frequency of attendance at religious services (ATTEND: 0 = never, 8 = several times a week), (2) strength of religious identification (RELITEN: 0 = somewhat or not very strong, 1 = strong), (3) belief in life after death (POSTLIFE: 0 = do not believe, 1 = believe), (4) frequency of personal prayer (PRAY: 0 = never, 5 = several times a day), (5) feeling of closeness to God (NEARGOD: 0 = does not believe in God, 4 = extremely close), (6) Biblical literalness (BIBLE: 0 = non-literal interpretation, 1 = literal interpretation), (7) membership in church organizations (MEMCHRCH: 0 = no, 1 = yes), (8) participation in church activities other than religious services (CHRCHACT: 0 = no, 1 = yes), (9) frequency of viewing religious programming on television (TVRELIG: 0 = none, 1 = one hour per week or more), (10) belief in God (GOD: 0 = does not believe, 5 = "I know God exists and I have no doubts about it"), (11) "Born again" experience (REBORN: 0 = no, 1 = yes), (12) proselytizing activity - encourage others to accept Christ as the savior (SAVESOUL: 0 = no, 1 = yes), (13) frequency of reading the Bible (READWORD: 0 = never, 5 = several times a day), (14) belief that "those who violate God's rules must be punished" (PUNSIN: 0 = strongly disagree, 3 = strongly agree), (15) belief that immorality corrupts society (ROTAPPLE: 0 = strongly disagree, 3 = strongly agree), (16) salience of the Bible in one's life (DECBIBLE: 0 = not very important, 4 = very important), (17) salience of religious teachings in one's life (DECCHRCH: 0 = not very important, 4 = very important), (18) salience of regular attendance at religious services (GOCHRCH: 0 = not very important, 4 = very important), (19) salience of a belief in God (BELIEVE: 0 = not very important, 4 = very important), and (20) importance of following church doctrine (FOLLOW: 0 = not very important, 4 = very important). Each of these twenty items have been coded such that higher values indicate greater/ stronger religiosity. More detailed information on these items (i.e., question wording, response categories and metrics, and their marginal distributions) are available upon request from the lead author, but they also appear in Davis and Smith (1988).

For each of these twenty religion items, responses of "don't know" and "no answer" as well as missing data were recoded at the value of the appropriate measure of central tendency given the variable's level of measurement (i.e., mode, median, mean). This value was rounded to the nearest whole number. Then all twenty items were transformed into standardized variables (i.e., Z-scores). A principal components factor analysis on these twenty standardized items produced a single factor solution based upon a scree test of those factors with eigenvalues greater than 1.00 (eigenvalues = 7.52, 1.53, 1.25 and 1.21). These twenty standardized items were then placed into a single, additive global religiosity scale (alpha = .91).

In addition to this global religiosity scale, five additional religiosity sub-scales were also created from these standardized items: (1) a six-item religious salience scale (SALIENCE = RELITEN + DECBIBLE + DECCHRCH + GOCHRCH + BELIEVE + FOLLOW — alpha = .85), (2) a five-item other worldliness scale (OTHWORLD = POSTLIFE + NEARGOD + BIBLE + GOD + REBORN — alpha = .69), (3) a two-item concern with sin scale (SIN = PUNSIN + ROTAPPLE — alpha = .43), (4) a three-item public religiosity scale (PUBREL = ATTEND + MEMCHRCH + CHRCHACT — alpha = .75), and (5) a four-item private religiosity scale (PVTREL = PRAY + TVRELIG + SAVESOUL + READWORD — alpha = .70). In the analyses which follow we examine the effects of the global religiosity scale, the five religiosity sub-scales, and religious affiliation on each of the eight AIDS items.

Intervening and Control Variables

To adequately examine the relationship between religion and support for AIDS policies, it is necessary to control for the effects of other potential correlates and mediating influences. With regard to the latter, mediating influences, we contend that most of the effect of religiosity is mediated through more entrenched political and socio-moral values. AIDS is too recent a phenomenon for religion to have established a clear stand on policy issues toward it. Instead, the religious meaning of AIDS is currently under construction and is probably being interpreted through preexisting constructs, such as political conservativism, support for national spending on health care, and symbolic values associated with homosexuality and drug use (two of the dominant modes of transmission for the spread of the AIDS virus).

The GSS provides items which measure each of these symbolic and instrumental mechanisms for interpreting AIDS policies. The first of these is political ideology, a seven-point index ranging from 1 = extremely liberal to 7 = extremely conservative. We argue that highly religious persons hold politically conservative views and that conservatives are more likely to oppose the non-intrusive AIDS policy initiatives and to support the more intrusive policies. The second intervening variable is support for national health spending, a trichotomous, ordinal measure (1 = spending too much, 2 = spending about the right amount, and 3 = spending too little). Our reasoning here is two-fold. First, if the above argument holds, then, as conservatives, highly religious persons would oppose expanding "big government," including increased spending for public health. Second, we believe that highly religious persons would tend to frame the AIDS problem as the product of immoral behavior rather than as a public health issue. Hence, they would oppose AIDS related policies consistent with a definition of AIDS as a public health issue (i.e., the "non-intrusive" policies), but might support those policies designed to control problem populations (i.e., the "intrusive" policies).

Because IV drug use and homosexuality are two of the dominant modes of transmission of the AIDS virus, and because each of these activities is morally proscribed by many mainstream American religions, a measure of each is also included in our analyses. Respondents were asked to report their attitude concerning the morality or wrongfulness of consensual sexual relations between adults of the same sex. This item is measured on a four-point ordinal scale (1 = homosexuality is not wrong at all, 4 = homosexuality is always wrong). Given that the GSS does not include any items dealing directly with IV drug use, we employ a proxy or surrogate measure to tap, albeit crudely, into the respondents' attitudes toward drug use. Respondents were asked, "Do you think the use of marijuana should be made legal or not?" (0 = yes, 1 = no). Here we suggest that highly religious persons will oppose non-intrusive policies but will support the more intrusive policies because of their tendency to frame the AIDS issue as a consequence of immoral activities which have historically been opposed by mainstream American religions (Cochran 1991; Cochran and Beeghley 1992).

Again, each of these four variables (i.e., political conservativism, support for national spending on health care, opposition toward homosexuality, and opposition toward drug use) are treated as mediators through which the religious meaning and social construction of AIDS is developing. Because two

of the primary modes for the transmission of the AIDS virus are considered
to be immoral (i.e., homosexuality and IV drug use), it is unlikely that religious
persons, who tend to be opposed to such activities, are likely to generate
significant empathy for AIDS victims. As such, they are more likely to support
efforts at identifing and isolating persons with AIDS than with helping them.
This religiously-based "victim-derrogation," justified by a belief in a "just
world" (Cialdini, Kenrick, and Hoering 1976; Gruman and Sloan 1983; Rubin
and Peplau 1975; Sorrentino and Hardy 1974), is expressed through opposition
toward increases in national health spending. Finally, this set of beliefs, that
is, intolerance for homosexuality, support for the continued criminalization
of drug use, and opposition toward government spending on health care, are
part-and-parcel with a social, moral, political, and economic conservativism
which, in turn, is likely to be opposed to spending tax dollars on assisting
persons with the AIDS virus but, rather, is interested in controlling such
persons.

Lastly, a wide variety of sociodemographic variables are employed as
statistical controls. They include respondents' age (coded continuously in
years), race (0 = black, 1 = white, others were deleted from the analysis), gender
(0 = female, 1 = male), marital status (0 = married, divorced, separated, or
widowed, 1 = single, never married), southern and urban residency status (0
= non-southern, 1 = southern; 0 = non-SMSA, 1 = SMSA), level of education
(coded continuously in years attained), occupational prestige (Hodge-Siegle-
Rossi scores), and yearly income (a twenty-point ordinal scale based upon the
GSS income categories).

Method of Analysis

Because our analysis employs dichotomous dependent variables and both
continuous and categorical exogenous variables, the statistical procedure used
is logistic regression. As is well known, logit models permit analyses of the
relative effects of a set of explanatory variables on a non-interval scale
dependent variable in a manner analogous to standard linear regression,
without violating the conditions necessary to satisfy least squares estimation
while also meeting the need for the appropriate sigmoid functional form
(Hanushek and Jackson 1977).

FINDINGS

Table 1 presents the level of support for each of the eight prospective AIDS
policy initiatives by categories of religious affiliation. Generally, the public
tends to give clear approval for AIDS testing of couples applying for marriage
licenses (AIDSMAR) and for promoting safe sex practices both in sex

education courses in public schools and on public service announcements on television (AIDSSXED and AIDSADS). Banning children with AIDS from attending public schools (AIDSSCH) is widely opposed, though one of four adult Americans do support such an initiative. Likewise, there is little public support for having the government pay the medical costs of AIDS patients (AIDSHLTH), though one of three adult Americans support this policy. Very mixed support is observed for policies which would permit insurance companies to test applicants for the AIDS virus (AIDSINSR), require AIDS patients to wear medical identification tags (AIDSIDS), or make AIDS patients eligible for disability benefits (AIDSFARE).

The most striking feature of these findings is the high consistency in the level of support across religious affiliations for the eight policies. The only significant differences are: (1) the low level of support among liberal Protestants (typically Episcopalians and Presbyterians) for having the government pay the medical costs of AIDS patients (AIDSHLTH) or for prohibiting children with AIDS from attending public schools (AIDSSCH), (2) the relatively lower level of support among conservative Protestants (typically Southern Baptists, fundamentalists, and evangelicals) for governmentally sponsored promotions for safe sex, such as the use of condoms, in sex education courses in public schools (AIDSSXED) and on public service announcements on television (AIDSADS), (3) the slightly lower level of support among the non-affiliated for mandatory AIDS testing as an element of marriage licensing (AIDSMAR); however, the non-affiliated are somewhat more likely to support policies making AIDS patients eligible for disability benefits (AIDSFARE) and which would require the government to pay the health care costs of AIDS patients (AIDSHLTH), and (4) the relatively higher level of support from both conservative and moderate Protestants (the latter are typically Lutherans and Methodists) for the required use of medical identification tags by AIDS patients (AIDSIDS) and to prohibit children with the AIDS virus from attending public schools (AIDSSCH). Other than these small exceptions, the level of AIDS policy support is quite similar across religious affiliations. Whether these small differences are due to religious affiliation or to differences in religiosity is an issue we take up below.

While Table 1 reveals few differences in levels of support for the eight AIDS policies across categories of religious affiliation, the bivariate correlations reported in Table 2 suggest that religiosity, whether measured as a single, global scale or as dimensional specific sub-scales, is significantly associated with support/opposition for these policies. All six religiosity scales are significantly and inversely related to the two policies which promote safe sex practices (i.e., AIDSSXED and AIDSADS). As religiosity increases, support for government sponsored promotions for safe sex decreases. On the other hand, highly religious persons are significantly more likely to support the intrusive policies; in fact, twenty of the twenty-four coefficients are significant and positive.

Table 1. Support for Various AIDS Policies by Religious Affiliation (1988 GSS).

	No Affil.	Catholic	Lib. Prot.	Mod. Prot.	Cons. Prot.	Total
			% Support			
Non-Intrusive Policies:						
AIDSFARE	72.9	62.0	60.2	56.0	56.7	59.8
$X^2 = 5.17$						
AIDSHLTH	44.7	37.2	17.0	33.3	31.8	32.2
$X^2 = 15.21*$						
AIDSSXED	93.0	91.7	90.0	89.9	79.8	86.9
$X^2 = 17.88*$						
AIDSADS	95.9	91.2	92.5	91.1	73.9	85.1
$X^2 = 38.68*$						
Intrustive Policies:						
AIDSINSR	56.8	59.1	63.9	61.0	64.9	62.1
$X^2 = 2.01$						
AIDSMAR	73.2	89.9	87.5	89.9	91.8	88.8
$X^2 = 16.50*$						
AIDSIDS	54.7	53.5	60.6	72.4	73.0	64.3
$X^2 = 21.26*$						
AIDSSCH	29.6	23.5	18.6	31.6	32.9	27.5
$X^2 = 8.92$						
N (range)	44-57	159-181	93-107	75-79	211-248	584-665

Notes: * $p < .05$ with 4 degrees of freedom.
Due to the split-halves methodology of the GSS on the AIDS items and to missing information, the Ns for each cell vary. Hence, we report the range of the Ns for each religious affiliation.

Key: AIDSFARE: Make victims with AIDS eligible for disability benefits.
AIDSHLTH: Have the government pay all of the health care costs of AIDS patients.
AIDSSXED: Require the teaching of safe sex practices, such as the use of condoms, in sex education courses in public schools.
AIDSADS: Develop a government information program to promote safe sex practices, such as the use of condoms.
AIDSINSR: Permit insurance companies to test applicants for the AIDS virus.
AIDSMAR: Conduct mandatory testing for the AIDS virus before marriage.
AIDSIDS: Require people with the AIDS virus to wear identification tags that look like those carried by people with allergies or diabetes.
AIDSSCH: Prohibit students with the AIDS virus from attending public school.

We speculate that these findings indicate that different methods of framing the AIDS problem are employed by highly religious and highly secular persons. The religious are more likely to define AIDS as the product of an "immoral lifestyle choice" (i.e., homosexuality or IV drug use) that should be contained and controlled before it reaches the general population. Hence the highly religious are more inclined to support policies which others argue are violative

Table 2. Zero-Order Correlations—Religion and Support for Various AIDS Policies (1988 General Social Survey)

	Non-Intrusive Policies				Intrusive Policies				Mediator Variables			
	AIDSFARE	AIDSHLTH	AIDSSXED	AIDSADS	AIDSINSR	AIDSMAR	AIDSIDS	AIDSSCH	Political Views	Health $	Gay Sin	Antidrug
Religiosity	-.069*	.019	-.290*	-.317*	.101*	.185*	.120*	.113*	.206*	.029	.199*	.231*
Salience	-.045	.052	-.278*	.252*	.097*	.188*	.117*	.096*	.194*	.018	.288*	.232*
Other World	-.063	.019	-.176*	-.220*	.027	.168*	.124*	.078*	.159*	.033	.238*	.191*
Sin	-.038	.013	-.219*	-.254*	.135*	.203*	.174*	.152*	.135*	-.052*	.285*	.156*
Public Relations	-.111*	-.093*	-.252*	-.278*	.100*	.033	-.033	.057	.151*	-.010	.103*	.175*
Private Relations	-.028	.045	-.234*	-.285*	.077*	.143*	.104*	.098*	.161*	.001	.202*	.149*
Political Views	-.157*	-.163*	-.194*	-.219*	.156*	.149*	.019	.091*	—	-.102*	.160*	.166*
National. Health $	.112*	.084*	.145*	.155*	-.100*	-.025	.054	-.063	—	—	-.006	.047
Gay Sin	-.200*	-.090*	-.110*	-.160*	.127*	.235*	.162*	.167*	—	—	—	.154*
Antidrug	-.068	-.065	-.081	-.113*	.056	.229*	.077	.080	—	—	—	—

Note: * p < .05

220

of civil liberties (i.e., the intrusive policies); they are significantly more likely to support government efforts to identify AIDS victims and isolate them from the general population. The weakly religious and more secular segments of the general population, on the other hand, are more prone to adopt a public health perspective on the AIDS problem. From their perspective, AIDS victims should be supported and AIDS prevention policies should be limited to those which help AIDS patients but do not intrude upon the privacy of individual citizens.

Also reported in Table 2 are the zero-order correlations between the four intervening or mediator variables (i.e., political ideology, support for increased national spending on public health, and intolerance toward homosexuality and drug use) and both the six religiosity scales (i.e., the global religiosity scale and the five sub-scales: religious salience, other worldliness, preoccupation with sin, public religiosity, and private religiosity) and the eight AIDS policy measures. All six religiosity scales are positively and significantly related to both political ideology and intolerance toward both homosexuality and drug use. Thus the highly religious also tend to be politically conservative and opposed to immorality. Religiosity is relatively unrelated to support for increased spending for public health (only one sub-scale, public religiosity, is significantly related to the health spending item).

Holding a conservative political ideology is inversely related to support for the non-intrusive AIDS policies as is intolerance for immoral activities, especially homosexuality. Both are positively correlated with support for the more intrusive policies. Those who support increased spending for public health support the non-intrusive AIDS policies and, with the exception of opposing efforts which would permit insurance companies to test applicants for the AIDS virus (AIDSINSR), support for increased public health spending is unrelated to the more intrusive AIDS policy initiatives.

Table 3 presents the findings of the logistic regression analyses which examine the effects of religious affiliation, the global religiosity scale, the four mediator variables,[2] and the nine sociodemographic control variables on each of the eight AIDS policy variables. Given the daunting number of coefficients presented in this table, we restrict our discussion to the effects of the religion and mediator variables. It is evident from these findings that the religion variables are for the most part unrelated to support for these policies. There are few significant differences observed across the categories of religious affiliation in the level of support for or opposition to these eight AIDS policies. However, conservative Protestants are significantly less likely than many of the other religious affiliation classifications to support either the teaching of safe sex practices in sex education courses in the public schools (AIDSSCH) or government sponsored public service announcements promoting safe sex practices (AIDSADS). Likewise, the global religiosity scale is significantly related only to these same two policies. Highly religious persons are opposed

Table 3. Logistic Regression—The Effects of Religion on Support for Various AIDS Policies (1988 General Social Survey)

| | Non-Intrusive Policies | | | | | | | | Intrusive Policies | | | | | | | |
| | AIDSFARE | | AIDSHLTH | | AIDSSXED | | AIDSADS | | AIDSINSR | | AIDSMAR | | AIDSIDS | | AIDSSCH | |
Religion	b	B	b	B	b	B	b	B	b	B	b	B	b	B	b	B
Variables:																
No Affil.	.833	.124	.858	.129	−.254	−.039	.175	.026	.305	.044	−.049	−.008	−.624	−.096	.929*	.135*
Catholic	.335	.082	.495	.123	.741*	.182*	.970*	.239*	−.007	−.002	.370	.091	−.725*	−.178*	−.097	−.024
Lib. Prot.	.316	.063	−.369	−.075	.535	.106	1.185*	.248*	.080	.016	.054	.011	−.310	−.061	−.154	−.031
Mod. Prot.	−.048	−.009	.383	.071	.665*	.119*	1.351*	.249*	−.026	−.005	.157	.028	.125	.023	.334	.062
Religiosity	.004	.024	.004	.025	−.086*	−.576*	−.068*	−.442*	.010	.063	.014	.094	.007	.049	.012	.077
Controls:																
Age	−.006	−.058	.011	.111	−.020*	−.192*	−.023*	−.232*	−.014*	.136*	−.002	−.018	−.004	−.036	−.010	−.098
Race	−1.129*	−.207*	−1.237*	−.235*	−1.417*	−.256*	−1.292*	−.244*	−.838*	.162*	−.121	−.022	.382	.068	−.016	−.003
Gender	−.640*	−.176*	−.014	−.004	−.497	−.136*	.107	.029	.169	.046	−.684*	−.187*	.157	.043	−.133	−.036
Single	−.318	−.071	.293	.066	−1.147*	−.253*	−.047	−.010	−.103	−.023	−.310	−.068	.509	.112	.000	.000
Southern	−.308	−.081	−.308	−.080	.217	.057	.377	.097	.428*	.112*	.152	.040	.273	.072	.221	.058
Urban	−.049	−.012	.133	.032	−.515	−.121*	.055	.013	.027	.006	−.746	−.176	−.150	−.036	.121	.029
Education	−.017	−.028	−.053	−.089	.109*	.179*	.083	.134	−.027	−.045	−.106	−.176	−.085*	−.140*	−.150*	−.249*
Occ. Prestige	−.001	−.011	.002	.014	−.022	−.166*	−.004	−.031	−.006	−.047	−.009	−.069	−.016*	−.120*	.006	.046
Income	.031	.072	−.051*	−.117*	.057	.132	−.008	−.018	−.012	−.028	.047	.109	.002	.005	.017	.040
Pol. Views	−.131	−.098	−.233*	−.171*	−.222*	−.165*	−.346*	−.253*	.163*	.120*	.246*	.183*	−.023	−.017	.118	.085
Nat. Health $	.366*	.116*	.336	.099	.745*	.238*	.744*	.217*	−.312	−.091	−.227	−.073	.121	.039	−.184	−.054
Gay Sin	−.507*	−.250*	.285*	.132*	−.218	−.106	−.438	−.204	.210	.096	.426*	.205*	.257*	.127*	.431*	.202*
AntiDrug	−.095	−.017	−.030	−.006	−.006	−.001	.131	.025	−.162	−.030	1.080*	.197*	.258	.048	.179	.034
Constant:	3.284		−.215		3.709		3.890		−.713		1.881		.979		−.936	
−2 Log L: (intercept)	824.730		733.862		515.981		501.971		780.507		463.936		817.387		689.043	
(model)	746.294		655.997		390.438		365.105		722.789		387.028		752.283		640.921	
Model X² (w/18 d.f.)	78.436*		77.865*		125.544*		136.865*		57.718*		76.908*		65.104*		48.122*	
Sommers' D	.409		.436		.664		.706		.379		.545		.393		.359	
N	612		584		665		617		588		663		627		586	

Note: * p < .05

222

Table 4. Logistic Regression—The Effects of the Religiosity Sub-Scales on Support for Various AIDS Policies (1988 NORC-GSS)

	Non-Intrusive Policies										Intrusive Policies					
	AIDSFARE		AIDSHLTH		AIDSSXED		AIDSADS		AIDSINSR		AIDSMAR		AIDSIDS		AIDSSCH	
	b	B	b	B	b	B	b	B	b	B	b	B	b	B	b	B
Variables:																
Religion:																
No Afil.	.936*	.139*	.901*	.135*	-.058	-.009	.360	.054*	.296	.043	.098	.014	-.611	-.094	.915	.133
Catholic	.546*	.133*	.523	.130	.952*	.234*	1.096*	.271*	-.080	-.020	.657	.161	-.617*	-.151*	-.137	-.034
Lib. Prot.	.405	.080	-.364*	-.074	.609	.120	1.192*	.249*	.031	.006	.237	.047	-.264	-.052	-.182	-.037
Mod. Prot.	.072	.013	.338	.063	.756	.135	1.428*	.263*	-.056	-.010	-.185	.033	.166	.030	.303	.056
Salience	.070*	.178*	.056	.136	-.108*	-.275*	.000	.001	.020	.050	.062	.158	.003	.008	-.003	-.006
Other World	-.040	-.076	.034	.060	.079	.150	.029	.051	-.073	-.132	-.008	-.016	.005	.009	-.035	-.063
Sin	.095	.084	-.020	-.017	-.141	-.125	-.205	-.178	.094	.082	.239*	.212*	.136*	.121*	.142	.125
Public Rel.	-.172*	-.238*	-.153*	-.204*	-.211*	-.290*	-.230*	-.304*	.079	.105	-.207*	-.285*	-.061	-.084	.048	.064
Private Rel.	.055	.087	.017	.027	-.091	-.141	-.080	-.129	.002	.004	.056	.088	.028	.043	.013	.021
Controls:																
Age	-.007	-.070	.012	.120	-.017	-.166	-.022*	-.219*	.012	.120	-.004	-.041	-.004	-.042	-.012	-.114
Race	-1.147*	-.210*	-1.235*	-.234*	-1.429*	-.258*	-1.369*	-.259*	.848*	.164*	-.264	-.047	.351	.062	-.013	-.002
Gender	-.694*	-.191*	-.009	-.002	-.509	-.140	.142	.039	.138	.037	-.766*	-.210*	.122	.034	-.163	-.044
Single	-.385	-.086	.257	.058	-1.243*	-.274*	-.035	-.008	-.083	-.019	-.451	-.099	.494	.109	.003	.001
Southern	-.377	-.099	-.311	-.081	.095	.025	.384	.099	.452*	.118*	.045	.012	.240	.063	.237	.062
Urban	-.104	-.025	.084	.020	-.508	-.119	-.056	-.013	.041	.010	-.823*	-.194*	-.198	-.047	.144	.034
Education	.011	.018	-.032	-.053	.142*	.234*	.109	.177	-.032	-.053	-.077	-.126	-.074	-.123	-.153*	-.254*
Occ. Prestige	.002	.012	.003	.025	-.021	-.154	-.003	-.022	-.008	-.060	-.007	-.051	-.014	-.107	.006	.045
Income	.039	.090	-.053*	-.122*	.057	.132	-.009	-.019	-.008	-.019	.059	.137	.007	.016	.021	.049
Pol. Views	-.118	-.089	-.245*	-.180*	-.221*	-.164*	-.379*	-.278*	.167*	.123*	.248*	.185*	-.014	-.010	.119	.086
Nat. Health $	.410*	.130*	.267	.079	.710*	.227*	.686*	.200*	-.280	-.081	-.160	-.051	.145	.047	-.144	-.042
Gay Sin	-.573*	-.282*	.260*	.120*	-.259	-.126	-.465	-.216	.200	.091	.401*	.193*	.223*	.109*	.405*	.190*
AntiDrug	-.175	-.032	-.049	-.009	-.035	-.006	.026	.005	-.154	-.029	.969*	.177*	.229	.043	.181	.034
Constant:	2.939		-.204		3.391		4.039		-.608		1.627		.860		-.881	
-2 Log L:																
(intercept)	824.730		733.862		515.981		501.971		780.507		463.936		817.387		689.043	
(model)	730.475		646.556		381.052		355.643		715.570		374.049		746.433		636.752	
Model X² (w/22 d.f.)	94.475*		87.306*		134.929*		146.643*		64.938*		89.887*		70.954*		52.291*	
Sommers' D	.445		.456		.689		.720		.388		.588		.404		.379	
N	612		584		665		617		588		663		627		586	

Note: * p < .05

223

to policies designed to promote safe sex, either in sex education courses in public schools or over public service ads on television. We suspect that these independent religion effects are due to the unique stand on "pro-family" values taken by deeply and conservatively religious persons (Hertel and Hughes 1987), a position which we take up in the discussion section below.

It appears that the observed bivariate effects of religiosity on support for the remaining AIDS policy initiatives, however, may indeed be mediated, as predicted, through political ideology, support for government spending on public health, and attitudes toward homosexuality and drug use. At least one of these items maintains a significant effect on each of these AIDS policies, especially political ideology and attitude toward homosexuality which are strongly related to religiosity, inversely related to support for the non-intrusive policies, and positively related to the more intrusive policies. Finally, support for increased public health spending is, as expected, positively associated with support for the non-intrusive policies.

In Table 4 we replaced the single, global religiosity scale with the five religiosity sub-scales. Doing so did not meaningfully alter the observed effects of any of the other variables; few differences in the level of support for the AIDS policies were observed across categories of religious affiliation and the four mediator variables retained their effects as observed in Table 3. Likewise, most of the religiosity effects (twenty-nine of forty) were statistically insignificant. Nevertheless, two patterns of religiosity effects are quite evident when the global scale is decomposed into dimensional sub-scales. First, public religiosity is significantly and inversely related with each of the four non-intrusive AIDS policy initiatives. Second, a religious concern with sin is positively and significantly associated with support for two of the four intrusive policies (AIDSMAR and AIDSIDS).

SUMMARY AND DISCUSSION

In this study, we have argued that the religious framing of AIDS is an emergent phenomenon in which the meaning of the disease, attitudes toward its victims, and support/opposition for various public health policies are based on more entrenched beliefs and values. Chief among these, particularly for members of the religious right, are traditional values associated with sexuality, especially homosexuality, substance abuse, and political conservatism. As such, we hypothesized that the effects of religious affiliation and religiosity on support for four "intrusive" and four "non-intrusive" AIDS policies are indirect and mediated primarily through these other more entrenched values. This is largely what we find. The consistently observed bivariate effects of the religion variables are reduced to nonsignificance when the influence of these mediator variables is controlled in the multivariate analyses. The only religion effects which continue to hold when these mediators are introduced are those for conservative Protestantism and the global religiosity scale on attitudes toward efforts to promote safe-sex practices (AIDSSXED and AIDSADS), the inverse effects of the public religiosity sub-scale on support for the non-intrusive policies (i.e., AIDSFARE, AIDSHLTH, AIDSSXED, and AIDSADS), and the positive effect of the religious concern for sin sub-scale on two of the four intrusive AIDS policies (AIDSMAR and AIDSIDS).

Of the the four mediator variables, political conservativism and anti-homosexual sentiments are positively related to support for the intrusive AIDS policy items and negatively related to support for the non-intrusive policies. Support for increased government spending on public health is positively related to support for the four non-intrusive AIDS policies, but is unrelated to the more intrusive policies. Finally, support for the continued criminalization of drugs, perhaps due to the surrogate nature of the item employed, is, for the most part, unrelated to the eight AIDS policy items.[3]

These findings are highly consistent with a number of other studies which have also shown that political conservativism and anti-gay sentiments directly affect both attitudes toward AIDS victims (Johnson 1987; Larsen et al. 1990; Stipp and Kerr 1989) and support/opposition for various AIDS policies (Jelen and Wilcox 1992; Le Poire et al. 1990; Price and Hsu 1992). However, our findings of largely indirect religious effects are not consistent with other works which have shown relatively powerful direct religious influences on attitudes toward AIDS victims/policies (cf. Greeley 1991; Johnson 1987; Jelen & Wilcox 1992; Le Poire et al. 1990).

Nevertheless, whether direct or indirect, the nature of the influence of religiosity and religious affiliation, particularly conservative Protestantism, toward AIDS appears to be rather moralistic and vengeful. Highly religious members of the religious right tend to view persons with AIDS negatively and to support those AIDS policies which attempt to identify, stigmatize, and segregate persons with AIDS from the general population. The retributivist tone taken toward AIDS by such persons is little different from that which they also show toward other "sinners" (Grasmick, Cochran, Bursik, and Kimpel 1993; Grasmick, Davenport, Chamlin, and Bursik, 1992). Such a stand, when combined with the political influence of the religious right, may have powerful implications for the effectiveness of public health policies aimed at preventing the further spread of this epidemic disease.

In 1980, Conrad and Schneider introduced social scientists to an emerging trend in the apparatus of social control congruent with the rise of the medical profession: the medicalization of deviance. Under this new trend, forms of behavior previously defined as deviant behaviors, such as alcohol abuse, opiate addiction, hyperactivity, and others, were successfully redefined as medical problems. There has also emerged an accompanying expansion of medical jurisdiction into areas of morality and a translocation of the arenas of social control. We suggest that a counter-trend is also evident—the *moralization of illnesses*. As in the case of AIDS, some illnesses, primarily because of their epidemic nature and/or the populations afflicted with them, are being reconstructed by some segments of society as deviant behaviors (cf. Sontag 1978). Such a trend, we argue, has great implications for public health policy. In the case of AIDS, a disease currently undergoing such a moralization process, many of the proposed prevention programs are likely to be undermined and rendered ineffective unless this counter-trend can be defeated.

ACKNOWLEDGMENTS

This research was supported by faculty research funds from the Office of Research Administration, University of Oklahoma. We would like to acknowledge the helpful comments of Drs. Mitchell B. Chamlin and Peter B. Wood. An earlier draft of this paper was presented at the annual meetings of the Association for the Sociology of Religion, Pittsburgh, PA, August 18-20, 1992. Please direct all correspondance to the lead author at the following address: Department of Criminology, University of South Florida, Tampa, FL 33620.

NOTES

1.   We are indebted to the work of Jakobi (1990) for much of the material presented in this section.

2.   With regard to the sociodemographic control variables, our findings reveal several significant age, gender, race, and education effects. Older persons, males, whites, and the less educated are less likely to support the non-intrusive policies and are more likely to support the more intrusive AIDS policies.

REFERENCES

Albert, E. 1989. "AIDS and the Press: The Creation and Transformation of a Social Problem."
    Pp. 39-44 in *Images of Issues: Typifying Contemporary Social Problems,* edited by J. Best.
    New York: Aldine de Gruyter.
Altman, D. 1986. *AIDS in the Mind of America.* Garden City, NY: Anchor Press.
Beauchamp, D.E. 1986. "Morality and the Health of the Body Politic." *Hastings Center Report*
    16:30-36.
Beckley, R.E. and H.P. Chalfant. 1992. "AIDS and the Church: A Texas Update." Paper presented
    at the annual meeting of the Southwestern Social Science Association, Austin, TX (April).
Bell, N.K. 1991. "Social/Sexual Norms and AIDS in the South." *AIDS Education and Prevention*
    3:164-180.
Brandt, A.M. 1988. "AIDS in Historical Perspective." Pp. 31-38 in *AIDS: Ethics and Public Policy,*
    edited by C. Pierce and D. VanDeVeer. Belmont, CA: Wadsworth.
Cialdini, R.B., D.T. Kenrick, and J.H. Hoering. 1976. "Victim Derogation and the Lerner
    Paradigm: Just World or Just Justification?" *Journal of Personality and Social Psychology*
    33:719-724.

Cochran, J.K. 1991. "The Effects of Religiosity on Adolescent Self-Reported Frequency of Drug and Alcohol Use." *Journal of Drug Issues* 22:91-104.

Cochran, J.K. and L. Beeghley. 1991. "The Influence of Religion on Attitudes toward Nonmarital Sexuality: A Preliminary Assessment of Reference Group Theory." *Journal for the Scientific Study of Religion* 30:45-62.

Conrad, P. and J.W. Schneider. 1980. *Deviance and Medicalization: From Badness to Sickness.* St. Louis: Mosby.

Davis, J.A. and T.W. Smith. 1988. *General Social Surveys: Cumulative Codebook.* Chicago: National Opinion Research Center.

Grasmick, H.G., J.K. Cochran, R.J. Bursik, Jr., and M. Kimpel. 1993. "Religion, Punitive Justice, and Support for the Death Penalty." *Justice Quarterly* 10:289-314.

Grasmick, H.G., E. Davenport, M.B. Chamlin, and R.J. Bursik, Jr. 1992. "Protestant Fundamentalism and the Retributive Doctrine of Punishment." *Criminology* 30:21-45.

Greeley, A.M. 1991. "Religion and Attitudes towards AIDS Policy." *Sociology and Social Research* 75:126-132.

Gruman, J.C. and R.P. Sloan. 1983. "Disease as Justice: Perceptions of the Victims of Physical Illness." *Basic and Applied Social Psychology* 4:39-46.

Hanushek, E.A. and J.E. Jackson. 1977. *Statistical Methods for Social Scientists.* New York: Academic Press.

Hertel, B. and M. Hughes. 1987. "Religious Affiliation, Attendance and Support for Pro-Family Issues in the United States." *Social Forces* 65:858-880.

Jakobi, P.L. 1990. "Medical Science, Christian Fundamentalism, and the Etiology of AIDS." *AIDS Public Policy Journal* 5:89-93.

Jelen, T.G. and C. Wilcox. 1992. "Symbolic and Instrumental Values as Predictors of AIDS Policy Attitudes." *Social Science Quarterly* 73:737-749.

Johnson, S.D. 1987. "Factors Related to Intolerance of AIDS Victims." *Journal for the Scientific Study of Religion* 26:105-110.

Johnson, S.D. and J. Tamney. 1984. "Support for the Moral Majority: A Test of a Model." *Journal for the Scientific Study of Religion* 23:183-196.

————. 1985. "The Christian Right and the 1984 Presidential Election." *Review of Religious Research* 27:124-133.

Kellstedt, L. and C. Smidt. 1991. "Measuring Fundamentalism: An Analysis of Different Operational Strategies." *Journal for the Scientific Study of Religion* 30:259-278.

Larsen, K.S., M. Serra, and E. Long. 1990. "AIDS Victims and Heterosexual Attitudes." *Journal of Homosexuality* 19:103-116.

Le Poire, B.A., C.K. Sigelman, L. Sigelman, and H.C. Kenski. 1990. "Who Wants to Quarantine Persons with AIDS? Patterns of Support for California's Proposition 64." *Social Science Quarterly* 71:239-249.

Marsden, G.M. 1977. "Fundamentalism as an American Phenomenon: A Comparison with English Evangelicalism." *Church History* 46:215-232.

Price, V. and M-L. Hsu. 1992. "Public Opinion about AIDS Policies: The Role of Misinformation and Attitudes toward Homosexuals. *Public Opinion Quarterly* 56:29-52.

Rothenberg, S. and F. Newport. 1984. *The Evangelical Voter.* Washington, DC: Free Congress Foundation.

Rubin, Z. and L.A. Peplau. 1975. "Who Believes in a Just World?" *Journal of Social Issues* 31:65-89.

Singer, E., T.F. Rogers, and M. Corcoran. 1987. "The Polls - A Report: AIDS." *Public Opinion Quarterly* 51:580-595.

Smith, T.W. 1990. "Classifying Protestant Denominations." *Review of Religious Research* 31:225-249.

Sontag, S. 1979. *Illness as Metaphor.* New York: Vintage Books.

Sorrentino, R.M. and J.E. Hardy. 1974. "Religiousness and Derogation of an Innocent Victim."
    Journal of Personality 42:372-382.
Stevens, L.A. and P.R. Muskin. 1987. "Techniques for Reversing the Failure of Empathy towards
    AIDS Patients." *Journal of the American Academy of Psychoanalysis* 15:539-551.
Stipp, H. and D. Kerr. 1989. "Determinants of Public Opinion about AIDS." *Public Opinion
    Quarterly* 53:98-106.
Tamney, J. and S. Johnson. 1983. "The Moral Majority in Middletown." *Journal for the Scientific
    Study of Religion* 22:145-157.

CONTRIBUTORS

John K. Cochran is Associate Professor of Criminology at the University of South Florida. Dr. Cochran took his PhD at the University of Florida. His research interests include the social control functions of religion and examinations of issues in macro-social deterrence and rational choice perspectives. He has recently published in the *Journal of Research in Crime and Delinquency* and *Criminology.*

Jill Garner received her MA in Sociology from the University of Oklahoma and is currently a Statistical Analyst I with the Oklahoma Department of Mental Health. She has an article forthcoming at *Youth and Society.*

C. Kirk Hadaway is Secretary for Research and Evaluation for the United Church of Christ in Cleveland, Ohio. He previously held several research positions in the Southern Baptist Convention. His PhD is in sociology from the University of Massachusetts, Amherst, and his most recent books are *Church and Denominational Growth* (Abingdon Press, 1993) and *Church Growth Principles* (Broadman Press, 1991). His current research interests include religious marginality, cultural change, and congregational studies.

Bernadette C. Hayes is currently a Lecturer in Sociology at Queen's University of Belfast, Northern Ireland. Previous appointments include Lecturer in Sociology at the University of Surrey and a Research Fellowship at the Australian National University. She has published widely in the area of gender and social stratification. Her most recent publications include articles in the *Journal of Marriage and the Family, Public Opinion Quarterly, British Journal of Sociology, Political Studies, Sociology,* and *Women & Politics.* Her current research interests focus on gender and politics.

Michael P. Hornsby-Smith is a Reader in Sociology at the University of Surrey, England. His main research has been concerned with the social and religious transformations in English Catholicism since the Second World War and the Second Vatican Council. His publications include *Roman Catholics in England* (Cambridge University Press, 1987), *Roman Catholic Beliefs in England* (Cambridge University Press, 1991), and numerous articles in *Archives de Sciences Sociales des Religions, Journal for the Scientific Study of Religion, Review of Religious Research, Social Compass,* and other journals. His current research interests include the completion of a co-authored book on The Politics of Spirituality and of one on the role of the Catholic Church in social policy formulation in the nations of Western Europe.

Matthew P. Lawson is a doctoral candidate at Princeton University. He earned a BA from Indiana University and an MA from the University of Chicago. His dissertation examines the relationship between ritual symbolism and practical worldly activity in the life stories of charismatic Catholics.

Adair Lummis is a Research Associate at Hartford Seminary. She holds a PhD in sociology from Columbia University. She has co-authored two books, *Women of the Cloth* (with Jackson Carroll and Barbara Hargorve; Harper and Row, 1983) and *Islamic Values in the United States* (with Yvonne Haddad; Oxford, 1987). Currently, she is completing a national study of women's spiritual support groups along with Allison Stokes and Miriam Therese Winter. She also is beginning a national cross-denominational study of clergywomen in the nineties together with other colleagues.

Monty L. Lynn is Associate Professor of Management Sciences at Abilene Christian University, Abilene, Texas. He earned an MS in human-environment relations at Cornell University, and an MOB (organizational behavior) and PhD (social-organizational psychology) at Brigham Young University. His primary research interests are in the organizational behavior and theory of religious, business, labor, and health care institutions. His publications have appeared in the *Journal of Organizational Behavior, Industrial Relations, Hospital and Health Services Administration, Organizational Behavior Teaching Review,* and *Decision Sciences.* He is a member of the Academy of Management, Society for the Scientific Study of Religion, and Religious Research Association.

Penny Long Marler is Assistant Professor of Religious Studies at Samford University with a joint appointment in Sociology. She holds an MSSW from the Kent School of Social Work, University of Louisville and an MDiv and PhD from Southern Baptist Theological Seminary. She has authored articles on religious marginality, congregational analysis, denominational mobility, church membership and participation trends, and the sociology of the family.

Augustine Meier is an Associate Professor at Saint Paul University, Ottawa, Ontario, Canada. He took his PhD, MA, and M.Ed degrees at the University of Ottawa. He is a member of the Ottawa University School of Graduate Studies and a registered psychologist in Ontario. His current research interests are counseling and Psychotherapy. Dr. Meier has published papers in *Canadian Journal of Psychiatry, Clinical Psychology, Journal of Cognitive Psychotherapy, Journal of Consulting* and *Clinical Psychology,* and *Pastoral Sciences.*

David O. Moberg is Professor Emeritus of Social and Cultural Sciences at Marquette University, Milwaukee, Wisconsin. His MA is from the University of Washington, and his PhD in sociology is from the University of Minnesota. He has held two Fulbright professorships (Netherlands and West Germany) and has taught and lectured at numerous colleges, universities, and theological seminaries besides his long-term appointments at Bethel College in Minnesota and at Marquette. He is the author of several books and numerous articles, is a former president of the Religious Research Association, Association for the Sociology of Religion, and Wisconsin Sociological Association, and has held leadership positions in several other professional organizations related to sociology, gerontology, and the study of religion.

André Nauta is currently a Visting Assistant Professor at Case Western Reserve University (PhD, Iowa State). Current research interests include perspectives on religion in multicultural congregations and the relationship of religiosity to older adult mental health. He is a member of the Society for the Scientific Study of Religion, the American Sociological Association, and the Gerontological Society of America.

H. Wesley Perkins (MDiv, Yale Divinity School; MA, PhD, Yale) is Professor of Sociology at Hobart and William Smith Colleges. His research on religiosity and social justice attitudes in England and the United States and on religion, well-being and drug abuse has been published in *Sociological Analysis, Review of Religious Research, Journal for the Scientific Study of Religion* and other journals. He was the 1992 Program Chair for the Association for the Sociology of Religion.

Allison Stokes holds an MDiv and a PhD in American Studies, both from Yale University. She is the Founding Director of the Clergywomen's Interfaith Institute in the Berkshires and also serves as pastor of the West Stockbridge Congregational Church. She is the author of *Ministry After Freud* (Pilgrim Press, 1985). In 1994 she was a Merrill Fellow at Harvard Divinity School.

Jeffry A. Will is Assistant Professor of Sociology at the University of North Florida. His Ph.D. is from the University of Massachusetts. Professor Will's current research interests include the use of factorial surveys to assess attributions of deservedness among the poor. He is the author of *The Deserving Poor* (Garland Press, 1993).

REVIEWERS

Many experts viewed manuscripts that were submitted for Volume 6 of *Research in the Social Scientific Study of Religion.* Their sixty evaluations significantly contribute to the quality of these volumes. The co-editors, authors, and readers are indebted to each of the following:

Robert Abelman   Cleveland State University

Jon Atack   West Sussex, England

Merlin B. Brinkerhoff   University of Calgary

Malcolm Brown   The William Temple Foundation and
                          Manchester Business School, England

Robert Chandler   Illinois State University

Mark Chaves   University of Notre Dame

John K. Cochran   University of South Florida

Walter E. Conn   Villanova University

Diana C. Dale   Institute of Worklife Ministry, Houston

Lorne Dawson   University of Waterloo

Michael Donahue   Search Institute, Minneapolis

Joseph A. Erickson   Augsburg College

Hans G. Furth	Catholic University of America
Anne M. Hallum	Stetson University
Tim B. Heaton	Brigham Young University
Russell Heddendorf	Covenant College
Evertt W. Huffard	Harding University Graduate School of Religion
Laurence Iannaccone	Santa Clara University
Patricia L. Jakobi	University of Texas Medical Branch at Galveston
Ted Jelen	Illinois Benedictine College
Benton Johnson	University of Oregon
Mary Johnson	Emmanuel College
Stephen D. Johnson	Ball State University
Stephen A. Kent	University of Alberta
Lee A. Kirkpatrick	College of William and Mary
Robert Liebman	Portland State University
Ronald Loxley	Essex Churches Council for Industry and Commerce, England
Bill J. Leonard	Samford University
H. Newton Malony	Fuller Theological Seminary
H. Leon McBeth	Southwestern Baptist Theological Seminary
A. I. McFadyen	University of Leeds
Paul Mojzes	Rosemont College

Richard Moline	Rosemead School of Psychology Biola University
Marie Augusta Neal	Emmanuel College
Michael Newcomb	University of California, Los Angeles
Richard Noll	Philadelphia, Pennsylvania
Wayne E. Oates	University of Louisville School of Medicine and Southern Baptist Theological Seminary
Janice A. Peck	University of Minnesota
Robin D. Perrin	Pepperdine University
Margaret M. Poloma	University of Akron
Lewis R. Rambo	San Francisco Theological Seminary
Anton Rauscher	University of Augsburg, Germany
James T. Richardson	University of Nevada, Reno
E. Burke Roachford, Jr.	Middlebury College
Thomas Robbins	Rochester, Minnesota
Rex Rogers	Grand Rapids Baptist College
Ellen Rosenberg	Western Connecticut State University
Walter W. Sawatsky	Associated Mennonite Biblical Seminaries
Michael J. Shapiro	University of Hawaii
Anson Shupe	Indiana University/Purdue University, Fort Wayne
Corwin Smidt	Calvin College
Henry E. Speck, III	Abilene Christian University

Phillips Stevens, Jr.	State University of New York, Buffalo
Ronald R. Stockton	University of Michigan, Dearborn
Rodney Stark	University of Washington
William H. Swatos, Jr.	Editor, *Sociology of Religion*
Darwin L. Thomas	Brigham Young University
Michael Weed	Institute for Christian Studies, Austin
Louis Jolyon West	University of California, Los Angeles
Patricia Wittberg	Indiana University/Purdue University, Indianapolis

AUTHOR INDEX

SUBJECT INDEX

Research in the Social Scientific Study of Religion

Edited by **Monty L. Lynn,** *Department of Management Sciences, Abilene Christian University* and **David O. Moberg,** *Department of Social and Cultural Sciences, Marquette University.*

Research in the Social Scientific Study of Religion functions as an outlet for major research reports, review articles, and theoretical papers in the social-scientific study of religion. This annual publication is interdisciplinary in nature including contributions from such fields as sociology, psychology, anthropology, communication, organizational behavior and theory, economics, and the human service professions.

Research in the Social Scientific Study of Religion allows the publication of longer manuscripts than journals permit. Thus, significant research-oriented theoretical studies, state-of-the-art surveys, and reviews of literature in the field can be accommodated in addition to briefer articles. Invited papers form the bulk of each volume but other articles making a significant contribution to the field are also considered.

REVIEWS: "a very original choice of research opening some very new perspectives"
— *Francis H. Houtart*
Editor, Social Compass

"Internationally minded, properly concerned to stimulate the comparative study of religion, and delightfully eclectic"
— *Charles Y. Glock*
Professor Emeritus of Sociology
University of California, Berkeley

Volume 1, 1989, 260 pp. $73.25
ISBN 0-89232-882-7

J A I P R E S S

JAI PRESS

Religion and the Social Order

Edited by **David G. Bromley,** *Department of Sociology and Anthropology, Virginia Commonwealth University*

Religion and the Social Order explorers seminal issues being addressed by social scientists studying religious institutions and religious behavior. The organization of each volume is thematic, with several contributors preparing theoretical statements or empirical research results on the same issue. A wide range of theoretical approaches, substantive issues, historical and cross-cultural analyses give the series both intellectual depth and breadth of perspective.

**J
A
I

P
R
E
S
S**

Revitalization Movement, *Helen Rose Ebaugh.* **The Church
and Modernization,** *Gregory Baum and Jean-Gay Vaillancourt.*
**PART TWO: CHANGES IN THE INTERNAL DYNAMICS OF
THE U.S. CHURCH. The Demographics of American
Catholics: 1965-1990,** *Andrew M. Greeley.* **Catholic Youth in
the Modern Church,** *Patrick H. McNamara.* **Changes in the
Priesthood and Seminaries,** *Dean R. Hoge.* **Full Pews and
Empty Altars: Demographics of U.S. Diocesan Priests, 1966-
2005,** *Richard A. Schoenherr and Lawrence A. Young.*
American Sisters: Organizational and Value Changes, *Marie
Augusta Neal, S.N.D.* **New Roles for Women in the Catholic
Church: 1965-1990,** *Ruth A. Wallace.* **PART THREE: THE
CHURCH AND SOCIAL ISSUES: INSTITUTIONAL COMMIT-
MENTS AND SHIFTING ATTITUDES OF CATHOLICS.
Catholic Sexual Ethics Since Vatican II,** *James R. Kelly.* **The
Church and Social Issues:Institutional Commitments,**
Joseph Fitzpatrick, S.J. **The Church and New Immigrants,**
Kevin J. Christiano. The Social Movement for Change Within the
Catholic Church, Katherine Meyer. **PART FOUR: CATHOLICISM
IN WORLD PERSPECTIVE. Western European Catholicism
Since Vatican II,** *Karel Dobbelaere and Liliane Voye.* **The Post—
Vatican II Church in Latin America,** *Madeleine Adriance.* **PART
FIVE: LOOKING TO THE FUTURE OF THE CATHOLIC
CHURCH IN THE UNITED STATES. U.S. Catholicism: The
Now and Future Church,** *Joseph H. Fichter, S.J.* **Vatican II and
the Reconceptualization of the Church,** *Helen Rose Ebaugh.*

Volume 3: The Handbook on Cults and Sects in America
1993, 2 Volume Set $146.50
ISBN 1-55938-477-8

Edited by **David G. Bromley,** *Virginia Commonwealth
University* and **Jeffrey K. Hadden** *University of Virginia*

**PART A - CONTENTS: Preface. Introduction. Exploring the
Significance of Cults and Sects in America: Perspectives,
Issues and Agendas,** *David G. Bromley and Jeffrey K. Hadden.*
**PART I. EMERGENCE AND DEVELOPMENT OF CULTS AND
SECTS. A. Maturing Inquiries. Historical Lessons in the
Study of Cults and Sects,** *Bryan Wilson.* **Charisma and
Leadership in New Religious Movements,** *Frederick Bird.*
Organizational Development of Cults and Sects, *Phillp E.
Hammond and David. W. Machacek.* **B. Emerging Issues. A
Rational Approach to the History of American Cults and
Sects,** *Rodney Stark and Roger Finke.* **Research in Social
Movements and New Religious Movements: Prospects for
Convergence,** *Armand L. Mauss.* **Explorations Along the
Sacred Frontier: Notes on Para-Religions, Quasi-Religions,
and Other Boundary Phenomena,** *Arthur L. Greil.* **PART II. THE
SOCIOCULTURAL ENVIRONMENT OF CULTS AND SECTS.
A. Maturing Inquiries. The Organization of Oppoistion to New**

Religious Movements, *David G. Bromley and Anson Shupe.*
Religious Movements and Church-State Relations, *Thomas Robbins and James A. Beckford.* **New Religions and the Family,** *Stuart Wright and William V. D'Antonio.* **B. Emerging Issues. Rational Choice Propositions About Religious Movements,** *Rodney Stark and Laurence R. Iannaccone.* **New Religions and the Political Order,** *Theodore E. Long.* **New Religions, Science and Secularization,** *William Sims Bainbridge.*

PART B - CONTENTS: Preface. Introduction. Exploring the Significance of Cults and Sects in America: Perspectives, Issues and Agendas, *David G. Bromley and Jeffrey K. Hadden.* **PART III. CULTS, SECTS AND THE INDIVIDUAL. A. Maturing Inquiries. Conversion to New Religious Movements,** *Richard Machalek and David Snow.* **A Social Psychological Critique of "Brainwashing" Claims About Recruitment to New Religions,** *James T. Richardson.* **The New Religions and Mental Health,** *John Saliba.* **B. Emerging Issues. Leaving New Religions,** *Stuart Wright and Helen Rose Ebaugh.* **Health and Healing,** *Meredith McGuire.* **Life Cycle, Generation, and Participation in Religious Groups,** *Wade Clark Roof and Karen Walsh.* **Feminist Perspectives on New Religious Movements,** *Lynn Davidman and Janet Jacobs.* **PART IV. THE ROAD TO MATURITY FROM EPISTEMOLOGY TO A COMPREHENSIVE RESEARCH AGENDA. Will the Real Cult Please Stand Up? A Comparative Analysis of Social Constructions of New Religious Movements,** *Eileen Barker.* **Problems of Research and Data in the Study of New Religions,** *James T. Richardson, Robert Balch and J. Gordon Melton.*

JAI PRESS INC.

55 Old Post Road # 2 - P.O. Box 1678
Greenwich, Connecticut 06836-1678
Tel: (203) 661-7602   Fax:(203) 661-0792